The Ancient Flame

THE WILLIAM AND KATHERINE DEVERS
SERIES IN DANTE STUDIES

Theodore J. Cachey, Jr., and Christian Moevs, editors
Simone Marchesi, associate editor
Ilaria Marchesi, assistant editor

———————

The
ANCIENT *F*LAME

*Dante
and the Poets*

WINTHROP WETHERBEE

*University of Notre Dame Press
Notre Dame, Indiana*

Designed by Wendy McMillen
Set in 10.8/14.2 Dante by Four Star Books
Printed on 60# Nature's Natural by Sheridan Books

Library of Congress Cataloging-in-Publication Data

Wetherbee, Winthrop, 1938–
    The ancient flame : Dante and the poets / Winthrop Wetherbee.
        p.   cm. — (The William and Katherine Devers series in Dante studies)
    Includes bibliographical references and index.
    ISBN-13: 978-0-268-04412-1 (pbk. : alk. paper)
    ISBN-10: 0-268-04412-0 (pbk. : alk. paper)
    1. Dante Alighieri, 1265–1321—Criticism and interpretation.
2. Dante Alighieri, 1265–1321—Knowledge—Literature.   I. Title.
    PQ4427.C53W484   2008
    851'.1—dc22
                                                          2008000420

Le passé n'est pas fugace, il reste sur place.

Proust

Contents

About the William and Katherine Devers Series in Dante Studies

The William and Katherine Devers Program in Dante Studies at the University of Notre Dame supports rare book acquisitions in the university's John A. Zahm Dante collections, funds an annual visiting professorship in Dante studies, and supports electronic and print publication of scholarly research in the field. In collaboration with the Medieval Institute at the university, the Devers program has initiated a series dedicated to the publication of the most significant current scholarship in the field of Dante Studies.

In keeping with the spirit that inspired the creation of the Devers program, the series takes Dante as a focal point that draws together the many disciplines and lines of inquiry that constitute a cultural tradition without fixed boundaries. Accordingly, the series hopes to illuminate Dante's position at the center of contemporary critical debates in the humanities by reflecting both the highest quality of scholarly achievement and the greatest diversity of critical perspectives.

The series publishes works on Dante from a wide variety of disciplinary viewpoints and in diverse scholarly genres, including critical studies, commentaries, editions, translations, and conference proceedings of exceptional importance. The series is supervised by an international advisory board composed of distinguished Dante scholars and is published regularly by the University of Notre Dame Press. The Dolphin and Anchor device that appears on publications of the Devers series was used by the great humanist, grammarian, editor, and typographer Aldus Manutius (1449–1515), in whose 1502 edition of Dante (second issue) and all subsequent editions it appeared. The device illustrates the ancient proverb *Festina lente*, "Hurry up slowly."

Theodore J. Cachey, Jr., and Christian Moevs, *editors*

Simone Marchesi, *associate editor*

Ilaria Marchesi, *assistant editor*

Preface

When a lifelong amateur Dantista tries in his golden years to make a contribution to Dante studies he is bound to need a lot of help. The friends who have sat through trial versions of my ideas or stimulated me with theirs are many, but I am especially grateful to Jay Schleusener, Tom Stillinger, Carol Kaske, Caron Cioffi, Disa Gambera, Suzie Hagedorn, and Richard Neuse. Warren Ginsberg read and provided valuable commentary on my attempts at defining Dante's debt to Ovid. Audiences at Dartmouth, Villanova, Southern Connecticut, Penn, and Virginia contributed helpful feedback on early versions of other chapters, and my Cornell colleagues Carol Rosen and Kora Battig von Wittelsbach have guided my faltering steps as a reader of Italian. My beloved Andrea allowed me an unconscionable amount of Dante time during a precious and long-awaited sojourn in Rome. Much of the writing was done there, in the library of the hospitable American Academy, most of the rest in Cornell's equally hospitable Olin.

Years ago it was my good fortune to have first John Freccero, then Giuseppe Mazzotta as Cornell colleagues, and my indebtedness to both is ongoing. Reaching further back, it is a great pleasure to finally acknowledge a debt of nearly fifty years' standing to Kenneth Reckford who, as my tutor at Harvard, taught me not just to construe and scan but also to *hear* Latin poetry. Whatever true resonances I may have detected between Dante's words and those of his classical forebears are a late harvest of the fruits of Professor Reckford's teaching.

1

Introduction

Dante and Classical Poetry

In the Old French *Eneas* there is an elaborate account of the tomb of the beautiful warrior Camille, Vergil's Camilla, slain while seeking to defend Italy against the Trojans. Suspended over the bier by a golden chain is a lamp filled with a rare oil, which, if undisturbed, will burn forever. The chain in turn depends from the beak of a golden dove set high on a pillar. In another part of the chamber stands the mechanical image of an archer, his bow drawn and an arrow pointing at the breast of the dove:

> Li archiers pot longues viser
> et toz tens mes l'arc anteser,
> mais ja li boldons ni trairoit,
> se primes l'arc ne destandoit
> le laz d'une regeteore
> qui aparoilliez ert desore,
> qui tenoit l'arc toz tens tendu.
> A un sofle fust tot perdu:
> qui soflast la regeteore,
> et al destandist anislore

et li archiers idonc traisist
droit au colon, se l'abatist,
dunc fust la chaene rompue
et la lanpe tote espandue.
(*Eneas* 7705–18)

[Long might the archer gaze, and hold the bow ever drawn,
but he would not release the arrow unless the bow were released from the noose of a snare. The snare had been arranged
above, and held the bow always drawn. At a breath all would
be lost: if one blew on the snare it would be immediately
sprung, and the archer would shoot straight at the dove and
strike it. Then the chain would be broken and the lamp would
be wholly destroyed.]

Nothing in Vergil corresponds to this passage, but its imagery recalls the archery contest which concludes the funeral games for Aeneas'
father, Anchises, in *Aeneid 5*. A dove is tethered by one leg to the top of
a long pole. The first contestant's arrow strikes the pole; as the bird beats
its wings in terror, a second arrow severs the cord which tethers it; the
happy bird flies upward, and a third archer, taking advantage of a dark
cloud which sets off the bird's white feathers, strikes it in midair. The
bird "leaves its life in the starry heavens" (517–18) and carries the arrow
back to earth.

This passage in turn is dense with echoes; most of all it evokes Vergil's painful account of the drawn-out final moments of the Euripidean
tragedy of Dido—the certainty of her death, her "infixum vulnus," and
the almost grudging deliberateness with which Iris, at the instigation of
Juno, severs the vital thread, allowing Dido's life to be borne away on the
wind (*Aen.* 4.688–705).

By framing the death of Camilla in imagery which so vividly evokes
the fate of Dido, the *Eneas* poet acknowledges and extends the chain of allusion that links the two Vergilian moments, inscribing into his own poem
that sense of loss which is perhaps Vergil's most distinctive feature as an
epic poet. The symbolic linkage of an impossible feminine purity and in-
supportable feminine suffering expresses the price of heroic conquest, the

destruction of a purer world and the remorseless subordination of human concerns that are necessary to the task of empire. And in the means by which the *Eneas* poet indicates his awareness of these things, a Byzantine invention that may please his drowsy audience while its true meaning remains sealed up with Camilla, there is a conscious naïveté, and the tacit acknowledgment of a fundamental conflict. As the dove who holds suspended the magic lamp is perpetually threatened, so in the description as a whole an impulse to fanciful transcendence that epitomizes the courtly idealism of romance is balanced against an underlying awareness of the historical and emotional realities of classical epic.

If he knew the *Eneas,* Dante will have understood perfectly the romance poet's intention in alluding to Vergil as he does, and the *Commedia* is charged with allusions of a very similar kind. And he would recognize as well, in the contrasting of the pathetic and fanciful treatment of Camilla with the Vergilian tragedy it evokes, the *Eneas* poet's acute awareness of all that his poem is not, and cannot be, the profound difference between medieval romance and classical epic. As his allusions are sure, so his pathos is finely balanced; but it is a perilous balance, and in responding to it we can all too easily be seduced into mere sentimentality, and reduce his complex representation to kitsch.

In the circle of the lustful in the fifth canto of Dante's *Inferno,* epic tragedy and courtly pathos are again brought into contrast; the canto has all the allusive force of the *Eneas* passage, but provides as well a vivid demonstration of the seductive power of romance. As Vergil identifies Dido, Achilles, and Paris, the Pilgrim's imagination involuntarily transforms them into romance figures, "donne antiche e cavalieri" whose role as lovers, for a Dante smitten by *pietà,* far outweighs their significance in world history.[1] His response to the story of Francesca, and the swoon which ends the episode, mark him as a connoisseur of the pathos of star-crossed love, and the poet's reminders that we are in the circle "ov'è Dido," set against the Pilgrim's stunted compassion, helps us realize the

---

1. Vergil, curiously and uncharacteristically, plays to Dante's courtly *pietà* in this scene, identifying "the great Achilles" only as the ill-fated lover of Dares and Benoit, and pairing Paris with Tristan.

distance that separates his world of "dolce amor" from the tragic universe of Vergil.[2]

The references to Dido are part of a larger pattern of allusions to the *Aeneid*, which frame the encounter with Francesca as the tomb of Camilla is framed by archer and dove. But Dante evokes the un-epic qualities of romance, its pathos and fantasy, only to exorcise them. The Pilgrim's swooning response to Francesca's story, in an atmosphere haunted by the memory of Dido, is only a stage in an engagement with classical poetry which grows steadily more complex as the *Inferno* unfolds.

Dante's poem incorporates the worldview of ancient epic more completely than any previous vernacular poem, and it is from the directness and honesty with which he both assimilates and challenges the tragic vision of the Roman poets that the *Commedia* and the transcendent experience it reports derive much of their extraordinary power. Throughout the poem Dante's engagements with these poets define a process of self-discovery that is in effect an existential counterpart to the spiritual journey which is his primary theme. Coming to terms with the poets of Roman epic is repeatedly shown to be the necessary precondition for the Pilgrim's attainment of genuine understanding, and the lessons they teach must be continually relearned. Even in the *Paradiso* their wisdom maintains a pervasive and often disturbing relevance to Dante's spiritual education, and to the very end reminders of their vision of history, the many paths that lead forward from the voyage of the Argo to the last days of Ulysses, remain essential to Dante's articulation of his experience of heaven.

---

2. Boccaccio understood the poet's complex intention here, and his *Esposizioni* of *Inferno* 5, dismissing the narrative Dante had created for Francesca as an improbable "fiction," offer an alternative version which sets the lovers' story in a more complex social context. Francesca's husband, Gianciotto, appears first in the role of King Mark to the lovers' Tristan and Iseult. His murder of Francesca, whom he loves "more than himself," occurs accidentally as he seeks to avenge himself on Paolo. He is left grief-stricken, and the lovers are buried together "con molte lacrime," thus completing what is unmistakably a romance plot, but one which, like the Tristan story and unlike that of Dante's lovers, approaches tragedy. Singleton's note to *Inferno* 5. 97 includes the entire story, prefaced by the comment, puzzling to me, that Boccaccio has "embroidered" his narrative "to exculpate Francesca as much as possible."

Dante's engagement with ancient poetry and the story it yields are what my book is about. As an emblem of my approach to this complex subject, I offer a passage from another twelfth-century poem, the *Anticlaudianus* of Alan of Lille. Alan, like Dante, was at pains to engage Latin epic in a meaningful way: His elaborate allegory, a spiritual odyssey culminating in a psychomachia, was, he claimed, truer to the traditions of ancient poetry than the pseudoclassical epics of his contemporaries Joseph of Exeter and Walter of Chatillon.[3] But he was also astute in recognizing the ways in which his poem must not only diverge from, but inevitably fall short of, the classical standard. His awareness of the true power of ancient epic appears clearly in one of his poem's many set pieces, a roll call of ancient practitioners of the Liberal Arts, climaxed by a tribute to the distinctive qualities of the great Latin poets:

> Ovidii flumen, Lucani fulmen, abyssum
> Vergilii . . .
>
> > (*Anticl.* 2.361–62)

[Ovid's great river, Lucan's thunderbolt, the depth of Vergil . . .]

The carefully chosen metaphors are a tribute to Alan's rhetorical powers as well as those of the poets he celebrates. Any reader of the *Metamorphoses* will recognize in *flumen* the sweep of Ovid's "perpetuum carmen," the endless song of continuity and transformation that articulates human history. The harsh style of Lucan's grim account of civil war and his lacerating anger at the death of Roman liberty are his *fulmen*, their thunder an ironic echo of divine retribution in a world from which the gods and justice are absent. The Vergilian abyss is the unfathomable sadness of the *Aeneid*, the sense of loss that is always an audible undertone in Vergil's celebration of Augustan Rome, a reminder that the price of empire is the alienation of nature and the destruction of primitive community.

Thus Alan's epithets seem to point deliberately to what is darkest in Latin epic, the relentlessness of fate and the inevitability of loss. They

---

3. See *Anticlaudianus* 1.165–70.

show him aware of how radically such poetry, where divine benevolence cannot be taken for granted and questions of order and justice evoke profound anxiety, differs from that of his own epic, the work of a Christian poet who can see himself as a pen in the hand of God (*Anticl.* 5.265–305), and whose poem aims to emulate the ordered fullness of God's handiwork. But they do something more: They suggest, vividly and concisely, how it *feels* to read the ancient poets, and it is in this respect most of all that they anticipate Dante's approach to his chosen *auctores*.

The *Anticlaudianus* was much admired: It was elaborately glossed, and imitated or adapted by various vernacular writers.[4] But Alan's astute intuition of the possibility of recovering the authentic classical tradition was largely ignored. The presumption inherent in the grand design of the *Anticlaudianus* is cruelly mocked by Jean de Meun, the first major vernacular author to confront the poem, and the vernacular poet whose use of classical poetry most nearly anticipates Dante's. The *Roman de la Rose* brings its vast narrative to a climax with the besieging of the castle of Jealousy by the forces of *Amors* and Venus, an action of epic scale which parodies both the later, Iliadic portions of the *Aeneid* (and more pointedly the *Eneas*) and the psychomachia which occupies the last books of the *Anticlaudianus*. The crude humor of Jean's concluding episode, the grotesquely literal defloration of the Rose by his lover-hero, is at once a coarse parody of the rage which impels the final acts of Vergil's Aeneas and a caustic response to the "triumph of Nature" which resolves the action of Alan's poem.

Dante, however, who knew Alan's poetry well, recognized the astuteness and sensitivity of his allusions to epic tradition, and saw in them a literary self-consciousness much like his own.[5] His allusions to his poetic role in the *Commedia* echo Alan's, and he shares Alan's sense of the challenge posed by ancient poetry, alien in character yet unquestionably authoritative, and inescapably a standard for the serious Christian writer. No poet save Milton, indeed, has been so concerned to measure up to this standard, and a major achievement of the *Commedia* is its coming to

---

4. See *Anticlaudianus,* ed. Bossuat, pp. 42–46.
5. See Dronke, *Dante and Medieval Latin,* 8–14; Vasoli, *Otto saggi,* 83–102.

terms with the great forebears to whom he grants the name of *poeta:*
Vergil, Ovid, and Lucan, the "bella scola" of Homer, and the "Christian"
poet Statius.[6]

Dante reminds us continually of his debt to these great Poeti, and
the uniquely intimate relation of his poetry to theirs:

> Elli givan dinanzi, e io soletto
> > di retro, e ascoltava i lor sermoni
> > ch'a poetar mi davano intelletto.
> > > (*Purg.* 22.127–29)

[They were going on in front, and I solitary behind, and
I was listening to their speech, which gave me understanding
in poetry.]

These lines refer specifically to Vergil and Statius, but they nicely define
Dante's engagement with the larger tradition the two poets represent.
His encounters with ancient epic are crucial to the story of the Pilgrim
as human being, as the retrospective and necessarily inadequate recorder
of his experience of the afterlife, and it is largely his constant awareness
of their informing presence that enables him to view that experience
with a certain detachment. By continually invoking the Poeti, and inviting us to view his poetic project in the light of theirs, Dante charts his developing awareness of his own artistic role, and the ethical and psychological challenges it involves.

Dante's engagements with the Latin tradition take widely different
forms. Vergil's poetry is powerfully present to the Dante of the *Inferno,*
and at significant junctures in the *Purgatorio* and *Paradiso.* Lucan's presence
is most evident in the *Inferno,* and in *Purgatorio* 1 (which, as I will suggest,
is in many ways a coda to the *Inferno*). Theirs is the poetry Dante experiences most fully and existentially, and in tension with which his sense of
his own status as poet takes shape. By contrast, his engagement with Ovid

---

6. In what follows I often refer to these poets individually as Poeta, and
collectively as the Poeti.

and Statius, crucial to the *Commedia*'s narrative of artistic experience, is oblique and selective. Ovidian motifs give form to imaginative tours de force at every level of the poem, and there is a sense in which Ovid is Dante's most important model, the greatest challenge to *aemulatio*, the poet he perhaps sees as most like himself. The very theme of the *Commedia* is metamorphosis. But Ovid is at once everywhere and nowhere in Dante's poem, present in innumerable echoes and allusions, verbal and structural, but never confronted directly. Statius' historical position, together with certain unique features of the *Thebaid*, gives rise to the myth of a latter-day disciple of the pagan Poeti, inspired at once by Vergil and by the newly disseminated Christian gospel to become the first Christian Poeta. Statius and Ovid are largely reinvented by Dante, though to very different effect. Vergil and Lucan, by contrast, remain unalterably, even obdurately themselves, and the limitations of their spiritual horizons are as important to Dante's conception of them as their poetic power.

These distinctions are important to my project, but equally important is the sense in which these great figures collectively represent poetry itself. It is in this capacity that Homer and the poets of Limbo honor Dante with admission to their company. And as Leonard Barkan remarks, Dante's introduction into their "bella scola" is not just a self-tribute, but "the keystone of the poetic world of the *Inferno*," a declaration of the depth and directness of Dante's engagement with classical culture. The appropriation and reworking of classical models that is crucial to the project of the *Commedia* as a whole occurs only after the pagan vision of the Poeti has been "respected, confronted, saved."[7] These well-chosen terms, defining as they do what Dante considered the essential precondition of meaningful *imitatio*, also define the subject of my book. What I want to isolate is Dante's experience, as reader and practitioner, of poetry as such, and the ways in which the significance of this experience reveals itself in his encounters with the Poeti—revolutionary encounters in which, "for the first time in nearly a thousand years, a Christian can see pagan civilization, not just through a glass darkly, but face to face."[8]

---

7. Barkan, *Gods Made Flesh*, 139–40.
8. Barkan, *Gods Made Flesh*, 138.

Marino Barchiesi has explored the implications of this confrontation in a classic essay. Focusing on the Dante who weeps at the sight of the distorted forms of the diviners of *Inferno* 20, he sees him as inviting the reader to join with him in a sympathy for their plight which approaches the catharsis evoked by classical tragedy.[9] For Barchiesi this is a momentary experience. Vergil's sharp rebuke of the Pilgrim's misguided *pietà* reawakens him to the stern logic of divine justice, and marks the limit of his susceptibility to the tragic view of life. For the Vergil who had allowed his Aeneas and Dido to share, not only passion, but a deep sense of the *lacrimae rerum* which express the human condition, is also the Vergil who affirms justice as Aeneas' defining characteristic, and dismisses the selfish and arbitrary gods of the *Aeneid* as "falsi e bugiardi" (*Inf.* 1.72–73). His harsh words to Dante in the valley of the false seers prepare us for an episode in which the blindness of paganism is exposed once and for all.[10]

I am not sure that *Inferno* 20 can be interpreted so decisively,[11] and I am quite sure that Dante's experience of what Barchiesi calls "human and classical catharsis" extends well beyond this episode. It is present in his response to Ulysses and even Ugolino, and it is an essential factor in the reading of the *Thebaid* on which his invention of the crypto-Christian Statius is founded. Even in Paradise he will temper a conventional denunciation of the lustful Dido by reminding us of her heroic qualities. Indeed nothing is more remarkable in Dante's dealings with the Poeti than his ability to preserve their human, tragic perspective on the personae of their poems while placing these figures in a radically new perspective. From beginning to end of the *Commedia* he views them face-to-face.

Barchiesi's view of Vergil seems to me similarly limiting. Where Barchiesi sees him wholly as a stable and stabilizing presence, one who teaches Dante to avoid the emotional and ethical pitfalls of his own poem, I would argue that his influence on Dante is as varied and complex as the *Aeneid* itself. One of the most startling, almost uncanny features of the *Inferno* is Dante's ability to show how a remembered moment in the *Aeneid*

---

9. Barchiesi, "Catarsi classica," 72–76.
10. Barchiesi, "Catarsi classica," 76.
11. See below, chap. 3, pp. 73–79.

can determine his response to his immediate situation. And we, too, if we are sufficiently attentive to how Vergilian echoes and undertones enrich and darken the tone of Dante's lines, can recover from them something of the complexity of Dante's experience as a would-be-Christian poet in hell. He has assimilated ancient poetry, and above all the poetry of Vergil, to the point at which it informs and sustains his own, justifying his claim to a place in the "bella scola"; again and again an attentive reader can experience the "hidden reserve of literary energy" that is released when one recognizes the dynamic relation between a passage in Dante and the ancient text to which it alludes.[12]

But this energy is hard to control, and resists, often powerfully, Dante's attempts to assert himself as the author of a comedy. When Dante's sense of his own larger purpose flags, the bleak spiritual horizons of paganism encroach on his vision, and his poetry becomes for a time the vehicle of a tragic and fatalistic view of history. Unable to muster in himself a Christian compassion for the suffering he encounters in the underworld (and finally forbidden even a purely humane *pietà*), he is drawn, by his deep but often misguided sympathy with Vergil, into darker emotions—other, more self-indulgent modes of pity, but also something like despair. His fascination with the representational powers of Lucan and Ovid provokes him to the indulgence of an anger that continually threatens to become merely cruel, and imitation that erupts into rivalry. Such moments can involve a radical loss of autonomy, and letting the ancient author dictate his course becomes dangerous. Though his careful placement of his encounters with the several Poeti suggests an orderly and definitive appropriation of the epic tradition, they are in large part a remarkably explicit dramatization of the anxiety of influence. Aspiring to a purity of vision impossible for a pagan poet, Dante is continually nagged by desire, anger, and violence in the archetypal forms in which the Poeti present them, for as their first true modern disciple he cannot avoid sharing their preoccupations.

In this uncertain state Dante shows himself responsive to ancient poetry at a level more profound than *imitatio*, but only gradually becomes

---

12. See Conte, *Rhetoric of Imitation*, 33.

capable of that full appropriation of the master texts which the medieval arts of poetry call *aemulatio*.[13] Though the "bella scola," recognizing the depth of his understanding of their poems, honor Dante by declaring him "sesto tra cotanto senno" (*Inf.* 4.102), effectively conferring on him the title of Poeta, it is only when his long pilgrimage is nearly complete that he is able to imagine claiming this title for himself (*Par.* 25.1–9). Only by completely subjecting himself to the authority of the "bella scola," learning, by a kind of negative capability, to view his own life, and human existence as a whole, through their eyes, could Dante realize the full power of their poetic art and the vision that informed it. Only through an experience of such immediacy and depth could he claim to be himself a true poet, his own appropriation of the ancient poets an authentic reconfiguring of the classical tradition such as they themselves had effected. And only when possessed of the authority of a poet in this highest sense could he genuinely claim the spiritual distance from these great forebears that is essential to his transformation of the tradition.

For many critics of the *Commedia,* Dante's undeniable distancing of himself from the Poeti has seemed to constitute an assertion of superiority. But this is a claim I do not believe Dante himself would have made. He would have been in full sympathy with Eliot's rejoinder to the charge that we "know so much more" than the classical authors did: "Precisely. And they are that which we know."[14] If there is a sense in which Dante is superior to the ancient poets it is because he has been permitted, through supervenient grace, to see beyond tragedy, to affirm truths that they in moments of quasi-religious inspiration had dimly intuited, and through this knowledge escape the tyranny of fatalism. Thoroughly schooled in classical ethics, he has learned through Christian humility the limits of the "magnanimity," stoic courage, and *pietas* that were the noblest attributes his Roman mentors could conceive.

But Dante is at the same time keenly sensitive to the ways in which the Roman poets had differed among themselves in their attitudes toward duty, destiny, and fate, and his assertion of a difference that is finally

---

13. See Picone, "Dante argonauta," 173–76; Farrell, *Vergil's Georgics,* 4–5.
14. Eliot, "Tradition and the Individual Talent," 16.

absolute coexists with a deep awareness of the continuity of his own trans-formative project with theirs. Whatever sense of a truly prophetic voca-tion he may have had, Dante knew that his ability to see more clearly than his great forebears was largely a matter of history. His conception of the distinctive qualities of the Poeti is grounded in his sense of the historical context in which each had written, and he saw Roman poetry as having evolved spiritually even in the absence of Christian revelation. The histori-cal significance of Vergil, the prophet of empire, is made explicit in vari-ous ways, and is of course fundamental to Dante's use of him, but history is a factor in his assessment of the other Poeti as well. It is no coincidence that the poets in Limbo are named in chronological order. Ovid, a genera-tion younger than Vergil, and unique in that his life bridged the divide between the pagan and Christian eras, plays a dynamic role in both the pagan and the Christian world of the *Commedia,* and is the one poet whose historical situation is not clearly demarcated. But Lucan, whose entire life was lived under the early emperors, is represented emblematically by the Cato of the *Purgatorio,* whose life and values, admirable though they ap-pear, reflect the futility of mere pagan virtue in a world which has lost faith in its gods. And Statius might well have borne witness, as Dante's Statius claims to have done, to the sufferings of the martyrs and the grow-ing influence of Christian preaching in the Rome of Domitian. His imag-ined conversion reflects Dante's response to strong spiritual undertones in the *Thebaid* which modern criticism is only now rediscovering.

But I am concerned most of all with *how* these poets are present to Dante, what was at stake for him as he sought a new kind of relationship with them. As I have suggested, taking their poetry seriously meant, first and foremost, experiencing it directly and as nearly as possible on its own terms, as the essential precondition for adapting it to his purposes. Like Alan of Lille, like Augustine and Milton, Dante conveys through his lan-guage what a fully appreciative reading of these poets involves, what it means to expose oneself as fully as possible to the forces that shaped their poetry, forces which remain latent in the texts that survive them. We can understand their value for him only when we have recognized how he reawakened these forces, participated in the limited historical and spiri-tual vision of his chosen Poeti through an act of sympathetic imagination, and underwent in his own literary persona the experience that they them-selves had sought to convey.

In emphasizing the existential aspect of Dante's engagement with the great Roman poets, I may seem to be arguing for a reading of the *Commedia* as something other than a religious poem, and in a sense this is true. I want to demonstrate that the story of Dante the spiritual pilgrim coexists with an equally coherent narrative of artistic development, a coexistence which is not peaceful and remains unresolved. In this respect, I would suggest, Dante is a profoundly Boethian figure, whose poem, like Boethius' great *Consolation,* records both profound growth in spiritual awareness and an all-too-human sense of the difficulties involved in seeking to transcend purely human concerns. The Dante who must descend again to the world after his experience of Paradise is at once the prophet-reformer of Cacciaguida's exhortations and a mere man, one who, like the Boethius whose silence is the most striking feature of the final stages of the *Consolation,* continues to harbor anxieties about the workings of providence and the dispensation of justice.

In arguing for a Dante whose ongoing earthly story both complements and disrupts his spiritual progress, I am aware of following in the footsteps of Teodolinda Barolini. From beginning to end of this project I have kept *Dante's Poets* within easy reach, and much of my argument is encapsulated in her observation that "the poets of the *Comedy* constitute a carefully fashioned narrative," Dante's reading of which is at the same time a "self-reading."[15] She speaks for me when she notes the care with which he deploys the term *poeta,* making clear by at last appropriating the title for himself that he is a poet in the epic sense, "fulfilling and completing a poetic itinerary that begins with the *Aeneid* and that finds in the *Comedy* . . . its last and highest form of expression."[16]

But for Barolini the importance of ancient epic as a standard of artistic achievement is largely emblematic. Dante's most significant encounters with poetry as such are with the vernacular, as represented both by earlier Italian and Provençal lyric and by his own *canzoni.* Vergil and Statius, who represent the classical tradition, are treated mainly in terms of the roles played by their *ombre* in the narrative of the *Commedia,* and with very little specific reference to their own poems. Statius' presence, indeed, is for

---

15. *Dante's Poets,* xiii.

16. *Dante's Poets,* 270–71.

Barolini a matter of convenience. His boundless admiration for the *Aeneid,* together with a historical situation which makes plausible his exposure to Christianity, serves to set off by contrast the uncertain position of Vergil, at once the artistic superior and the spiritual inferior of his disciple.[17]

I have aimed to tell the other side of the story, by emphasizing the intimacy of Dante's engagement with the texts of the Poeti, the extent to which his gradual discovery of his own mission as a vernacular poet depended on a close and attentive reading of his Latin models. And I am aware that in arguing, as I do, that Dante encountered ancient epic as nearly as possible on its own terms, I may seem to be rejecting the well-established typological approach to the classical elements in his poetry. This approach, which aims to show how classical poetry is subsumed and made to serve Dante's Christian purposes, has produced some of the finest modern criticism of the *Commedia,* and I hope that my study may help to provide a richer context and a more solid grounding for such criticism. But I am also concerned to demonstrate the need for a less exclusive application of this approach, which has tended to more or less neutralize the power inherent in ancient poetry as Dante received it, in the process of demonstrating its value as a foil to his Christian vision.

Seminal for this critical method is of course Auerbach's argument that the classical concreteness of Dante's characters provides the basis for a "figural" reading, similar to that whereby the events and personae of the Old Testament are related to those of the New.[18] Giuseppe Mazzotta, refining this approach, views the relation of Dante's classical personae to his religious vision as more nearly reciprocal. By assigning a typological role to a Cato or an Aeneas, Dante is not isolating the character and his telos from their secular context, but inviting us to view their position in that context from a redeeming perspective in which the concrete events of pagan history assume an integral relation to the pattern of spiritual history.[19] Whereas in Auerbach's readings there is always something arbitrary about the relation of the figure to its meaning—a gap between concreteness and figurality that he does not seek to bridge—for Maz-

---

17. *Dante's Poets,* 256–62.
18. "'Figura,'" 60–76.
19. Mazzotta, *Dante, Poet,* 3–4, 58–68, 170–80.

zotta the more we know of the original context from which the figure derives, the richer the typological reading it can be made to yield.

But a certain arbitrariness is perhaps inevitable when a biblically grounded theory of representation is applied to secular texts, and Mazzotta's readings, too, are selective, privileging certain details and suppressing others. The Poeti are suspended between pagan and Christian history, and everything depends on our ability to read them with sensitivity while resisting the seduction of the alienated desire that lurks in pagan texts. To avoid "the trap of narcissistic literary identification" we must open the text to new meaning by a "violent" act of interpretation. In practice this means accepting the allegories of the grammarians at one moment and rejecting them at another, now affirming and now dismissing the religious intuitions of the pagan author, and thus constituting for ourselves the *sensus proprius* of the text.[20]

The practice of letting the objectives and procedures of typological reading determine our understanding of Dante's use of the Poeti is deeply ingrained in modern criticism of Dante. It pervades an excellent recent collection of essays that address Dante's "poetry of allusion" as it engages Vergil and Ovid. The authors conceive allusion in broad terms, taking account of "'dialectical' and 'synecdochical' cross-references, oblique echoes, and even 'screened' or suppressed allusions."[21] This volume has been essential to my own reading of Dante, as my notes will make clear. But here, too, typological thinking too often preempts a fully objective approach to the classical texts. The authors aim to acknowledge the depth of Dante's understanding of the *Aeneid,* comparing his reading to the body of recent criticism that has emphasized the poem's darker aspects, and they recognize a dialogic element in his engagement with Vergil. But by defining the purpose of this dialogue as "remotivating the idea of Vergil as a proto-Christian prophet," and stressing the quasi-scriptural status of the *Aeneid* in Dante's canon of chosen texts,[22] they tend to foreclose the possibility of our viewing Dante as first and foremost a sympathetic reader of Vergil's poetry for its own sake and on its own terms.

---

20. Mazzotta, *Dante, Poet,* 188–91.
21. Jacoff and Schnapp, eds., *Poetry of Allusion,* "Introduction," 2.
22. Jacoff and Schnapp, "Introduction," 3–4, 10–12.

It is certainly the case that the historical narrative fashioned by Vergil enjoys a privileged status in Dante's worldview, and in the *Commedia* Vergil himself is granted a power of understanding that can seem to approach the prophetic. But the full significance of the *Aeneid* as a "provisionally sacred text" can emerge only when we have recognized how fully Dante himself experienced it as a compelling and authoritative text in its own right.[23] The truth of the *Aeneid* to the pattern of sacred history must clearly be determined by the external standard of a religious vision which, for Dante, ultimately subsumes it, but Dante makes equally clear the importance, for himself and for his readers, of experiencing the human truth of Vergil's vision of human existence, and in particular the ways in which his representation of the underworld expresses this vision, before imposing any such judgment. For Dante's Vergil is held to a stricter standard than the Statius of the *Purgatorio,* and his special role depends fundamentally on the truth of the *Aeneid* in its historical context. If Vergil's damnation is a spiritual tragedy, it is the insights and intuitions of his poetry that constitute his claim to salvation, as only the limitations of the vision embodied in his poetry can finally justify the denial of that claim. Both the insights and the limitations of the Vergilian vision are probed again and again in the *Commedia,* and by giving careful attention, not just to their potential figural significance, but to their immediate effect on Dante, as reader and disciple, we can perhaps gain a better understanding both of why Dante reveres Vergil as he does and of why he must nonetheless let him remain in Limbo.

Ovid, too, plays a more complex and immediate role in the *Commedia* than the prevailing tendencies of recent criticism would suggest. For the authors of *The Poetry of Allusion* he is the ideal foil to Dante the typological poet. The *Metamorphoses* exhibit a "poetics of exemplarity," a narrative mode that culminates in memorable images of the effects of passion that lend themselves to allegorization. Thus in dealing with Ovid's tales of erotic violence, Dante "revises the equation of Eros and death" by

---

23. In this Dante differs significantly from Augustine, in other respects the ideal model of the reader, but a reader for whom an "aesthetic" engagement with pagan texts is always to be mistrusted. See Stock, *Augustine the Reader,* 26–33.

supplying the teleological purpose that is missing in Ovid, superimposing a Christian narrative of "sublime and sublimated" love.[24] In themselves the *Metamorphoses* have none of the provisional sanctity of the *Aeneid*. One contributor to *The Poetry of Allusion* has suggested elsewhere that Ovid is "a poet happily going nowhere," refusing the responsibilities of epic and taking each new fable as a fresh challenge to his *ingenium*.[25]

The asssumptions underlying this approach have been stated more explicitly by Warren Ginsberg. In Ovid, he says, "metamorphosis is a device that locates the meaning of a text exclusively in its surface." In rewriting Ovid's great poem, Dante aims "to show that under God's inspection, its sole ethical import consists in the fact that its changes are only superficial, that they have no inner meaning, but continually look to further change" while in Dante's hands metamorphosis "changes from fiction to a figure of allegory, the soul's impaired form, justice, conversion, the Incarnation, and the Resurrection."[26]

Dante clearly found in Ovid an ideal foil to his own dramatizations of ethical and spiritual crisis. But has he simply exploited the two-dimensionality of Ovid's representations of change to set off his own images of more profound transformation, or has Ovid helped him see his way to this new perspective? Determining the spirit and purpose of Ovid's poetry is of course a fundamental problem, probably unresolvable. Is the *Ars Amatoria* a handbook for seducers, a kamasutra, a parodic affront to the official Roman virtues, a shrewd and sensitive commentary on the importance and difficulty of intimacy? Is it all of these? None of these? Does the point of the *Heroides* inhere in its comedy, the seemingly inexhaustible energy with which Ovid's abandoned ladies show themselves deluded by passion or ignorance? Or is it a tribute to Euripides and the Vergil of

---

24. Jacoff and Schnapp, "Introduction," 10–11.

25. Hawkins, *Dante's Testaments*, 149–50. This view of Ovid as essentially a stylist who "celebrates himself and his own sustained tour de force" is balanced by a subtle and sensitive reading of Dante's interaction with Ovid in Hawkins' essay "Watching Matelda" (Jacoff and Schnapp, eds., *Poetry of Allusion*, 181–201; *Dante's Testaments*, 159–79).

26. Ginsberg, *Dante's Aesthetics*, 116, 134, 146, 150. See also Barolini, *Dante's Poets*, 223–26; Cioffi, "Anxieties of Ovidian Influence," 92–96.

Aeneid 4, an appeal for a reassessment of the conventions of heroic poetry? Ovid clearly knows the *Aeneid* more or less by heart: Does he deeply admire Vergil, or does he find his utter seriousness amusing?

As many as the stars in the sky are the readings of Ovid's poems. This is true above all of the *Metamorphoses,* and perhaps the beginning of wisdom about this work is to recognize that it defies moral judgment. Metamorphosis, as Joseph Solodow observes, "is the opposite of morality."[27] Charles Segal, in a study which did much to enlarge our view of the poem, nicely defines the problems one meets in trying to determine Ovid's moral outlook. Where Hermann Fraenkel and other sympathetic readers see Ovid as affirming the value of "the concerns of the mind and heart" in the face of force and natural law, Segal notes that purely physical forces prevail again and again in the *Metamorphoses.*[28] We may, if we choose, see Ovid as expressing, consciously or not, a more or less political attitude, "a sense of the helplessness and vulnerability of the individual in the vast Roman *imperium.*"[29] But the continual emphasis on suffering and loss is not always easy to read. We may hesitate to see Ovid himself as the quasi-sadist some readers have found him, the connoisseur of suffering whose rhetoric toys with our emotions, daring us to identify with his characters and then mocking our sentimentality.[30] But he can often seem to have created more suffering than he can fully control, so that the world of his poem appears dominated by arbitrary and purposeless cruelty.[31]

It is also, of course, possible to read Ovid's position, his apparently deliberate refusal to let the meaning of his text be rendered finite, as a principled stand against interpretation, an invitation to his readers to let sheer human sympathy determine their response. Such a reading enables Ralph Johnson to declare the *Metamorphoses* "among the most charitable poems in western literature."[32] But perhaps no major poem

---

27. *World,* p. 157.

28. Segal, *Landscape,* 86, citing Fraenkel, *Ovid,* 89.

29. Segal, *Landscape,* 92.

30. For this view, see Galinsky, *Ovid's Metamorphoses,* 63, 129–38; Williams, *Change and Decline,* 188–90, 254–61; Richlin, "Reading Ovid's Rapes."

31. Segal, *Landscape,* 92–93.

32. "Counter-classical Sensibility," 147; also Fraenkel, *Ovid,* 20 -23, 83–84, 90, 95; Pucci, *Full-Knowing Reader,* 197–222.

in the western tradition is harder to read, *in bono* or *in malo,* in a consistent way.

Dante acknowledges Ovid's complexity in various, and at times un-
expected, ways. One of the more subtle, though it appears at first glance
the most obvious, is the famous moment in *Inferno* 25 when he explicitly
claims to have outdone the poet of the *Metamorphoses* as an engineer of
transformation. We are bound to be struck by the recklessness of Dante's
artistry here, his evident fascination with the sheer power of his description and his disregard for the dangers inherent in the imagining of cruelty.
There is no point in the *Inferno* at which the serious issues involved in the
passing of judgment are more flagrantly ignored, and the depiction of punishment more clearly an end in itself. The problem of passing judgment
will become more complex as the Pilgrim descends to the lowest circles of
Dis, and Dante will be tempted with other opportunities to test his powers
by imitating the Poeti, but here he carries sheer artistic presumption to an
extreme. His claim to have redefined the poetics of metamorphosis seems
almost to reduce divine judgment itself to a matter of artistic skill.

But while these are issues about which Ovid could teach him a great
deal, Ovid in fact is not clearly implicated in Dante's overreaching. Though
Dante borrows details from several Ovidian metamorphoses, the descriptions against which he explicitly pits his own, the transformations of
Cadmus and Arethusa, are notable for their lack of the cruelty on display
here.[33] Cadmus, long haunted by the fear of having been guilty of impiety
in slaying the serpent that had killed his companions (*Met.* 3.32–94), prays
in old age to become himself a serpent; his prayer is granted, his wife is
similarly transformed, and the two live on in a tranquillity that recalls the
Golden Age (*Met.* 4.602–3).[34] The transformation of the nymph Arethusa
into a stream is again the response to a prayer, uttered as she flees the lust
of the river god Alpheus, who then resumes his own watery shape to
mingle with her (*Met.* 5.618–38). In both episodes the gods and the natural world seem to regard human *pietas* with benevolence.

---

33. See Pucci, *Full-Knowing Reader,* 211–13.

34. Kirkpatrick, *Dante's "Inferno,"* 320–22, argues that transforming a human
being into a serpent would have offended Dante ipso facto, as a degradation of the
human figure. But this seems to ignore both Ovid's lines and Cadmus' relation to
Theban history.

As the *Commedia* proceeds, it is a humane Ovid that we encounter, the Ovid whose crises of transformation often suggest a spirituality which cannot find fulfillment in the world of his poem, whose sensitivity to the disruptive power of desire models Dante's experience at crucial stages. Ovid's acute awareness of the implications and dangers of artistic creation also significantly informs Dante's reflections on his own project. And the world Dante views from the enlightening distance of Paradise is essentially an image of Ovidian mythic history.

It is Lucan who, in depicting the horrible deaths inflicted on the soldiers Sabellus and Nasidius by venomous serpents, displays the seemingly pointless, virtuoso cruelty to which Dante surrenders himself in *Inferno* 25. But Lucan's descriptions, while deliberately fantastic as well as brutal, have a definite purpose within the larger economy of the *Pharsalia*.[35] Dante's violence is ostensibly purposeful, and his victims are simultaneously destroyed and reconstituted, but as he will later confess, the reason for his long account is the "novità" of what he describes (*Inf.* 25.144), and its relation to the economy of the *Inferno* remains obscure: Dante acknowledges that he did not recognize the three figures whom he transforms (*Inf.* 25.40), and it is from the commentators that we possess our largely conjectural knowledge of their identities and crimes.

That Lucan should be the instigator here is very much of a piece with his larger role in the *Inferno,* but it is significant that it is Ovid whom Dante challenges most directly. It is an implicit judgment on Dante's proud gesture that he is engaging Ovid at a superficial level, and his own creativity is operating in a correspondingly meaningless way. By making it clear through his allusions that it is Lucan's poetry rather than Ovid's that provides the real provocation for his tour de force, Dante obliquely acknowledges an Ovid who is far more than the cynical virtuoso his challenge seems to address, and whose role will become more meaningful as the *Commedia* progresses.

Lucan, too, plays a larger role in the *Commedia* than this brief encounter would suggest. Study of Dante's dealings with the *Pharsalia* has centered on what Auerbach, Mazzotta, and many others have seen as the

---

35. See below, chap. 4, pp. 106–8.

finest example of Dante's assimilation of pagan poetry and history, his re-creation of the Roman statesman and general Cato, who had committed suicide rather than submit to Caesar, but whom Dante makes the guardian of the shores of Purgatory. There is almost universal agreement among Dantisti that Cato is a pagan saint, a Roman Moses, the embodiment of the many virtues attributed to Lucan's hero in the *Convivio*. But this reading of Cato is based on an uncritical reading of Lucan himself. For Dante the *Pharsalia* is always the caustic and despairing chronicle of the demise of the Roman republic, and he was well aware that its characterization of Cato is significantly more complex than the *Convivio* portrayal would suggest. Lucan's Cato is not just the embodiment of Stoic virtue and loyalty to the republican ideal, but an extremist whose principles, as enunciated by himself, are self-centered, politically shortsighted, and inhumane. Dante's view of Cato is somewhat more benign but significantly ambiguous. The Pilgrim's encounter with Cato is a liminal event, in which the laws of the *Inferno* give way grudgingly to the liberative spirit of Purgatory. It also marks a complex and ambiguous stage in the reclaiming of poetry from a nether world where it had existed largely as what Vergil calls "scritta morta" (*Inf.* 8.127).

Dante's Cato is also the final exercise in a Lucanian mode which first emerges in Canto 9 of the *Inferno,* where Vergil makes the oddly casual announcement that he was once summoned forth from Limbo by the witch Erichtho, and made to descend to the lowest circle of Dis. Dante knew Erichtho from her role in the *Pharsalia,* where, though she makes a single memorable appearance, she can be seen as emblematizing Lucan's poetic enterprise in its cynical, subversive aspect. Her intrusion into the *Commedia,* on the basis of a fable which is surely Dante's own, marks a significant shift in the relations of the Pilgrim with Vergil, whose authority is questioned in various ways in the ensuing cantos, which can be seen as the Lucanian portion of the *Inferno.* Her spell is decisively broken only when the travelers have met with Cato and moved on.

Dante's reading of Vergil, Ovid, and Lucan seems remarkably unaffected by the allegorizing tradition of the medieval schools, whose methods are clearly reflected in his more or less typological treatment of these authors in the *Convivio.* The case of Statius is different, in that here Dante can appear to be practicing typological criticism of the most radical kind.

Making a Christian of the author of the *Thebaid* would seem to require, among other things, suppressing the Statius whose Thebes provides the standard by which political treachery is judged in the *Inferno*, and making the most of a small store of potentially allegorizable details. But Dante's Statius is not just the embodiment of an allegorization of the *Thebaid*, as many Dantisti would have him, and Dante's invention involves a good deal more than the privileging of a few fleeting moments of spiritual intuition in Statius' poetry. Dante, always a superbly attentive reader, has discovered in the *Thebaid* a deep, and for the pagan Statius an irresolvable, conflict between epic purpose and a total repudiation of epic in favor of a narrative centered on private and largely feminine virtues. In his oscillation between these two perspectives he resembles the Ovid who moves freely between cruelty and pathos, but his view of the world of his poem is finally closest to the benign reading of an Ovid who "takes the part of the personal and subjective against what is grand and universal."[36]

My project, then, is to show that Dante's engagement with his pagan sources is more intimate, more closely responsive to the distinctive qualities of their poetry, and far less violently interpretive than even the most thoughtful modern studies would suggest. It depends on a "self-transposition," an imagining of the particularity and otherness of their worldview that depends on seeing the world as nearly as possible through their eyes. When he achieves this without losing sight of himself and his present situation, he achieves a "higher universality," a breadth of vision that transcends both his own particularity and that of the ancient poet.[37] When, on the other hand, he merely abandons himself to the influence of the poet's vision, the result is a profound disorientation; it is at such moments that Dante becomes "smarrito," unable to speak or act, and even loses consciousness.

---

36. Solodow, *World*, 158.

37. The terms within quotation marks in this and the previous sentence are those of Gadamer, *Truth and Method*, 300–307, a discussion of "consciousness of being affected by history" which has been important to my thinking about the workings of poetic tradition.

In what follows I have aimed to show that Dante's dealings with epic tradition are integral to the narrative of the *Commedia*. At several points I will be charged with having explored an allusion at unecessary length— Arachne in *Purgatorio* 12, for example, or Juno and Iris in the opening simile of *Paradiso* 12. But I have done so to demonstrate as fully as possible the richness of Dante's understanding of the Poeti, the depth to which his allusions plumb the archive of poetic knowledge embodied in their texts. I have highlighted the presence of individual Poeti at different points in the poem in order to suggest the character of the influence exercised by each, but I hope it will be clear that their interaction in Dante's artistic consciousness is the crucial determinant of their importance for him. And I hope it will be clear as well why I have emphasized the importance of Dante's unmediated response to the texts of the Poeti, and largely ignored the contributions of the grammarians and mythographers in determining the format in which he read these texts. For we can understand the role of ancient poetry in establishing the distinctive horizon of Dante's private experience, the world-historical perspective of the *Commedia,* and the basis this history provides for allegory, only by first studying Dante the reader as he submits himself to the power of precisely the "seductive and unredeemed" qualities of this poetry, and so deliberately opens his own poem to what Barolini calls a "detheologizing" reading.[38] The implications of this poetic experience remain a central concern throughout the *Commedia,* and its importance is clear from the opening episode, where Dante encounters Vergil and begins his ongoing engagement with that great "text of desire," the *Aeneid.*[39]

---

38. See Barolini, *undivine Comedy,* 17: "Detheologizing is . . . a way of reading that attempts to break out of the hermeneutic guidelines that result in theologized readings whose outcomes have been overdetermined by the author."

39. See Mazzotta, *Dante,* 150–59.

2

Vergil in the *Inferno*

Scritta morta

The power of poetic language, and the language of Vergil in particular, plays a crucial role in our introduction to Dante's underworld. Canto 3 of the *Inferno* has rightly been called the "canto virgiliano per eccellenza"[1] for it not only inaugurates the descent into hell, but brings to its climax a reading of Vergil that is a central concern of the opening cantos. It begins, however, with a wholly anonymous passage whose power seems almost self-generated, the lines which Vergil himself will later recall as "scritta morta" (*Inf.* 8.127), the inscription over the gate of hell:

> Per me si va ne la città dolente,
> > per me si va ne l'etterno dolore,
> > per me si va tra la perduta gente.

---

1. Padoan, "Il canto III," 50; Paratore, "Canto III," 27–28.

Giustizia mosse il mio alto fattore;
   fecemi la divina podestate,
   la somma sapïenza e 'l primo amore.
Dinanzi a me non fuor cose create
   se non etterne, e io etterno duro.
   Lasciate ogne speranza, voi ch'intrate.
                       (*Inf.* 3.1–9)

[Through me you enter the woeful city, through me you
enter eternal grief, through me you enter among the lost.
Justice moved my high maker: The divine power made
me, the supreme wisdom, and the primal love. Before me
nothing was created if not eternal, and eternal I endure.
Abandon every hope, you who enter.]

We cannot know who speaks these lines, or to whom. We learn that they
appear above an entrance, but their function remains unclear. They are "of
an obscure color," and their effect for Dante is "duro" (10, 12), terms which
may refer to the physical inscription or to its ominously depersonalized
rhetoric, and in either case reinforce an effect of ruthless and alien authority. The somber eloquence of the first few lines, each a self-contained
syntactic unit, resists the coordinative influence of terza rima, and suggests
the movement of spondaic hexameter. The passage exerts a strange control, forcing us to submit ourselves imaginatively to an experience we will
come to recognize as a vicarious form of damnation.

The inscription has an undeniably epic quality. But as we will learn, its
somber menace is illusory: The very force which created hell has already
demonstrated the vulnerability to assault of this seeming barrier, and the
power of God to free those within. Hence the gate and the inscription are
an appropriate introduction to the ruined monumentality of the underworld, and the dominant effect of the inscription is irony. Its language, like
the people whose fate it proclaims, is alienated from purpose and meaning, what Vergil will call "il ben de l'intelletto" (18).[2] Its repeated use of the

---

2. See Freccero, *Poetics*, 100–101.

first person anticipates the futile self-assertions of the damned, and its declarations are really negations. That it has endured unaltered since the beginning of time attests to its authority but exposes the lifeless, negative character of that authority, which, like the proud inscription on the pedestal of Shelley's Ozymandias, mocks itself by its very affirmation. The eternity it claims is not that of the "belle cose" of the primal creation but a secondary manifestation of divine power, occasioned by sin.[3] Like every created thing, it is a work of "il primo amore," yet it attests only the alienation of those within from any participation in that love.

In describing the gateway to Dis Vergil had emphasized its massiveness, and the impregnability of the citadel itself (*Aen.* 6.552–54). Dante's inscription, presumably graven in stone, seems to claim a similar substantiality. It recalls as well the inscrutable portentousness of the great stones and stone monuments that are part of the landscape of epic, reminders of the heroic past. But the endurance of such monuments is subject to the power of nature and the gods, who work inexorably to obscure and finally obliterate that past,[4] and the authority declared by the inscription is similarly subject to the divine will. The power it claims is utterly negative, dependent on the demoralization of the human will by ignorance or sin. In this respect its role resembles that of the Old Law in the economy of salvation: since the passion of Christ this Law is "dead" ("mortua") in that it is no longer binding; since the promulgation of the Gospel it is also "deadly" ("mortifera"), in that its continued observance denies the truths of faith.[5] To accept the authority of the inscription is to commit essentially the same fatal historical error. It thus provides a first intimation of how the process of damnation works, and how we collaborate in it, a process which we will see enacted as Dante moves forward, keenly aware of the precedent of Vergil's underworld, and with Vergil's language reverberating in his mind.

---

3. On this eternity that is not quite eternal, see Boccaccio's gloss on *Inf.* 3.8, *Esposizioni* 3.5–7; Thomas Aquinas, *Summa Theologiae* 1.10.3 ad 2.

4. See Ford, *Homer,* 138–57.

5. See Thomas, *Summa,* 1.2. 103.4, 104.3. Thomas distinguishes "ceremonial" from "judicial" precepts. The latter are still valid insofar as their authority does not depend on their being identified with the Law.

The lifeless poetry of the inscription is a distillation of what Dante will experience as the negative power of pagan poetry in its tragic aspect, the extreme fatalism toward which such poetry gravitates in the absence of hope. It echoes the grim warning of Vergil's Sibyl, that the descent into hell is all too easy, and its somber power is lurking throughout the *Aeneid*, the poem which, more than any other, has opened the infernal depths to Dante's imagination. Throughout Canto 3, Vergilian language will exhibit a power that resembles the awful, demoralizing power of the inscription. Vergil is, of course, the bearer of salutary doctrine, but as the opening cantos emphasize repeatedly, he is first and foremost a source of poetic language, the "parlare onesto" of the *Aeneid*. And an important consequence of Dante's profound sensitivity to Vergilian language is that the darkness which surfaces at crucial moments in the *Aeneid*—profound misgivings about the meaning and value of human life and history, the temptation of fatalism that burdens both the poet and his hero—is audible as well at the most Vergilian moments in the *Inferno*. It is suggested at several points that the inscription's proclamation of the finality of damnation has an authority for Vergil that at times seems to contradict his assurances to Dante.[6] But before looking closely at Vergil's role and that of his poetry it will be helpful to consider how Vergil first emerges into the world of the *Commedia*.

Reading Vergil

The initial encounter of Pilgrim and poet in Canto 1 is preceded by a description of dawn, and its effect on the Pilgrim as he begins to ascend the mountain:

> Temp' era dal principio del mattino,
> e 'l sol montava 'n sù con quelle stelle
> ch'eran con lui quando l'amor divino

---

6. Vergil knows of Christ's descent into hell, but sees "antichi spiriti" like himself as irrevocably damned ("perduti," "sanza speme," *Inf.* 4.41–42), and later fears that Medusa may prevent Dante's return to the world (9.56–57).

mosse di prima quelle cose belle;
  sì ch'a bene sperar m'era cagione

  . . .

l'ora del tempo e la dolce stagione.
                    (*Inf.* 1.37–42)

[It was the beginning of the morning, and the sun was
mounting with the stars that were with it when Divine Love
first set those beautiful things in motion, so that the hour of
the day and the sweet season gave me cause for good hope.]

The significance of this Edenic moment is emphasized by contrast when
Dante, harassed by the lion and wolf, retreats downward, toward a region
"dove 'l sol tace" (60). The obvious reference of this phrase is to the darkness from which Dante had emerged, and toward which he now reverts.
But it refers also to a state of consciousness in which the order of the universe can no longer, as in the lines quoted above, speak to him. Where
the sun is silent, the world presents itself devoid of meaning. And it is in
this uncertain state or place, where meaning has been suspended, that
Dante encounters a figure whom "long silence" has rendered "faint" or
"indistinct" ("fioco," 1.63).

It is significant that the same synesthetic formula, a failure of vision
defined as an absence of articulate sound, expresses the artistic as well as
the cosmic aspect of Dante's crisis. Whatever else Vergil's "lungo silenzio"
may mean, it clearly refers to a time during which the true character of
Vergil's poetry has been lost—that character which Dante will revive in
the *Commedia*.[7] For it is language, the "bello stilo" of Vergil, that Dante
stresses in defining their relationship. It is through Vergil's "parola ornata,"
his "parlare onesto," that Beatrice hopes to draw Dante back to the true
path (*Inf.* 2.67, 113). And it is the mediating power of Vergil's words that
will enable Dante to set forth on his journey confident that divine powers are at work on his behalf (2.136–38). Mastery of Vergil's "bello stilo,"
already realized in his *canzoni,* will now enable him to express more fully

---

7. See Consoli, *Significato del Virgilio Dantesco,* 34–45.

the "buono ardire" which love of Beatrice arouses in him. Vergilian poetry will emerge from long silence wrought into a new, spiritual design, as the visible universe assumes a deeper meaning when recognized as ordered by divine love, and through this design Dante will reestablish himself in his right relation to that love.

As Vergil presents himself to the Pilgrim, he seems clearly to be the vessel of a poetry that will readily serve the purposes of the Christian poet. The *Aeneid* affirms the continuity and purpose of history and Rome's divinely sanctioned role as legislator of world order. Vergilian language is a unique instrument, able to express the highest human aspirations and the sacrifices they require. Under Vergil's influence Dante will become both a new Aeneas and the poet of a new, Christian Rome where all are fellow citizens with Christ (*Purg.* 32.102).

But before all this can happen Dante must come to terms with a Vergil who has a history of his own. Before responding to the Pilgrim's hapless "'*Miserere* di me'" Vergil reconstitutes himself as he had existed in the world (Mantua, Lombardy, Rome), in history (the era of Julius and Augustus Caesar), and as the poet of Aeneas' journeying after the fall of Troy (*Inf.* 1.67–75). Only then does he acknowledge the Pilgrim, and his abrupt first question seems detached and imperceptive, a dismissal of Dante's plight as mere folly:

> "Ma tu perché ritorni a tanta noia?
>   perché non sali il dilettoso monte
>   ch'è principio e cagion di tutta gioia?"
> (Inf. 1.76–78)

> ["But you, why do you return to so much woe? Why do you
> not climb the delectable mountain, the source and cause of
> every happiness?"]

Vergil knows only too well the "noia" toward which the Pilgrim's ruinous descent is tending, but seems to have no sense of the gravitation of spirit that prevents him from reversing his course. His words echo the infernal guide of his own *Aeneid,* the Cumaean Sibyl, who, like Vergil here, will prove capable of prophecy and sympathetic counsel, but is at first only puzzled by Aeneas' apparently mad desire to descend to the underworld.[8]

Dante seems not to hear Vergil's question, but reacts directly to what the shade has said about himself. Identifying the other as Vergil, the Pilgrim goes on to redefine him as in effect a resource of his own poetry:

> "Or se' tu quel Virgilio e quella fonte
>   che spandi di parlar sì largo fiume?"
> rispuos' io lui con vergognosa fronte.
> "O de li altri poeti onore e lume,
>   vagliami 'l lungo studio e 'l grande amore
>   che m'ha fatto cercar lo tuo volume.
> Tu se' lo mio maestro e 'l mio autore,
>   tu se' solo colui da cu' io tolsi
>   lo bello stilo che m'ha fatto onore."
>
>   (*Inf.* 1.79–87)

["Are you, then, that Vergil, that fount which pours forth so broad a stream of speech?" I answered him, my brow covered with shame. "O glory and light of other poets, may the long study and the great love that have made me search your volume avail me! You are my master and my author. You alone are he from whom I took the fair style that has done me honor."]

Dante's words underline the concession which had prefaced Vergil's first speech: "'No, [I am] not a living man. Once I was'" (*Inf.* 1.67). The Vergil to whom Dante responds ("*quel* Virgilio") is no longer a man who lived and wrote but a source, a fountain of powerful language.[9] The verb *spandi*, which describes the activity of this source, expresses its power but denies it a self-determining character, relegating it to a constant, depersonalized

---

8. *Aen.* 6.133–35: "quod si tantus amor menti, si tanta cupido est / . . . et insano iuuat indulgere labori." On the role of the Sibyl see Brooks, "*Discolor Aura,*" 266–68.

9. Cf. *Purg.* 21.125–26, where Statius meets "quel Virgilio" from whom he too had gained "forte a cantar."

function. Dante's zealous love for Vergil, his "maestro" and "autore," has been devoted to a book, the "volume" from which he "took" his famous style. The title "autore" is high praise, and with "volume" hints at the quasi-biblical status of Vergil's text.[10] But "maestro" suggests a more practical kind of authority, and the verb *togliere,* which describes Dante's appropriation of the master's language, is commonly used in the *Commedia* to denote deprivation, dispossession, even robbery.[11]

Dante's attempt to reduce Vergil, and to a lesser extent the other Poeti, to resources of his own poetry, models to be exploited and transcended, will be ongoing. There will remain, however, an aspect of Vergil's role, in which his poetry is neither a secular Testament nor simply a source and model for Dante's, but harbors its own character and power. Vergil the man no longer exists. The ghost who speaks to Dante bears only a remote relation to the volume Dante so values. The Vergil of the *Commedia* is a function of Dante's love for the *Aeneid,* his role determined by the status Dante has assigned that poem in conceiving his own.[12] But the *Aeneid* retains a certain latent power of its own, and already in this opening scene Dante's experience is framed by allusions which suggest the complex influence of his engagement with Vergil's poem.

The moment at which Vergil appears to Dante recalls several moments of ambiguous prophetic reassurance in the *Aeneid,* but it is controlled by a specific allusion. The verb which describes the Pilgrim's rush toward the depths ("rovinava," *Inf.* 1.61) echoes Aeneas' account of reentering the burning city of Troy in search of his wife Creusa, there to wander in a near-frenzy, "tectis urbis sine fine *ruenti*" (*Aen.* 2.771).[13] In a moment

---

10. On *volume* and *autore* see Hollander, "Dante's Use of *Aeneid* I," 144–45, and his *Allegory,* 77–79. On *maestro* and *autore* see Mazzotta, *Dante, Poet,* 154–55.

11. *Togliere* will be used again to describe Statius' appropriation of the poetic power of Vergil, "dal qual tu togliesti / forte a cantar" (*Purg.* 21.125–26). In the *Inferno* it often denotes the removal of the damned from earthly life, as in Francesca's reference to "la bella persona / che mi fu tolta" (*Inf.* 5.101–2). See also *Inf.* 7.59; 13.105; 24.135; 33.130.

12. In letting the *Aeneid* play so prominent a role in defining his own poetic mission, Dante is both acknowledging Vergil's modernity and revealing his own. See Mazzotta, *Worlds of Petrarch,* 17–18.

13. Given the allusive context I assume that Dante read "ruenti" in line 730, though the variant "furenti" is attested by Servius and others.

Creusa is before his eyes ("ante oculos," 773), as Vergil's shade suddenly appears "dinanzi a li occhi" of Dante (*Inf.* 1.62). And Creusa's words reveal that Aeneas' impending journey will be overseen by divine powers (777–78) as Vergil will recount the heavenly impetus of his mission to the Pilgrim.

But the most striking similarity between the Dantean and Vergilian moments is their fascination with a certain kind of despair. Aeneas' rush through the ruins of Troy is prompted not only by the loss of his wife but also by a strange, Hamletlike desire to reexperience the disaster of the city's fall:

> stat casus renouare omnis omnemque reuerti
> per Troiam et rursus caput obiectare periclis.
> (*Aen.* 2.750–51)

> [It seemed good to reenact the whole disaster, to go back
> through all of Troy, and again expose my life to danger.]

Creusa will recognize in the impulse represented by the noncommital "stat" the madness of desperation. Her rebuke to her husband will be closely echoed in the Sibyl's skeptical response to Aeneas' wish to enter the underworld.[14] The link reinforces the parallel role of Dante's Vergil, who sees in the Pilgrim's downhill flight a confused desire to return to the horrors he had fled. In all three situations love, memory, and guilt have aroused a deeply self-destructive impulse. In the Pilgrim this impulse is intensified by the memory of the Vergilian episodes. The full power of the *Aeneid* to control the Pilgrim's behavior will emerge only gradually, but Dante is already close to another keenly sensitive reader of Vergil, the Augustine of the *Confessions,* who had disdainfully recalled his youthful susceptibility to the sadness of the *Aeneid* only to find himself still hypnotized by Vergilian images—the burning city, the beloved woman speaking from beyond the grave—and by the rhythms of Vergilian poetry: "et Troiae incendium 'atque ípsius úmbra Creúsae.'"[15]

---

14. Cp. *Aen.* 2.776–77: "quid tantum insano iuuat indulgere dolori, / o dulcis coniunx?" with *Aen.* 6.133–35 (quoted above, n. 8, p. 31).

15. *Confessions* 1.13.22; the final words echo *Aen.* 2.772.

The most unnerving of those moments in which the Pilgrim is confused or demoralized by the memory of Vergil's poem occurs at the end of Canto 3. It is the most sustained reminiscence of Vergil in the *Commedia,* but it has received relatively little attention, perhaps because the allusion is so obvious as to seem perfunctory. Dante's arrival at the shore of Acheron closely recalls the corresponding moment in *Aeneid* 6. Its centerpiece is the double simile which describes the souls of the damned, who hurl themselves from the shore at the command of Charon:

> Come d'autunno si levan le foglie
> l'una appresso de l'altra, fin che 'l ramo
> vede a la terra tutte le sue spoglie,
> similemente il mal seme d'Adamo
> gittansi di quel lito ad una ad una,
> per cenni come augel per suo richiamo.
>   (*Inf.* 3.112–17)

[As the leaves fall away in autumn, one after another, till the bough sees all its spoils upon the ground, so there the evil seed of Adam: one by one they cast themselves from that shore, at signals, like a bird at its call.]

We must recognize the care with which Dante has made the impulse of the damned souls the climax of the episode. We have been told that the catalyst of their despairing action is the voice of the "demon" Charon, who bids them abandon hope and prepare to enter hell (*Inf.* 3.84–87). His cruel words ("parole crude," 102) precipitate the self-abandonment in which the souls curse "God, their parents, the human race, the place, the time, the seed of their begetting and of their birth" (103–5) and actively collaborate in their final damnation.

In the *Aeneid* Charon is less demonic than simply old, and the Latin adjective *cruda* describes the strange, supernatural energy which enables him in old age to keep ferrying the endless procession of souls to the farther shore.[16] Dante's Italian cognate, which points to the savage rather than the

---

16. *Aen.* 6.304: "iam senior, sed cruda deo uiridisque senectus" ("though he was now old, the old age of a god is tough and green").

vital aspect of the quality it names, locates Charon's demonic energy in his speech, and the displacement epitomizes the role of language in Canto 3 as a whole. In the opening lines of the canto, as we have seen, the verbal force of the inscription is substituted for the massive material strength of Vergil's citadel. Charon's inveighal against the damned souls, echoing the inscription in its promise of eternal darkness and its denial of hope (85, 87), is a similar substitution of deadly language for physical force.[17]

The culmination of the work of language in the canto is the pair of similes quoted above, for their imagery illustrates not only the final self-abandonment of the damned souls, but its effect on Dante, and they make it plain that he is responding not only to what he sees and hears, but to his vivid memory of the words in which Vergil had described essentially the same scene:

> quam multa in siluis autumni frigore primo
> lapsa cadunt folia, aut ad terram gurgite ab alto
> quam multae glomerantur aues, ubi frigidus annus
> trans pontum fugat et terris immittit apricis.
>
> > (*Aen.* 6.309–12)

> [as many as the leaves which fall in the forest at the first chill of autumn, or as the birds which flock from the deep water to shore, when the cold of the year drives them over the sea and bids them flee to sunny lands.]

Dante's similes recall Vergil's, but his alterations show him enthralled by the spectacle, as if he had been seized by the same demonic force that drives the damned souls.

> . . . si levan le foglie
> l'una appresso de l'altra, fin che 'l ramo
> vede a la terra tutte le sue spoglie.

> [. . . as the leaves fall, one after another, till the bough sees all its spoils upon the ground.]

---

17. See Kirkpatrick, *Dante's "Inferno,"* 67.

Everything is particularized. The image of the falling leaves is here augmented by that of the bough, which "sees" them as they lie on the earth. The leaves, moreover, fall one by one, "l'una appresso de l'altra," an unnatural detail that diverts us from the beauty of the image in itself, and points toward its significance in the context of the *Inferno*.

The "ramo," despoiled of its leaves,[18] is the Pilgrim, exposed and powerless as he observes the despair of the damned. The leaves which fall in sequence mirror the sequentiality of his imaginative and verbal response to the controlling memory of the words of the *Aeneid*.[19] This control is evident again as Vergil's migrant birds, fleeing instinctively before the winter wind, are reduced by Dante to a single bird, trained to respond to its master's signal. The similes in their new context express not just the despairing spirit's collaboration in its own damnation, but the vicarious identification of Dante the pilgrim with this impulse. This in turn is Dante's powerful metaphor for the challenge of imitating his great poetic forebear. So deeply has he felt the power of Vergil's language that he has momentarily assimilated also the profound sadness that lies behind it, thus giving an added point to the final term of the comparison. For the action of "the evil seed of Adam" represents not only the self-destructive impulse of the damned souls, but the self-diminishing effect of Dante's identification with them. The leaves, Dante's own words, are the seed he spends in an ejaculation of vicarious self-abandonment. Like the bird drawn to the master's lure, he has suspended his own flight and let himself be seduced into reenacting the bleak finality of the Vergilian moment. The words of the *Aeneid* have themselves become "parole crude," completing a process inaugurated by the "scritta morta" of the canto's opening lines.

This act of imaginative self-damnation is at the same time an extraordinary act of artistic courage. Dante has made himself experience in its

---

18. *Spoglie,* as *E.D.* notes, are what clothes or covers us, and so can be *tolte.* As used here and in *Inf.* 13.103, the word implies both body and "identity," the self or *persona* which is lost (*tolto*) through damnation. See above, p. 32, n. 11.

19. The same sense of an informing yet alien power is present in a more benign form in the likely source of Dante's tree which "sees" its own foliage, *Georgic* 2.82, where a newly grafted tree "miratur . . . nouas frondes et non sua poma." See Ronconi, *Filología e linguistica,* 207.

full power a pagan, tragic view of life. His submission to what is most
alien in the spiritual universe of the *Aeneid* suggests the complexity of
the process by which literary tradition is formed, the ambiguous continuity that links the modern poet to his ancient forebears. To emulate the
Poeti as Dante does is the highest aspiration a poet qua poet can have,
and the most dangerous. To accept at least momentarily, to *feel* the spiritual limitations of paganism is an essential preparation for Dante's underworld journey, offering a unique sense of the horror of damnation,
but jeopardizing what should be a correspondingly vivid awareness of the
sustaining love of God.

Assimilating a poetry as powerful as Vergil's is an experience in
which the inspirational and the destructive can be hard to distinguish.
Hence the Pilgrim's violent reaction when Vergil intrudes to remind him
of the spiritual meaning of what he sees, and his true status as one over
whom Charon has no power (3.127–29). The shock of the contradiction
between his real and his imagined condition is overwhelming, and as the
scene disintegrates around him he falls unconscious. Despite its shocking psychological impact, this moment, like every moment in the *Commedia,* has its place in the providential scheme; Dante's descent into hell
is a miraculous event, and the tremors, winds, and flashing light which
herald his crossing over Acheron represent the suspension of natural law
that any miracle involves. But the simultaneity of the divine with the
psychological event is crucial, and one purpose of the scene is to emphasize the chasm that separates the levels at which the two events are
enacted.

The power of the remembered *Aeneid* to shape Dante's experience is
shown more subtly in Canto 5. The Pilgrim is again overwhelmed by his
imaginative involvement in a situation he fails to understand, and Vergil
is again the mediating presence. The canto unfolds, as we are twice reminded, in the circle "ov' è Dido" (*Inf.* 5.85), and reenacts Augustine's description, in the same passage cited above, of the effect on his younger
self of Vergil's powerful account of Dido's suicide.[20] As the young Augustine had dwelled on Dido's suffering to the exclusion of any sense of the

----

20. See p. 33, n. 15; and Mazzotta, *Dante, Poet,* 165–70.

larger meaning of the *Aeneid,* so the Pilgrim is here very much the love poet who had worked into Beatrice's first speech an allusion to Ovid.[21]

If Augustine is an important presence in this scene, the Vergil of the *Aeneid* is equally so. The Pilgrim's response to Paolo and Francesca is shaped not only by Augustine's experience but also, like Augustine's, and to a much greater extent, by the guilty compassion with which Aeneas, meeting the shade of Dido in Vergil's underworld, seeks to reaffirm a bond totally at odds with his own larger mission. As he acknowledges Dido's terrible fate, in the words which Augustine will cite as having evoked his own response to the scene,[22] Aeneas is reduced to tears, and speaks words of "sweet love" (*Aen.* 6.455). So Dante discovers in the lovers he beholds a reflection of his own tender feelings. For both the indulgence of these feelings is primary, and both episodes end with their heroes wholly absorbed in reflection on the sorrows of love. But while Dido's unresponsiveness shocks Aeneas into a partial awareness of her suffering, her "casu . . . iniquo" (*Aen.* 6.475), Dante's pity remains wholly self-indulgent, and it is under the pressure of this pity that he succumbs to a deathlike swoon.

The final line of the canto is nearly identical to the account of Dante's swoon at the end of Canto 3. But where that earlier lapse was compared to sleep, Dante here falls "like a dead body." Both the repetition and the variation, concluding an episode which has been charged from beginning to end with Dante's feelings of love and pity, suggest a personal significance absent in the earlier episode. The suggestion is already lurking in the beautiful Vergilian simile which describes Paolo and Francesca as they respond to the Pilgrim's call:

> Quali colombe dal disio chiamate
> con l'ali alzate e ferme al dolce nido
> vegnon per l'aere, dal voler portate;

---

21. Several commentators note that Beatrice's reference to "l'amico mio, e non de la ventura" (*Inf.* 2.61) evokes Abelard's commentary on *Romans* (7.13): "fortunae potius . . . amici quam hominis." It is closer to Ovid, *Ex Ponto* 1.9.15–16; see Paratore, "Ovidio," 227.

22. "extinctam ferroque extrema secutam," *Aen.* 6.457, quoted verbatim by Augustine in the passage cited above p. 33, n. 15.

cotali uscir de la schiera ov' è Dido,
  a noi venendo per l'aere maligno,
  sì forte fu l'affettüoso grido.
                    (*Inf.* 5.82–87)

[As doves called by desire, with wings raised and steady, come
through the air, borne by their will to their sweet nest, so
did these issue from the troop where Dido is, coming to us
through the malignant air, such force had the compassionate cry.]

The paired souls' response to the Pilgrim's appeal recalls the twin doves
who appear to guide an anxious Aeneas through the ancient forest to the
tree that bears the golden bough (*Aen.* 6.185–211). Vergil's doves are Venus'
answer to her son's half-conscious prayer, and thus have a quasi-religious
significance, but Dante's are "summoned by desire," and it is this that an-
imates them. In both cases the doves' behavior is precisely adapted to the
eager responsiveness of the human seeker. But Venus' doves, pacing their
flight to ensure that Aeneas can keep them in sight (199–200), are portents, whereas Dante's dove-spirits simply mirror his desire:

"Di quel che udire e che parlar vi piace,
  noi udiremo e parleremo a voi."
                    (*Inf.* 5.94–95)

["Of that which it pleases you to hear and to speak, we will
hear and speak with you."]

The allusion embodied in the dove simile frames the encounter with
Francesca as in effect a second descent into hell, Dante's personal introduction to the psychological and moral testing of the underworld journey, a
test very different from the exercise in stoicism to which Vergil had subjected Aeneas. Aeneas is the public hero, his life a continual schooling in
the sacrifice of private desire to "virtue and the true task" (*Aen.* 12.435).[23]

---

23. This aspect of Aeneas' role and the contrast with Dante's are well
brought out by Ball, "Theological Semantics," 19–36, 249–58.

To the extent that desire clouds his judgment, he risks the failure of his divinely ordained mission.[24] The lesson he is to derive from his underworld journey is beautifully conveyed in the words with which the shade of Deiphobus, whom he meets shortly after his vain appeal to Dido, concludes their exchange:

> "discedam, explebo numerum, reddarque tenebris.
> i decus, i nostrum; melioribus utere fatis."
>
> > (*Aen.* 6.545–46)

> ["I leave you, to resume my allotted place among the shades.
> Go, glory of our people, and may you enjoy a better fate."]

Aeneas can go forward, the lines suggest, once Deiphobus' shade and the memories with which their encounter has been charged have withdrawn and assumed their place in the coherent fabric of a realized and distanced past.

For Dante, however, realization and coherence are yet to come. He must enter the very citadel of Dis, forbidden to Aeneas, and pursue self-understanding by seeing himself implicated in the situations he beholds. Like Aeneas, he must keep his distance, and accept the justice of the sinners' punishments, avoiding both the contamination of their despair and the indulgence of sentimentalizing their pain, though to this point he has conspicuously failed on both counts. He is in a realm where sympathy can have no legitimate place, where "vive la pietà quand' è ben morta" (*Inf.* 20.28).[25] But he must also learn that the act of defining the situation of

---

24. Dante's Virgil perhaps tacitly corrects the one great lapse in his proto-Roman hero's emotional austerity when, seeing Dido among the victims of desire (*Inf.* 5.61–62), he identifies her only as a suicide and an unfaithful wife. Dante's view is very different: see below, chap. 7, pp. 221–22; chap. 8, pp. 246–49.

25. By *pietà* here Vergil does not, of course, mean "charity." See Ball, "Theological Semantics," 20–36; and *Conv.* 2.10.6, where Dante distinguishes *pietade* as the "volgar gente" understand it, a passion caused by others' suffering, from that habitual *pietade* which is "a noble disposition of the mind, capable of experiencing love, pity (*misericordia*), and other charitable passions."

the sinners, and his own privileged relation to it, is fraught with dangers. He shares the desires that provoked their fatal errors, and in imposing on them the standard of divine judgment he will be committing an act of violence that will violate as well his own deepest human instincts.[26] The *pietà* that draws him to Francesca or Pier della Vigna, like his filial affection for Brunetto Latini, or the disdainfulness for which he is praised by Vergil, and which he grudgingly admires in Farinata, is the imperfect version of a quality of spirit which, fully developed and rightly understood, would enable him to distinguish what is admirable or worthy of sympathy in the sinners from the sin which distorts it. For the moment, however, he must depend on Vergil's ethical sense and Vergil's humanity, and his deepest and truest feelings are obscured for him by this dependence.

To Dante, then, Vergil is meaningful in radically different ways. His most obvious and most positive significance is as the medium through whom the Pilgrim experiences the constant concern of Beatrice for his well-being. The desire, the "buono ardire," with which he responds to Vergil's revelation of his commission expresses itself as a feeling of unanimity with his fellow poet:

> Tu m'hai con disiderio il cor disposto
>   sì al venir con le parole tue,
>   ch'i' son tornato nel primo proposto.
> Or va, ch'un sol volere è d'ambedue.
>   (*Inf.* 2.136–39)

[By your words you have made me so eager to come with you that I have returned to my first resolve. Now on, for a single will is in us both.]

But the appearance of common purpose is deceptive. Despite the final phrase, it is important to remember that the "sol volere" here is Dante's

---

26. On this aspect of Dante's role in the *Inferno* see Teskey's reading of the Francesca episode, *Allegory and Violence*, 25–31.

alone; it is his will that "moves" Vergil here,[27] and Dante himself who actively embarks on "the deep and savage path."[28]

Meanwhile the shadowy Vergil who authored *Aeneid* 6 is present as well, though only insofar as Dante's imagination, actively or involuntarily, conjures him up. He emerges into language only at moments of crisis, and it is important to recognize the different ways in which his textual presence manifests itself. As we have seen, there are moments when his influence is in virtual collaboration with the horrors of the underworld, overwhelming Dante's spiritual awareness and forcing him to come as close as possible to the experience of damnation, but even these crises confirm Dante's initial claim to have appropriated Vergil's linguistic power and caused it to inform his own poetry.

The fullest demonstration of this is another intensely Vergilian moment, the encounter with Pier della Vigna. The episode is pervaded by the memory of Aeneas' encounter with Polydorus (*Aen.* 3.22–48), and marked by a heavy emphasis on "credence" and "credibility." The Pilgrim is assured by Vergil that he is to see things which, simply reported, would "take away" his power to believe Vergil's words (*Inf.* 9.20–21).[29] Bewildered by the wailings of people he cannot see, he becomes self-conscious, sensing that Vergil is closely observing his reaction (25–27); then at Vergil's prompting he acts out a tentative version of Aeneas' assault on the plant that harbors the spirit of Polydorus, breaking a twig from a bush which then cries out in pained rebuke of his lack of "pietade" (36). While Dante stands suspended, "like one who is afraid" (45), Vergil explains to the "wounded soul" what has happened:

---

27. In *Inf.* 2.141, after Dante's impassioned speech, Vergil is "moved" to proceed ("mosso fue"), and he describes himself as moved, again with reference to Beatrice, in *Inf.* 12.88–92. At *Inf.* 1.136, he himself had moved ("si mosse"), or appeared to Dante to do so, as also at 7.99 and 10.124. On the thematics of motion, see Barolini, *undivine Comedy,* 30.

28. The active verb, *intrai* (142), suggests Dante's impetuosity at this point. *Intrare / entrare* will carry an ominous significance in the next few cantos, as immediately in 3.9. See also 5.19–20; 8.26, 90; 9.26, 33; and Barolini, *undivine Comedy,* 30–31.

29. Again the verb ("torrien") is a form of *togliere,* with its implications of dispossession and loss of autonomy. See above, p. 32, n. 11.

"S'elli avesse potuto creder prima,"
    rispuose 'l savio mio, "anima lesa,
    ciò c'ha veduto pur con la mia rima,
non averebbe in te la man distesa;
    ma la cosa incredibile mi fece
    indurlo ad ovra ch'a me stesso pesa."
                              (*Inf.* 13.46–51)

["If he, O wounded spirit, had been able to believe before,"
replied my sage, "what he had never seen save in my verses,
he would not have stretched forth his hand against you;
but the incredible thing made me prompt him to a deed
that grieves me."]

Vergil, here as elsewhere, assumes total understanding of what Dante has undergone, and why he has reacted as he has. If we accept his reading we must indeed see the Pilgrim as "tutto smarrito" (24), programmed by Vergil at a level where questions of belief and ethics are less to the point than the power of a remembered Vergilian pathos, which both dictates Dante's behavior and neutralizes his judgment. Vergil can seem to express compassion for the wounded spirit, but he has had no hesitation in subjecting Pier to added torment to demonstrate his authority. He provides no insight into the meaning of Pier's suffering, and as the episode runs its course we learn nothing about its meaning for the Pilgrim.[30] As Vergil foresees (30), Dante's thoughts are "broken off" ("monchi") by Pier's reproaches; his psychological state mirrors the physical plight of sinners who, once men, have become "sterpi" (37), "stumps" or stocks, and the barrier of metamorphosis points up his alienation as well as theirs. He cannot reach out to them verbally or spiritually, and in their presence feels

---

30. The Pilgrim is sometimes charged with a lack of trust that makes him act in spite of his memory of the Polydorus episode; thus Boyde, "*Inferno* XIII," 8, compares him to the apostle Thomas. But from the outset Vergil has assumed the necessity of Dante's learning the nature of the *bosco* for himself, and encouraged him to do so.

only the self-regarding "pietà" that had overwhelmed him on hearing Francesca (84).

But if Dante's response is inadequate, Vergil's limitations are equally in question.[31] The Polydorus episode is one of the most disturbingly ambiguous moments in the *Aeneid,* and nothing in Vergil's account of it has prepared the Pilgrim to come to terms with his own experience. He has absorbed the horror of the episode, and has it very much in mind as he confronts Pier, but whereas for Aeneas it had been enough to remain steadfast in the face of this horror, Dante must seek to derive knowledge from it. Vergil serves as mediator of the experience, but Vergil himself had not discovered in it what Dante now experiences as a challenge to his essential humanity. "Perché mi scerpi?" the wounded spirit asks; "non hai tu spirto di pietade alcuno?" ["Why do you tear me? Have you no spirit of pity?"] (35–36).[32] Behind the question is the more fundamental issue of how Dante the man of flesh and blood will be affected by his role as the imagining agent of the many and various forms of suffering displayed in lower hell. In depicting this suffering, he will continue to remain subject to the authority of ancient poetry. But in the meeting with Pier we are shown the limits of that authority, for here, though the mediating presence of Vergil and his poetry is essential, Dante clearly goes beyond Vergil, and the poetry of the *Aeneid* is reduced to an imperfect foreshadowing of Dante's more complex experience.[33]

---

31. See Biow, "From Ignorance to Knowledge," 45–61, 261–64.

32. A mark of difference between the Vergilian and Dantean perspectives here (though the latter remains latent) is the replacement of the admonitory "parce . . . parce" of Polydorus (*Aen.* 3.41, 42) by Pier's more probing "Perché? . . . Perché?" (*Inf.* 13.33, 35). Polydorus assumes Aeneas' essential virtue ("parce pias scelerare manus," *Aen.* 3.42), while Pier, unaware of Vergil's controlling presence, questions the *pietade* of Dante.

33. More complex, but not as absolutely distinct from Vergil's as Biow, "From Ignorance to Knowledge," 57, suggests. For him Vergil's "pain" as witness of Dante's action ("mi pesa," 51) is due to his recognizing "the superior power of Dante's Christian art." But Dante's art is nowhere more dependent on Vergil's poem than here, and part of Vergil's pain is surely at realizing that his own art had expressed more truth than he himself could possibly have seen in it, and more than Dante could have seen without his aid.

What Vergil Knows

Clearly a reading which emphasizes the dark undertones of the *Aeneid* cannot be a complete reading of Vergil's role in the *Commedia*. He is not only the source of Dante's Charon and Tisiphone, but the creator of Aeneas, the archexample of a life that is "onesta, laudabile . . . e fruttuosa."[34] He is the sage who, in the poem's central cantos, speaks clearly and truly of the nature of love, and whose authority is sufficient to declare Dante's will "libero, dritto, e sano" at the summit of Purgatory. And he is first and last the poet with whom Dante feels himself most profoundly in tune, the poet whose unique purity and spiritual dignity make manifest the "aetherial sense and pure flame of spirit" innate in the human soul (*Aen.* 6.747).

Perhaps the clearest indication of Vergil's unique status is his ability to intuit the transcendent power of the "virtù" revealed in Beatrice:

> "O donna di virtù, sola per cui
> l'umana spezie eccede ogne contento
> di quel ciel c'ha minor li cerchi sui."
> > (*Inf.* 2.76–78)

> ["O Lady of virtue, through alone mankind rises beyond all
> that is contained by the heaven that circles least."]

This initial, dazzling insight into the significance of Beatrice seems to anticipate the *Paradiso* and Dante's final affirmation of her Christlike role (*Par.* 31.79–90). But we must recognize that Vergil's words echo Anchises' account of the human soul's posthumous journey beyond the spheres.[35] Remarkable as Vergil's knowledge and spirituality are shown to be, here and throughout the *Commedia* they have their source in ancient poetry,

---

34. *Conv.* 4.26.8, in the course of a chapter devoted to the virtues embodied in Vergil's hero.

35. For Dante's Vergil (*Inf.* 2.77–78) as for Anchises the final stage of the soul's purification is its ascent beyond the moving spheres to the *convexa*, the vault of heaven (*Aen.* 6.241, 750).

chiefly his own, and in ancient philosophy.[36] The unique mission of Beatrice, moved by love to enlist Vergil's artistic powers on behalf of her friend, and Vergil's instant response to her appeal rewrite the scene in which the "divine" love of Venus arouses the creative powers of Vulcan to fashion the arms that will enable Aeneas to complete his "durum laborem" in Italy (*Aen.* 8.370–406). And as in the *Convivio,* beneath what can seem to be a redemptive spiritual vision are the transcendent yearnings of Stoic physics and the *Timaeus.*

Even in the *Purgatorio* it is not Christian doctrine but the psychology of Aristotle that both shapes Vergil's teaching on love and, despite the lucidity and beauty of his exposition, finally circumscribes it. When it touches on religious issues, Vergil's teaching becomes a kind of negative moral theology. He knows that all sinners have lost the Good as Aristotle defines it.[37] Though the sense in which he is a "rebel" against divine law is perhaps beyond our power to understand (*Inf.* 1.125),[38] he knows how the sinner offends against God. He has heard of the punishment of the rebel angels (*Inf.* 7.11–12), and knows that the punishment of all sinners will become most intense when they are "perfected" by reunion with their earthly bodies (*Inf.* 6.106–11). *Inferno* 11 is a veritable anthology of the ways in which malice and the "mad bestiality" of the violent can be explained as rejections of God's will.

"Love," for Vergil, remains part of the natural order; he recognizes that evil, according to its degree, tends toward the center of the universe (*Inf.* 11.64–65), but he has only an imaginative sense of the spiritually dynamic love that is capable of transcending the inexorable laws of gravity, moral and physical, by which the universe as he understands it is gov-

---

36. As Foster observes, *Two Dantes,* 244, Vergil has his own kind of piety: "It is always in character; never Christian; always at a certain remove, like those points of doctrine which he has to leave to Beatrice to instruct Dante in." See also his analysis of Dante's treatment of the ideas of human nobility and self-realization, 200–219.

37. Vergil's reference to the damned as having lost "the good of intellect" is based ultimately on Aristotle, *Nichomachean Ethics* 6.2.1139a. The phrase itself is a gloss of Thomas Aquinas on this passage, and it is presumably via Thomas that Dante in the *Convivio* credits Aristotle with having called truth "lo bene de lo intelletto." See *Conv.* 2.13.6, and the commentary of Vasoli, *Otto Saggi,* 218.

38. The most satisfying explanation I know of is Foster's, *Two Dantes,* 243–53.

erned.[39] And an extraordinary passage in Canto 12, in which he imagines the universe reduced to chaos by a "love" that would destroy the vital tension among the elements (12.40–42), shows him translating the violent effects of Christ's Crucifixion and descent to hell into the terms of Empedoclean cosmology. There is a genuine insight here, and a syncretizing impulse that Dante himself displays at a number of points,[40] but Vergil's conclusion, utterly at odds with the providentially ordered universe of the *Commedia,* demonstrates again his limited capacity to imagine a love transcending the natural order.

Vergil's limitations involve more than false doctrine, and there is a certain ambiguity in even the most seemingly positive aspects of his role. In this regard it may be helpful to compare the *Commedia* with another work highly valued by Dante, Boethius' *Consolatio.* Together, the descent of Beatrice to Vergil, suspended within the confines of Limbo, and Vergil's ensuing apparition to Dante clearly evoke the opening episode of Boethius' dialogue. The Pilgrim, like the Prisoner, has been so demoralized by ill fortune that he can no longer pursue the destiny that his inherent abilities and the uplifting influence of a uniquely empowering patroness had seemed to promise.

Like Boethius' Prisoner, Dante's Pilgrim will be guided to the threshold of a new spiritual awareness, but for both the journey will be fraught with uncertainty and frustration: Boethius allows his human interlocutor to give expression, not just to his growing understanding, but to the labor involved and the anxiety to which it gives rise.[41] His difficult progress is punctuated by poems whose hortatory exempla often seem to harbor

---

39. Vergil is perhaps closest to a transcendent intuition in *Inf.* 11.61–63, where he speaks both of natural love and of "quel ch' è poi aggiunto, / di che la fede spezïal si cria" (and that also which is added to it, and which creates a special trust). Cf. his declaration that the mysteries of Purgatory are the work of a "Virtù" whose purposes are veiled, and that humans must be content to know only the *quia* (*Purg.* 3.32–33, 37), juxtaposed to his knowledge that God is one substance in three persons and that the bearing of a child by Mary has a crucial significance (35–36, 38–39).

40. See the note of Durling and Martinez, eds. *Divine Comedy,* vol. 1, *Inferno,* on 41–43; Botterill, "*Inferno* XII," 159–60; Goffis, "*Inferno* XII," 223–24.

41. On this existential aspect of Boethius, see Miller, *Philosophical Chaucer,* 111–30.

a calculated ambiguity, and his last contribution to the dialogue is a poetic declaration of his lingering doubt and confusion. His silence during Philosophy's long concluding discourse on providence, fate, and free will is perhaps as telling as the power of Philosophy's arguments.

Dante will harbor many similar doubts, and while they will of course be authoritatively resolved, his progress will be far less orderly than that of Boethius' Prisoner. Much of his difficulty, like that of the Prisoner, will be caused by the intellectually and emotionally demanding nature of his experience,[42] but much of his difficulty will have to do with the limitations of the guidance Vergil is capable of providing. Philosophy had begun her ministrations to Boethius by banishing the Muses of poetry, whose persuasions only intensified his grief by inviting him to indulge it. Like the pathetic romance of Francesca, the Muses of Boethius, "usque in exitium dulces," exert a seductive power that is potentially fatal. But Vergil as he first appears to Dante is in effect poetry itself, and perhaps the greatest challenge Dante faces in the *Inferno* is that of learning how to integrate poetry in its full power and complexity into the larger scheme of the *Commedia*.

The neutralizing of Vergil's power that occurs so strikingly in the encounter with Pier is in fact the culmination of a gradual process of which the symptoms begin to appear as early as Canto 8.[43] The crossing of the Styx and the entry into the "basso inferno" (8.75) are marked by the curious retrograde movement with which the canto begins. Canto 7 had ended with Vergil and the Pilgrim at the foot of a tower, after a journey in which their eyes had been focused on the wrathful spirits sunk in the mire around them (7.127–29). The opening of Canto 8 retraces this journey, emphasizing now their first glimpses of the approaching citadel (8.1–6). The notorious "Io dico, seguitando . . . ," which begins the new canto calls attention to this disjunction, and its ostentatiously casual tone suggests the apparent ease with which Dante has, in this one instance, offered two versions of the same portion of his narrative,[44] overlapping but different in effect.

---

42. As Kirkpatrick observes, *Dante's "Inferno,"* 2–3, "The distinctive contribution of the *Inferno* to the plan of the *Commedia* as a whole is to demonstrate what our minds—and words—must suffer in developing any such plan."

43. See Barolini, *Dante's Poets*, 203–8.

44. See Sanguineti, *Dante reazionario*, 89–93.

The centerpiece of Canto 7 had been Vergil's lecture on the work of Fortune. This is commonly taken as a definitive statement on the power of the "goddess," but what it exhibits most strongly is the fatalism by which Vergil's vision is constantly threatened. Vergil seems to assign Fortune a place among the Intelligences who govern the movement of the heavenly spheres,[45] but his emphasis is on her inexorability rather than her divinity. Though one of the gods (86–87), she is at the same time subject to necessity (89), and while her role as governor and judge are mentioned repeatedly, the comparison of her "giudicio" to a snake in the grass points to its perversity (84). At no point is it suggested that there is an order to the changes she effects.[46] That she is "blessed," and rejoices in her blessedness, suggests that impunity is her main claim to divine status, and the "sphere" over which she presides belongs to no legitimate cosmology. Vergil offers, moreover, only a hint of the canonical view of Boethius' Philosophy, for whom an acceptance of Fortune's power is finally only a stage in the liberation of the mind from her dominion;[47] and as if in answer to Dante's assertion in the *Convivio* that to be governed by reason is to be freed from the tyranny of Fortune,[48] Vergil declares flatly that "your wisdom cannot withstand her" (*Inf.* 7.85).

Vergil's assertion of the fatal power of Fortune is quietly answered by Dante's reinvention of the figure of Phlegyas at the beginning of Canto 8. Vergil had made his Phlegyas, who had set fire to the temple of Apollo after the god had raped his daughter, the archvictim of fate. He is the centerpiece of the Sibyl's account of Dis, unique among the damned not only in being the most wretched of all ("miserrimus"), but as the one

---

45. On the *Intelligenze* (or "angels"), see *Conv.* 2.iv–viii; and Singleton's notes to *Inf.* 7.74–94.

46. Kirkpatrick, *Dante's "Inferno,"* 108–20, emphasizes the positive and original in Dante's treatment of *fortuna* as representing "divine order in the realm of physical matter" (113), but his argument applies only to Dante's own view of fortune, which is beyond Vergil's power to conceive.

47. Vergil's passing remark that those who blame Fortune should rather praise her (*Inf.* 7.91–92) recalls *De consolatione Philosophiae* 2. Pr.8, but in general his view is a resigned fatalism.

48. *Conv.* 4.11.9, where Aristotle is cited. Dante is perhaps recalling *Physics* 2.5.197a, but again, as Foster shows, "Tommaso Aquino," 634, the idea is more clearly expressed in Thomas, *Exp. Phys.,* 2.1, lect. 8.216.

prisoner of Dis who speaks, crying out to urge others to see in his utter misery a warning of the power of divine vengeance (*Aen.* 6.618–20). Dante's Phlegyas, who ferries the travelers across the Styx, has been reduced to a second, lesser Caron, comic in his eagerness to usher sinners to their doom, and enraged as if by "some great deception" ("grande inganno") as he comes to understand that the Pilgrim will evade his clutches (8.13–24). Dante emphasizes the "inganno," twice noting how Phlegyas' boat is weighed down by his living body (27, 29–30).

The transformation of Phlegyas, emblem of doom, into Dante's lively demon heralds a new departure. Not only does it place a renewed emphasis on the capriciousness of Fortune, but it announces a stage of the journey that will be less governed by canonical deference to Vergil, more inventive in its treatment of the "maggior pieta" of lower hell. The most striking illustration of this new perspective is also the strangest, and seems to call Vergil's controlling power into question more radically than anything we have previously been shown. In *Inferno* 9, as he and the Pilgrim await the angel whose power will enable them to enter the citadel of Dis, Vergil speaks of having once been "conjured" by the necromantic powers of the witch Erichtho, who had sent him to summon a soul from the lowest circle of Dis (*Inf.* 9.22–30).[49]

The timing of this revelation is disturbing, for it occurs at a moment when Vergil has come close to doubting the divinely sanctioned status of his present mission, and in an atmosphere which, like the central scene of Canto 3, is charged with reminiscences of the underworld of the *Aeneid*. Anxious because the promised heavenly aid has not appeared, Vergil is reduced to viewing the situation as it had presented itself to Aeneas. But here there is the added challenge of actually entering the citadel, and this, Vergil declares, cannot be accomplished "sanz' ira" (33), a phrase which may denote either the hostility of the guardians of Dis or the aggression

---

49. With Benvenuto and Boccaccio I take Erichtho's conjuring of Vergil as Dante's invention. Schnapp, "Lucanian Estimations," 122–23, cites critics who would assign the invention to Vergil himself—and who thereby, in my view, introduce a pointless complication. The question whether Erichtho could still have been alive at Vergil's death, almost thirty years after the battle at Pharsalia, is a red herring; Lucan says nothing about her age.

necessary to overcome them, but in either case presents these powers as a serious threat. Vergil fears lest the gaze of Medusa cause the travelers to be permanently imprisoned in Dis (56–57) and with his own hands covers Dante's eyes lest they encounter hers.[50]

John Freccero has argued that the threat posed by Medusa has a personal significance for Dante. To be fascinated by Medusa is to be arrested in the quest for meaning, to be "petrified" at the level of idolatry and spiritual alienation. In Vergil's protective gesture, he suggests, we can see the poet of the *Aeneid* warning the vernacular love poet that certain passions are inimical to the quest for self-understanding.[51] But it is hard to see Vergil's role here as positive. The first few lines of the canto show Dante attempting to read Vergil—to discern his state of mind; to understand his "broken" speech; perhaps most of all to fathom the significance for Vergil of the scene in the *Aeneid* which this canto so deliberately invokes, and which must be the key to Vergil's uncharacteristic anger and anxiety. For at the threshold of the Dis of the *Aeneid,* the Sibyl, the figure who corresponds most closely to Dante's Erichtho, but stands in a very different relation to the horrors the citadel contains, had given Aeneas an authoritative account of Dis.

Vergil's Dis remains closed to Aeneas, as to all who are pure,[52] but the Sibyl has been shown by Hecate all that it contains (*Aen.* 6.563–65). She is thus able to provide the awestruck Aeneas with a vivid panorama of its physical and moral horrors, thereby confirming her own authority and doing justice to epic tradition while sparing Aeneas the rigors of a direct confrontation. There is in her account, moreover, an emphasis on the presence in Dis of a controlling order, an assurance that a divinely ordained punishment awaits all who have "dared to be greatly wicked, and achieved what they dared" (*Aen.* 6.624), that is utterly at odds with the mood of *Inferno* 9. And when Dante, like Aeneas, expresses concern about what lies ahead, Vergil's attempt at reassurance ("però ti fa sicuro," 30)

---

50. On Vergil's anxiety here, see Mark Musa, *Advent at the Gates, 69–77.*

51. *Poetics,* 129–33.

52. Vergil himself claims to tell only what he has heard: "sit mihi fas *audita* loqui" (*Aen.* 6.266).

consists in the relating of his own hapless descent to the depths of Dis it-self at the bidding of Erichtho.

It is by no means clear that Vergil is ready to deal with what lies ahead, and the action of protecting Dante from Medusa's gaze, an improvised re-course at a moment when Dante has conspicuously ceased to pay atten-tion to his words (34–36), is perhaps an indication of his unpreparedness. When Dante calls attention to the "versi strani" which describe Vergil's gesture, he is perhaps suggesting that both the gesture and the fear which prompts it are signs of Vergil's inability, conditioned as he is by his own imagining of hell, to recognize the deeper level at which Dante's journey is sanctioned. In momentarily blinding Dante he is expressing his own blind-ness, and its inhibiting effect on Dante's understanding of his experience.

It is worth noting that when "strani" is used again, it refers to the trees of Canto 13, trees which once were men (*Inf.* 13.15). On these trees the Harpies sit lamenting, recalling to Dante's mind the episode in *Aeneid* 3 in which, after the Harpies have defiled a Trojan feast, and Aeneas' men have made a futile attempt to drive them off, their leader, Celaeno, utters the "announcement of future ill" to which Dante refers here (13.12; cp. *Aen.* 3.209–57). Like the uprooting of Polydorus earlier in *Aeneid* 3, attack-ing the Harpies involves an act of unwitting impiety on the part of Aeneas, and again, as in the Polydorus episode, the meaning of the encounter is left obscure, as the deeper human significance of the "alberi strani" of *In-ferno* 13 is obscure to Dante's Vergil. The allusion to *Aeneid* 3 at the open-ing of Canto 13 thus constitutes a sort of preface to the central episode, Dante's reworking of Aeneas' wounding of Polydorus, insofar as it fore-shadows the failure of communication that will again make plain the lim-its of Vergil's understanding.

Indeed to compare the *Inferno* with the *Aeneid* at this point is to re-alize how abruptly and radically Dante has made Vergil a foil to his own purposes. In Canto 9 he invents a basis for Vergil's knowledge of the lower regions that displaces the authority of Vergil's own poem; and he goes to elaborate lengths to show Vergil suspended between a wavering trust in the promise of divine aid and an enduring fear of the horrors of his own (and perhaps Lucan's) legendary underworld.[53] Even here, to be sure,

---

53. See Barolini, *Dante's Poets,* 204–7.

Vergil continues to exert a strong influence. When Dante acknowledges that he may have "drawn" too dark a meaning from Vergil's broken speech (14–15), he uses the same verb, *trarre,* which Vergil himself will use to describe his "drawing forth" of a spirit from the circle of Judas (27). Vergil had acted at the command of Erichtho, whose power cannot be resisted.[54] Dante, though he can seem to be exercising a radical control over his Vergil, is nonetheless dependent for guidance on the authority he himself has assigned to his guide, an authority which, as we have seen, has its demonic aspect. Dante continues to follow Vergil's lead unquestioningly, but his portrayal of his *maestro* raises doubts about Vergil's ability to sustain him at this critical juncture.

In the cantos that follow the Pilgrim gradually, and to some extent unwittingly, emerges from his earlier dependence on Vergil, and the significance of his fable of Vergil's conjuration by Erichtho becomes clearer. Erichtho's role is a grotesque parody of the elaborate mediation of divine authority that enables Beatrice to enlist Vergil as Dante's guide.[55] She is called "cruel" ("cruda," 23), and her cruelty, like that of the damning "parole crude" of Caron, is in effect pitted against the power of Lucy, "the enemy of all cruelty" (*Inf.* 2.100), at whose bidding Beatrice had summoned forth Vergil to become the Pilgrim's guide. Vergil himself on the threshold of Dis speaks of his disorientation in terms of the struggle between two powers, one a harbinger of divine assurance, the other the agent of a demoralizing downward gravitation which recalls to Vergil's mind the "scritta morta" over the gate of hell (8.121–30).[56]

By making Vergil recall his earlier descent at Erichtho's command, Dante invites us to reflect on the broader implications of the epic *descensus ad inferos,* and of Vergil's role as a poet of the underworld. The sixth book of the *Aeneid* is in one sense a powerful affirmation of the purpose

---

54. See Balducci, *Classicismo dantesco,* 41–45.

55. For an alternative reading, see Quint, "Epic Tradition," 202–7: noting the opposition of Erichtho and Beatrice, he reads the episode as affirming Vergilian over Lucanian poetics, and sees Vergil's authority "decisively reaffirmed" by the action of the heavenly messenger.

56. See Dragonetti, *Dante, pèlerin,* 57: "Béatrice et Erichto, la grâce et la magie, deux formes de puissance qui s'excluent. . . . Dans l'episode de Dité, Virgile est le lieu de ce terrible combat."

of the mission of Aeneas, punctuated with favorable comparisons to earlier heroes and culminating in a vision of cosmic order and a prophecy of the greatness of Rome. But it also reveals the limits within which human destinies are enacted in Vergil's universe. Through death one passes from life to what is for some a kind of purgatory, but purification requires a total forgetting, and prepares the soul only to return to the world. The multitude of souls thronging the banks of Lethe in anticipation of rebirth is a grim mirror image of the earlier scene on the shores of Acheron, and Aeneas, distilling a lifetime's experience into his words, expresses only horror at the "dira cupido" that impels them to seek to be born again (*Aen.* 6.721).

The spiritual horizons of Dante's Vergil are similarly circumscribed. Michael Putnam has suggested that in making his Vergil return at last to the underworld, Dante is responding to the sense of entrapment that the *Aeneid* conveys, of human life as "caught in the cycle of hell, purgatory, hell."[57] Vergil's final doom is clear in the very terms of his commissioning by Beatrice: The nobility of his style, which is perhaps what Beatrice refers to in calling him "courteous" (*Inf.* 2.58), is recognized on high, and for putting his noble language at the service of the court of Heaven she will praise him before the Lord of Heaven (73–74), but this patronage will leave the situation of Vergil's "anima cortese" (58) unaltered. Beatrice is immune to the misery of his condition (91–92), and his meaning for her, as largely for Dante himself, lies in the mediatory power of a body of language over which Vergil has ceased to exercise control.

It is a measure of the haplessness of Vergil's condition that he should be equally available to the designs of the heavenly *donne,* which have as their end Dante's salvation, and those of Erichtho, which aim to resurrect a spirit condemned to the lowest circle of hell.[58] Neither power does anything to free him from the "suspended" condition of those in Limbo (*Inf.* 2.52), and he describes that condition in terms that apply equally well to both situations. At the time when Erichtho forced him to enter Dis, he says, "my flesh had been but short while divested of me" ("di poco era di me la carne nuda," *Inf.* 9.25), and the vivid "nuda" expresses the ruthlessly depersonalizing effect of death as Vergil has experienced it, his reduction to a ves-

---

57. "Virgil's *Inferno*," 110.
58. See Hawkins, *Dante's Testaments,* 112–13.

sel for animation by whatever power may require the special qualities of his language. Any act of imagination that renews his "morta poesia" must involve a kind of necromancy, the revival of a "body" which is in reality a mere text; it can never re-create the living energy that produced that text, and remains wholly alien to the Vergil who was once a man. Erichtho's action represents the extreme form of this alienation. Whereas Vergil's eligibility to serve the court of Heaven is a function of his role as "Vater des Abendlands," an acknowledgment of elements in his poetry which have enriched the ethical and spiritual life of others, Erichtho's power isolates and exploits what is darkest in the *Aeneid,* and brings out undertones that the poet himself might have wished to suppress. By forcing him to enter "within the wall" (*Inf.* 9.26) she has violated the barrier he himself had defined, and made him behold things which the Sibyl had professed herself unable to relate (*Aen.* 6.625–27).[59] And at this liminal moment on the threshold of Dis, Dante seems for a moment to come close to suspending his adherence to Vergil's authority. Both his explicitly noted inattention to Vergil's words as he lifts his eyes to view the Furies and Vergil's awkward intervention to ward off the gaze of Medusa raise the question of whether Vergil's poetry provides an adequate model for the representation of human evil as the later cantos of the *Inferno* must expose it.[60]

Despite this brief crisis, the Pilgrim for the time being shows no further sign of doubting Vergil's authority, but in the next few cantos the character and extent of that authority is explored in various ways, and Dante's dependence on Vergil comes at times to seem a potential danger. After the two have entered Dis, the Pilgrim addresses his guide in terms which seem clearly to reaffirm his quasi-divine status:

> "O virtù somma, che per li empi giri
>   mi volvi," cominciai, "com' a te piace, . . ."
>   (*Inf.* 10.4–5)

> ["O supreme virtue," I began, "who lead me round as you will through the impious circles, . . ."]

---

59. See Schnapp, "Lucanian Estimations," 126–27.
60. See Kirkpatrick, *Dante's "Inferno,"* 134–35; Quint, "Epic Tradition."

As we hear these lines, and particularly the concluding "com' a te piace," we should recall Vergil's own account of his descent at Erichtho's bidding to the circle of Judas (*Inf.* 9.27):

> "ch'ella mi fece intrar dentr' a quel muro,
>   per trarne un spirto del cerchio di Giuda.
> Quell' è 'l più basso loco e 'l più oscuro,
>   e 'l più lontan dal ciel che tutto gira:
>   ben so 'l cammin; però ti fa sicuro."
>
> (Inf. 9.26–30)

> ["She made me enter within that wall to draw forth a spirit
> from the circle of Judas. That is the lowest place, and the
> darkest, and farthest from the heaven that encircles all.
> Well do I know the way, so reassure yourself."]

"The heaven that encircles all" is indeed very far, and Dante by his own account is utterly dependent on a Vergil who can never truly travel "as he will," whose less than divine capacities have been made plain.[61] His knowledge of the path ahead and the "security" it provides are the product of witchcraft. At this stage the Pilgrim's willing submission to Vergil's pleasure is at the least disturbing.

Other details in the next few cantos suggest a gradual loss of controlling authority on Vergil's part, and an emerging independence in Dante. Vergil is clearly impressed, perhaps even awed by the pride and bearing of Farinata, and fears lest Dante by some impropriety of speech incur his disdain (10.35–39),[62] but Dante himself, while courteous, has no hesitation

---

61. Dante's lines on the supreme virtue that enables Vergil to guide him through hell, "com'a te piace" (10.5), are echoed in a rather humble way by Vergil himself, who, anxious about the passage of time and the difficulties that lie ahead, tells Dante, "'l gir mi piace" (11.112).

62. Vergil has a curious respect for disdain, perhaps considering it an attribute of great men like the *magnanimo* Farinata, who seems to scorn not only the socially inferior Dante but also hell itself (10.36, 41). Vergil's attitude here recalls his warm response to the "alma sdegnosa" Dante had displayed in rebuffing

in standing up to Farinata's scorn. Vergil's encounters with the Minotaur, the Centaurs, and Capaneus, and even his recalling of the harrowing of hell, pass without comment from Dante, who seems increasingly involved with his own reflections (e.g., 12.49–51; 14.16–18; 16.10–12). When Vergil interrupts Dante's thoughts again, it is again to urge him to respond in a manner appropriate to the noble rank of those he meets (16.14–18), and the well-intended counsel has the effect of causing Dante for a moment to wholly abandon moral judgment (16.46–57).

The centerpiece of this section of the poem is Vergil's extraordinary description of the "gran veglio," the colossal figure whose composition from a hierarchy of metals and clay, together with his ruined state, expresses the course of human history (*Inf.* 14.94–114). The passage has a complex function. On the one hand it conveys a message as powerfully emblematic as that of the inscription over the gate of Canto 3, and announces the profound concern of the later *Inferno* with politics and history, placing human sovereignty in the larger perspective of sacred history.[63] But if we recall how the sense of a lost Golden Age pervades the later books of the *Aeneid*, we may see the account of the Veglio as a summarial expression of Vergil's worldview, profoundly true to human experience, but radically circumscribed by the fatalism which clouds his vision.

Vergil's limited perspective is suggested by the stream which provides the occasion for Vergil's account. The waters of this stream—which Vergil puzzlingly declares the most "notable" sight Dante has encountered (14.88–89)—are of a horrifying color (78), but the stream is otherwise unprepossessing, a "picciol fiumicello" (77) which recalls to Dante's mind the foul-smelling spring that supplies bathing water for the prostitutes of Viterbo (14.79–81). After Vergil has ended his portrait of the Veglio, he reverts again to the stream. The importance of the anonymous "fiumicello" in itself remains puzzling, but it is perhaps possible to intuit its importance

---

Filippo Argenti (*Inf.* 8.43–45), and anticipates his evident pride in his own disdainful facing down of the *disdegno* of Capaneus (14.61–72). It is perhaps Vergil's influence that prompts Dante's admiring "Ahi" for the disdainful bearing of the angel (9.88), though Villani, *Nuova cronica* 10.136, reports that Dante himself was "alquanto presuntuoso e schifo e isdegnoso."

63. See Mazzotta, *Dante, Poet,* 23–37.

for the poet of *Aeneid* 6. Since the stream channels the tears which flow downward from the world to form the rivers of hell (*Inf.* 14.112–17), it gives final expression to the long tragic course of human history as Vergil understands it. If the ruined Veglio is history itself, the stream is in some sense the "lacrimae rerum," the tears that are finally the truest expression of Vergil's vision: "mentem mortalia tangunt."[64]

The discussion which concludes the canto makes no reference to the meaning of the colossal figure, but provides instead a matter-of-fact lesson on the geography and hydraulics of hell. The same factual emphasis marks the opening of Canto 15, which underwhelmingly compares the earthworks of the seventh circle to those made by the Flemings and the Paduans, and finds them "neither so high nor so thick" (15.11). By the time we encounter Brunetto Latini, we have been distanced from the Old Man by a stretch of purely physical description whose significance is doubtful, leaving Vergil's powerful image in a sort of Limbo.

Vergil is nearly silent in Canto 15, but the canto bears on his role in significant ways. The meeting with Brunetto suggests several moments in *Aeneid* 6. Brunetto's first question to Dante clearly echoes the last words of Deiphobus to Aeneas (*Inf.* 15.46–48; cp. *Aen.* 6.531–34), though he cannot, like Deiphobus, accept his fate with a simple "discedam" (545). Instead he aspires to the role of a Palinurus or even, despite his jaundiced view of the fate of Roman values, an Anchises.[65]

The first details we are given concerning Brunetto are his "cotto aspetto" and his "viso abbrusciato." The first participle had been used of the foot of the Veglio (14.110), and the second will describe the effect of purifying fire on the spirits of the lustful (*Purg.* 25.137). When in the following canto Dante thinks of reaching out to embrace the Florentine (16.49), he is checked by the fear of being both "brusciato" and "cotto," thus mirroring in imagination the moment of his recognition of Brunetto. These carefully chosen terms,[66] which imply the mutuality of the ambiguous bond

---

64. *Aen.* 1.462.

65. Freccero, *Poetics,* 64–65, compares Brunetto's role with the reading of Anchises in the *Aeneid* commentary of Bernardus Silvestris. For Palinurus, see Havely's excellent "Brunetto and Palinurus."

66. These are the only uses of (*ab*)*brucciare.* In *Inf.* 22, the barrators are described as *cotti,* but the image is clearly of food rather than clay.

between Brunetto and Dante, at the same time link Brunetto with the ruined monument, and contrast his eternal punishment with the progressive purgation of the penitents in Purgatory.

The role Brunetto had imagined for himself in the realization of Dante's destiny is now unmistakably Vergil's. Brunetto resembles Palinurus only in having failed to complete his mission, and he has now been left, like Palinurus, naked on the strand (*Aen.* 5.871). In Vergil Dante has found a master whose art and wisdom can be assimilated and brought to a new fulfillment. In contrast, if we accept what seems to me the most plausible interpretation of his sin, Brunetto, desperately commending his *Tesoro* to his former protegé, is eternally trapped in that pedagogical sodomy which had found its self-interest in the programming of innocent minds.[67]

But while the image of the Veglio can be read as a striking illustration of Dante's responsiveness to the tone of Vergil's poetry, and the Brunetto episode as a backhanded expression of *pietas* toward his mentor, both cantos in their different ways show Vergil as an uncertain and misleading guide. His one contribution to the dialogue of Canto 15 is an apparently approving comment on Dante's too enthusiastic response to Brunetto's prophecies (99). Though he has displaced Brunetto as Dante's guide, his values and his sense of Dante's proper goal remain not clearly distinguishable from Brunetto's. Despite his apparent practical knowledge of the structure of the underworld—which is not always easy to reconcile with the infernal geography of *Aeneid* 6—he remains the Vergil whose earlier descent into Dis was the result of Erichtho's necromantic conjuration, and the implications of this strange journey continue to unfold as the *Inferno,* for a time, becomes less and less Vergilian.

The portentous allusion to Erichtho, which exposes so vividly the limitations of the Vergilian model, also recalls Erichtho's prominent role, and the very different treatment of things infernal, in Lucan's *Pharsalia.* The Thessalian witch makes a spectacular appearance in Book 6 of Lucan's

---

67. Such a reading does not of course exclude the possibility of physical sodomy, and more than one critic has suggested that Brunetto had a pederastic interest in Dante. For all that can be said on the subject of Brunetto's possible homosexuality, see the essays of Armour, Kay, and Boswell.

poem, where she summons forth a recently dead Pompeian soldier to foretell the outcome of the great battle at Pharsalia. The episode is worth examining in some detail at this point, since its uniquely grotesque poetry embodies both a forceful critique of the *Aeneid* and a veritable poetics of hell. Dante was deeply impressed by both, and his Erichtho episode reflects his astute reading of how Lucan in his own poem had exploited Vergil.

3

Lucan and Vergil

Judgment and Poetic Authority in Dis

As suggested by Lucan's fleeting appearance as the last of the "bella scola" in Limbo and the dismissive naming of him in *Inferno* 25, Dante's appropriation of Lucan differs fundamentally from his use of Vergil, but Lucan plays an important role in his imagining of hell. Dante's representation of infernal punishment draws heavily on Lucan's virtually inexhaustible supply of images of cruelty and monstrosity, and the prophecies of political misfortune delivered by several of Dante's sinners clearly recall the *Pharsalia*.[1] But Lucan is present in the *Commedia* principally as the source of Dante's Erichtho and Cato, figures whose roles depend very largely on their function in the *Pharsalia*. For Lucan they serve in their very different ways to emblematize the futility of the poem's action and the anger and despair which lie behind it, qualities crucial to Dante's use of them. Often identified as essentially a historian by medieval commentators,[2]

---

1. See Bon, "Lucano all'*Inferno*," 78–96.
2. Moos, "*Poeta* und *historicus*." Quint, "Epic Tradition," 205–6, refines this view: "Paradoxically, the *Pharsalia* makes history its subject matter in order to demonstrate the inauthenticity of poetic interpretations of history."

Lucan is for Dante a major poet, but a poet who claims to be so utterly at the mercy of the history he narrates that epic turns involuntarily to satire as he writes, and no redeeming perspective is possible. As with Vergil, Dante will come at last to a tentatively redemptive understanding of Lucan's undertaking but only after he has exploited to the full the bitter irony that pervades the *Pharsalia*.

Erichtho

Lucan's aggrandizing presentation of Erichtho vividly exemplifies the pessimism which expresses itself most plainly in his vision of the political situation of Rome and in a profound religious skepticism. It is, moreover, part of a sustained attack on Vergil. The *Pharsalia* aims to use recent Roman history to expose as false the high hopes embodied in the historical prophecies of the *Aeneid*, by showing that the triumph of Julius Caesar entailed the death of Roman liberty and paved the way for the horrors of *imperium* enacted during Lucan's own brief lifetime. This historical vision is framed by a bizarre, stunted version of epic convention in which the traditional gods play no significant role, and are effectively displaced by fortune, fate, and various kinds of magic. All these peculiarly Lucanian features converge in the Erichtho episode, introduced by a survey of Thessalian magic which refers again and again to the impunity with which its practitioners ignore the sacred authority of the gods, usurp or arrest their cosmic functions, and compel them to submit to its power. Erichtho, the most wicked of these witches, is also the most powerful. Though she offers neither prayer nor sacrifice, the gods accede to any wicked design at the first sound of her voice, fearful of what a second incantation might produce (*Phars*. 6.527–28).

What is realized in the art of Erichtho is precisely what religion denies and the highest poetry refuses to countenance, an utterly godless communion with death through control of the physical laws of nature. It is all the truth Lucan allows his hapless Rome. The prophecies Erichtho extorts through her magic are doubly circumscribed, by religious despair and by the grim *contemptus mundi* of the prophesying shades, whose only desire is never to be made to live again. Inevitably, the resulting vision of

Rome's future is a nightmare, Lucan's bitter rejoinder to Vergil's Augustan pageantry.

In effect Lucan's Erichtho episode rewrites *Aeneid* 6 as "scritta morta,"[3] and thereby declares the suitability of Lucan to serve, not as a guide, but as a sort of conditioning agent for Dante's descent into Dis. Vergil remains present to the Pilgrim as the journey proceeds, but the invocation of Lucan sanctions an indulgence of anger and an emphasis on horror and the grotesque for which Vergil offers no precedent. There is no discrediting of Vergil in this; indeed Dante's recourse to Lucan is a covert acknowledgment that it is the very high seriousness of the "altissimo poeta" that makes the *Aeneid* an inappropriate model at this stage, and the *Pharsalia* an apt one. For if Dante unquestionably admired Lucan, as a poet of great power and a profound student of the *Aeneid,* he also recognized a dark humor in Lucan's bitterness, a hint of mockery in his deployment of epic machinery, qualities which become important resources in the later cantos of the *Inferno.* And the Erichtho episode, where the horrific and the comic continually interact, provides perhaps the fullest illustration of how these resources function in the *Pharsalia.*

Both the power of Erichtho and its limitations are made clear in this description of the murky cave within which she practices her art:

Marcentes intus tenebrae pallensque sub antris
longa nocte situs numquam nisi carmine factum
lumen habet. Non Taenariis sic faucibus aer
sedit iners, maestum mundi confine latentis
ac nostri, quo non metuant admittere manes
Tartarei reges. Nam, quamuis Thessala uates
uim faciat fatis, dubium est, quod traxerit illuc,
aspiciat Stygias, an quod descenderit, umbras.

(Phars. 6.646–53)

[Within the cave are dank shadows and pallid decay; there is never light unless produced by incantation. Not in the very

---

3. For a full account of Lucan's anti-Vergilian project, see Danese, "L'anticosmo di Eritto."

jaws of Taenarus is the air so heavy. It is a grim barrier between
the other world and our own, and the rulers of Tartarus do not
fear to allow shades to come here. For although the Thessalian
witch has the power to control [the shades], it is not plain
whether she is so empowered because she has drawn them
forth, or because she has herself descended into the Stygian
darkness.]

The *Aeneid* offers no equivalent to Lucan's emphasis on the atmosphere
of his scene; the creation of horror is here an end in itself. Once we accus-
tom our eyes to its lurid glow, we can see in this passage a virtual allegory of the production of classical poetry, considered as "scritta morta."
Erictho's involvement with the Stygian realm is as much as anything else
a matter of representation, of the "carmen" which illumines a place of
utter spiritual darkness, mysterious only so long as we remain in doubt
regarding the uncertain balance of conjuration and participation through
which she makes present the shades of the dead.

The portentous question raised in the final lines of the passage—
does Erichtho draw forth the shades by incantation, or does she herself
descend into the underworld?—undermines the effect of terror, for its answer is already clear. Erichtho is an earthbound, human creature, no more
capable than any other of crossing the "maestum confine" that separates
the natural from the infernal world.[4] If we cannot absolutely deny the
reality of the space within which her conjurations are realized, we may
at least recognize that it exists largely through the act of an imagination
driven by anger and despair. The only border that is transgressed here is
that which separates *fas,* the mores and *pietas* that culture and social order
require, from *nefas,* a compulsion to inhumanity and sacrilege. And Lucan's
narration cannot conceal the futility of Erichtho's elaborate gestures in the
face of the inexorable gravity of mortality and fate. A sense of effort accompanies each new horror, and there are no sudden manifestations of
divine power like the Sibyl's prophetic rage; everything is the product of
Erichtho's tireless and obsessive energy. The powers of hell are present
only as names to conjure with, and all her art can achieve is a temporary

---

4. See Danese, "L'anticosmo di Eritto," 227–32.

suspension of the laws of death; imagination and language give a shape and local habitation to a realm which is finally hopeless.

Dante is well aware of Erichtho's limitations, and he has provided his own answer to Lucan's mock-portentous question about the scope of Erichtho's power. This power, we should note, aims to challenge, not just the traditional gods, but the poetic tradition that affirms their power. For the Erichtho of the *Pharsalia* owes her very existence to Lucan's intense need to exorcise the spirit of Vergil, to rid the world of his poem of any trace of the hope for Augustan Rome expressed in the *Aeneid*. As Lucan declares, the space where she works has "no light but that provided by song," and Dante's invention of her conjuring of the shade of Vergil is a gloss on these words. The underworld itself is in a fundamental sense "carmen," a literary tradition which each new poet adapts to his own cultural vision. The poetic imagining of this realm can generate language that has the power to stun the spirit, and subvert its will to hope and aspire, and it is this power in Vergil's poetry that Lucan, through Erichtho, has isolated and carried to a bizarre extreme. And while Dante's poetic project is grounded in his conviction that the art of a strong poet can remake this language and give a new life to the "scritta morta" of the past, he is keenly aware that the ability to do this involves more than art, and that his own appropriation of Vergil, if considered purely as an act of poetry, has a great deal in common with Lucan's.

Lucan's peculiar perspective, however, is ideally suited to Dante's purposes at this stage, for Lucan is fully aware of his own limitations as a poet in the great tradition. His power to rewrite Vergil is as inexorably circumscribed as Erichtho's power over the hapless spirits she commands. Indeed her project is largely a parodic comment on his, as is made clear by the gratuitous anti-Vergilian touches that litter the prophecy which a hapless ghost is finally induced to utter at Erichtho's command. The triumphs of Roman power and justice foretold by Vergil's Anchises are panoramically undone, and a depopulated Elysium is overrun by the ghosts of the wicked (6.782–99), in an almost childish mockery of the authority of the *Aeneid*.

By invoking Lucan on the threshold of Dis, Dante is preparing for the deeper descent by recalling a poet whose moral seriousness is beyond question, yet who refuses to acknowledge that the outrages he condemns have a spiritual meaning, and whose poetry achieves its most powerful effects by its caustic exploitation of the epic tradition. In the later cantos of the *Inferno,* as in the *Pharsalia,* the ridiculous, grotesque, and disgusting will all have their place, and Dante makes us aware of the risk he runs in emulating Lucan—the temptation to rival his tours de force of horror and, Erichtholike, make the depiction of infernal punishment an occasion for self-indulgence.[5]

Dante's representations of suffering and violence are ordered and purposeful in comparison to those of the *Pharsalia,* where futility is the intended effect of Lucan's inventiveness. But Dante, too, makes plain in various ways the unfulfilling nature of the task of judging and dispensing punishment. As with the opening books of *Paradise Lost,* what renders the later cantos of the *Inferno* memorable is not just the awfulness of the judgments enacted in them but their ambiguous engagement with ancient culture at its most serious, their demonstration of both the power and the limitations of pathos and tragedy.

Vergil is of course the master of these modes, and the dignity he confers through them is precisely what Lucan consistently denies his characters. Like Achilles or Aeneas, Lucan's generals bear the fate of nations on their shoulders, but they are political animals, self-centered, unheroic, and fallible. When Erichtho grudgingly acknowledges in the history of their actions an order whose inexorability exceeds her power to alter, she refers, not to destiny, but to fortune (*Phars.* 6.611–15). Dante, with lower hell as his setting, creates characters who are necessarily and profoundly flawed, as willfully blind as Lucan's to the responsibilities they have neglected in their preoccupation with their own unsatisfied desires, but he manages to endow them with qualities which call into question the adequacy of the judgments he has imposed on them.

Lucan versus Vergil

Though Vergil and the Pilgrim descend into Dis under the sign of Erichtho, Lucan is present only sporadically in the cantos that follow. But he can be

---

5. Terdiman, "Problematical Virtuosity."

said to sanction Dante's project insofar as the representation of lower hell is an indictment of the flawed characters of those who have determined the fortunes of the "civitas terrena," the blind world, a political and moral order which, if capable of magnificence, has always been contaminated by egotism, greed, and misguided ambition. It is a dangerous undertaking, for Dis, we know, cannot be fathomed "sanz' ira" (*Inf.* 9.33), and it will become clear that this phrase has a special meaning for Dante, portending the necessity that he maintain for himself the kind of emotional control and stability of perspective that Vergil had provided, however imperfectly, in the earlier cantos. The risk of contagion involved in working with the *poetae* is all the greater in Dis, and like Erichtho's onslaught on *Aeneid* 6, every imitation of an ancient model now brings with it the temptation of rivalry. In the lower depths Dante's own inventive powers will play a new, larger role, and the precedents provided by the *poetae* to the extent that they are present, will become a challenge rather than a source of guidance.

Lucan is explicitly named in the episode which provides the most obvious example of the sort of gratuitous virtuosity this challenge can elicit, the elaborate metamorphosis of *Inferno* 25. Though it is Ovid whom Dante challenges directly, it is Lucan whom his own elaborate description plainly recalls,[6] and he makes clear that it is the grotesque extreme to which Lucan carries his depictions of suffering that have fascinated him. The body of Lucan's Sabellus is first decomposed, then liquified and cooked by a serpent's venom, and reduced at last to "a little slimy puddle" ("minimum . . . virus," *Phars.* 9.776). Dante describes a victim's face reduced to mere raw matter but then remolded (*Inf.* 25.124–28). In describing Nasidius' wound Lucan seems close to losing himself in hyperbole; it is "greater than his whole body, greater than anything human," so that finally "the man himself was wholly buried within this swollen thing" (*Phars.* 9.793–96). Dante's assertion that Agnello's transformed body acquired "such limbs as have never been seen," so that his "perverted" shape appears "two things and no thing" (*Inf.* 25.74–78), is only a little less incoherent in its excitement. Dante's victims are not only destroyed but also reconstituted, so that his description has the continuity that Lucan

---

6. See above, pp. 20–21.

deliberately abandons, and as Warren Ginsberg has made clear,[7] there is a deeper level at which Dante's grotesques conform to a coherent moral-theological pattern. But as the scene unfolds he shows himself as fascinated as the sinner-spectators by the process itself.

Here again Erichtho provides an important model. The power to punish, almost always by the infliction of physical pain, is her great resource, and at the same time a measure of the futility of her enterprise. Its finite scope is made clear at the critical moment when the shade of a dead soldier whom Erichtho has compelled to prophesy is on the point of reentering his body, and her activity comes to center in the abuse of a single corpse:

> adspicit adstantem proiecti corporis umbram,
> exanimes artus inuisaque claustra timentem
> carceris antiqui. Pauet ire in pectus apertum
> uisceraque et ruptas letali uulnere fibras.
> A miser extremum cui mortis munus inique
> eripitur, non posse mori! Miratur Erictho
> has fatis licuisse moras, irataque Morti
> uerberat inmotum uiuo serpente cadaver.
> (Phars. 6.720–27)

> [she sees before her the ghost of the unburied corpse,
> fearful of the lifeless limbs and hateful confinement of
> its former prison. It is afraid to enter the opened breast,
> its flesh and sinews torn by a fatal wound. Wretched one,
> unjustly robbed of death's final gift, the assurance that
> one will not die again. Erichtho marvels that such delays
> were allowed to doomed souls. Raging against death,
> she lashes the unmoving corpse with a living serpent.]

There is a terrible absurdity in the contrast between the mind-boggling idea of a witch so powerful as to launch a direct attack on fate and death themselves and the vaudevillean gesture of beating a dead body with a live snake. There is of course a more serious point here: Erichtho's furious

---

7. Ginsberg, *Dante's Aesthetics*, 115–26.

activity expresses the limitations of a world with no spiritual dimension, where the very gods exist only to be dishonored by the chants of necromancers, and human dignity counts for so little that the autonomy of the physical body is virtually all that is at stake. This is the realm into which the challenge of Lucan's horrors has led Dante. The power to punish and the power of poetry are here one and the same, and Dante's own words have become "parole crude."

Viewed in this aspect the episode raises a more general issue with which the later cantos of the *Inferno* are deeply concerned. From the moment at which Vergil praises in the Pilgrim the "alma sdegnosa" that has repudiated Filippo Argenti (8.44–45), we are alerted to the ease with which praise and blame converge in the rhetoric of hell, and how readily Dante is drawn into the process of judgment and condemnation. The Dante of lower hell, moreover, is Dante the political exile, deploying the fiercest energies of pagan art to express his detestation of political corruption, and capable of assuming himself uniquely empowered to judge the sins and declare the political destiny of Italy. But lower hell also records the Pilgrim's dawning realization that the burden of judging the greatest sins is a responsibility no mere human being has the right to assume, that no human ethical system or standard can make adequate allowance for the forces which govern human experience and determine human acts.

The point is not simply that to understand all is to be obliged to suspend judgment: Dante recognizes evil when he sees it, and his detestation of it is real and solidly grounded. But as he contrives the torments of the archsinners he is aware of the real danger inherent in the imagining of cruelty, and aware also that in the earthly fates of these figures are expressed the grandness of human aspiration, albeit in the stunted form that a fatalistic view of human destiny allows, and the tragic circumstances that can give rise to barbaric actions. The tour de force of Ulysses' account of his final voyage and the grim power of Ugolino's narrative of the fates of his sons expose deep human failings, but no moral judgment, however penetrating, can give the full measure of their meaning for Dante. They are exercises in a poetry that resists the constraint of a providential view of human destiny.[8]

---

8. Dotti, *Divina Commedia*, 17.

Lucan is hardly an adequate model for engaging these deeper questions, but it is in something like the spirit of Erichtho that Dante describes the major transition which occurs at the very center of the *Inferno*, the descent of the travelers on the back of the monster Geryon. The appearance of this creature is apparently the result of Vergil's enigmatic gesture of casting into the abyss the cord which Dante had worn around his waist, and which apparently represents an earlier intention of self-discipline that he has since abandoned (16.106–14). It is heralded by the poem's first reference to dreaming ("sogna," 122), and by Dante's first reference to his poem and his ambitions for it. Geryon himself first appears via the simile of one who dives to free an anchor caught on a reef (or on "something else hidden in the sea"), then swims back to the surface (133–36).

John Freccero has suggested that the casting of the cord represents "a surrender of self-reliance," and that learning to make this surrender is the essence of Dante's formative experience in the *Inferno*. The anxious but ultimately secure descent on the back of Geryon, marked by allusions to the disastrous flights of Icarus and Phaeton, shows Dante's imagination submitting to a controlling providence, the "epic presumption" of his former, illusory self gradually undergoing a "novelistic conversion" to humility.[9]

I am not sure the *Inferno* as a whole effects this conversion as decisively as Freccero's reading would suggest, and certainly something very different seems to me to be taking place in this episode. Rather than a reining in of imagination and a renunciation of lofty artistic pretensions, I would argue that surrendering the cord represents a necessary freeing of Dante's imaginative powers, and that the conjuring up of Geryon is an initiatory exercise in the very epic presumption which Freccero would see him leaving behind. It is significant, I think, that it is Vergil who, apparently at Dante's bidding, casts the cord into the abyss. For he, too, is being drawn into a new realm, the darker, Erichthonian hell which his own poem had declined to enter.[10] Though we know that their flight will end safely, mythological allusion suggests a sense in which Vergil is Apollo to Dante's Phaethon, Daedalus to his Icarus.

---

9. Freccero, *Poetics*, 174–76.

10. Barolini, *undivine Comedy*, 63, sees the episode as heralding a "poetics of the new" but as marking a transition "from the lyric to the epic—'Vergilian'—mode."

Geryon is "dreamed" by Dante. The diver who frees the vessel to move forward is both Dante's imagination, compelled to explore uncharted depths, and the product of his imagining, a wholly original invention which emerges as if from nowhere to effect an unprecedented transition, then abruptly vanishes.[11] In the larger context of the *Commedia* (named for the first time in 16.127–28, as if to remind us that the terrors of the *Inferno* will pass), the creation of Geryon and Dante's insistence on the veracity of his account of this truthful emblem of falsehood invite us to recognize the complex forms that verisimilitude must take in a poem so largely concerned with the unnatural and the supernatural.[12] Though hardly undertaken in the spirit of Erichtho, the imagining of Geryon, monstrous, terrifying, and disdainful of the travelers, yet wholly subservient to their need,[13] seemingly uncontrollable yet ultimately as just as his human face might suggest, exhibits the same initial effect of reckless conjuration, the same indulgence in an ultimately innocuous horror, which are all Erichtho's powers amount to.

Lucan can be seen as having provided a clearer precedent for the role Dante assumes in Canto 19, perhaps the most radical instance of self-invention in the *Commedia*. The position Dante adopts here to address the corruption of the Church resembles in many ways the stance of Lucan as commentator on the disintegration of republican Rome.[14] Both poets describe the utter degradation of a cherished ideal, speaking from the vantage point of a still darker time when the institutions to whose decay they bear witness have been replaced by their antitheses, an empire organized around the cult of its ruler[15] and a Church held captive by the king of France. And as Lucan's pain and anger find expression again and again in violent invective against the impotence of the traditional gods and the

---

11. The arrow image which describes Geryon's sudden disappearance (17.136) had been used also of the emergence of Phlegyas, another product of radical imagining, from the fumes of the Stygian marsh (8.13–14).

12. On this issue, see Macfie, "Ovid, Arachne," 166–67.

13. Geryon's "disdain" is implied by that of the falcon to which he is compared (17.127–32). Like the bird's imagined aloofness, and like his own terrifying appearance, it is part of the illusion he creates, and coexists with full obedience.

14. See Bon, "Lucano all'*Inferno*," 73–77.

15. A ruler whose "divinity," as Lucan declares in his bitter eulogy of Nero, justifies the crimes and impiety of imperial power (*Phars.* 1.37–38).

false piety that has replaced them, so Dante lets his denunciation of the corrupted papacy verge on sacrilege.

There are of course significant differences. Whereas for Lucan the civil war had meant the death of Rome itself (*Phars.* 7.632–40), Dante distinguishes the sanctity of the Church from the sinful acts of its leaders (*Inf.* 19.100–103). Lucan takes pains to define his role as futile. His work will be valued only by those who refuse to acknowledge that the battle is lost, and Pompey dead (*Phars.* 7.210–13), and their only recourse in the face of "divine" imperial power will be to make gods of their own out of the fallen heroes of the republic (*Phars.* 9.601–4). Dante, by contrast, claims an extraordinary degree of authority. His posture is that of a "vox clamantis in deserto," like the San Giovanni whose holy place he admits to having damaged, by breaking a baptismal font to rescue "one who was drowning" (*Inf.* 19.16–20). By naming the third bolgia, and praising the "somma sapienza" whose wisdom created it (*Inf.* 19.6, 10–12), he tacitly interweaves his own art with the plan of divine judgment, anticipating the quasi-priestly role he will assume in addressing the shade of Nicholas III. By the end of the canto the question of Dante's authority has become the central concern.

The boldness of the self-invention in this canto coexists with several reminders of Dante's reliance on the will and judgment of Vergil, whose concern for the Pilgrim's well-being takes the form of literally carrying him from stage to stage, and culminates in the embrace of line 120. But the emphasis on the purely practical nature of Vergil's assistance makes it plain that his role extends only this far, and that Dante is in other respects very much on his own. And it is clear as he approaches Nicholas' tomb that he does not know how to proceed. He first compares himself to the friar whom a condemned thief compels to hear an extended confession (49–51), an image in which, as throughout the dialogue which follows, disdain for the sinner is balanced by respect for sacramental authority. Bewildered by Nicholas' first speech he is unable to reply until prompted by Vergil, who puts the very words in his mouth. After this emphasis on his uncertainty and need for support, his powerful response to Nicholas' rehearsal of papal corruption seems to come out of nowhere, and as his brief preface makes plain, he, too, does not understand the impulse that makes him speak (88–89). The convulsive movements of Nicholas during Dante's harangue are attributed to "ira o coscienza" (119), and though the terms seem to probe Nicholas' suffering, they can just as well be read as pointing to Dante's powerful but confused motives for speaking.

Vergil responds warmly to Dante's "parole vere" (123), and the phrase is significant, for he is in effect the vehicle of Dante's eloquence, as is shown emblematically by the repeated emphasis on his literal transporting of the Pilgrim. And as with his physical role, the limits of his role in enabling Dante's words are carefully defined. It is the "sound" ("suon," 123) of Dante's words to which he responds, words whose cadence and tone Dante himself calls to our attention (89, 118). Vergil shows no sign of being affected by or concerned with the substance of Dante's speech.[16]

Here again the comparison of Lucan suggests itself. For the Lucan who assails the corruption of Augustan Rome is, like Dante, deeply influenced by Vergil's poetic art, and at the same time, again like Dante, he is radically distanced from Vergil's vision of Rome. The historical disasters that both poets confront can be traced to the rise of the very empire that Vergil had heralded in quasi-religious terms, but whose consequences he did not live to see. As Lucan's "saeva indignatio" had taken the form of a grotesque rewriting of *Aeneid* 6, so Nicholas' prophecy of the further contamination of the papacy by its involvement with secular power and the galvanizing effect of this prophecy on the Pilgrim are like a bitter, Erichthonian reenactment of Anchises' vision of the future greatness of Rome. The paradoxical role of Vergil in authorizing two such powerful denials of the divinely sanctioned destiny he had proclaimed for Rome is also, again paradoxically, a forceful assertion of the authority of poetry itself. Vergil alone sanctions Dante's assumption of the stance of the prophet, and in emphasizing their relationship even as he makes this radical new departure, Dante reaffirms his fundamental dependence on the tradition of the Poeti.

Canto 20, an equal and opposite reaction to Canto 19, is Vergil's, and its theme is the flawed historical vision of pagan culture and its poets. But while Vergil emphatically takes charge here, the canto exposes, as clearly as any moment in the *Commedia*, the limits of his vision. His account of

---

16. The one other occurrence of "parole vere" in the poem is *Inf.* 2.135, where Dante praises Vergil's conveyal of the "vere parole" of Beatrice; there too Vergil had been the vehicle of language whose full meaning he could not know.

the seers and diviners is marred by mockery, pedantry, and a questionable reading of his own *Aeneid,* and comes as close as any passage in the poem to revealing human weakness in his character.

Dante is deeply moved by the spectacle of human creatures whose bodies have been so cruelly distorted, whose endless tears recall Vergil's account of the Veglio, and whose slow, silent movement reminds Dante of a religious procession. Comparing their deformity to the effect of an attack of palsy such as he has never seen, he introduces an important theme of the canto, namely, that the seers, far from being necromancers or Promethean overreachers, had their prophetic powers thrust upon them, and committed no clear impiety.[17] As he weeps, leaning on the rocky wall of the valley, his identification with the seers is clear, and Vergil's first harsh words are all the more shocking.

> Qui vive la pietà quand' è ben morta:
> > chi è più scellerato che colui
> > che al giudicio divin passion comporta?
> > > (*Inf.* 20.28–30)

[Here pity lives when it is altogether dead. Who is more impious than he who sorrows at / willfully intrudes on God's judgment?[18]]

Whatever Vergil's intention, his final words clearly implicate Dante, who, though he has allowed himself, with Vergil's approval, to become deeply involved in the process of passing judgment, now gives way to a sorrow which, like his hapless pity for Francesca, seems to ignore the justice at work.

---

17. The helplessness of the seers is further suggested by "scese" in line 10, normally used of bodily movement up or down, but here applied to sight, so that Dante's view of the sinners takes on something of the effect of the Barthesian "gaze."

18. In line 30 Singleton reads "*comporta,*" where others have preferred "porta." If we read "porta," which my second translation assumes, we may hear an echo of the chagrin of Statius' Amphiaraus at having "forced his will upon a forbidding heaven" ("caelo mentem insertasse vetanti"), *Theb.* 3.550.

But Dante's tears respond to aspects of the scene to which Vergil himself, in his uncharacteristic hostility, seems willfully blind.[19] Amphiaraus, one of the Seven who laid siege to Thebes, and whom Vergil imagines being mocked by the Thebans as he is swallowed up by the earth, is depicted by Statius as exemplary in his piety, the worthy priest of Apollo, who loves him and appears on the battlefield to lament his fate (*Theb.* 7.771–77). In the underworld Amphiaraus challenges the judgment of Pluto, and affirms his innocence so effectively that he is spared the torments of Dis (*Theb.* 8.85–126), while those on earth who mourn his loss are comforted by the conviction that he will continue to exercise a benign influence as a quasi-divinity (*Theb.* 8.206–7, 335–38). There is no hint of mockery.[20] Tiresias' fortunes, compressed by Ovid into fifteen sardonic lines (*Met.* 3.324–38), attest to the arbitrariness of fate and divine judgment; the striking of two mating serpents, the act for which he was transformed into a woman, was apparently not impious, since by repeating it he regained his masculinity. (Vergil, we may note, merely reports the two transformations and offers no judgment.) Tiresias became a seer only later: compelled to judge between Jove and Juno, his decision caused Juno to strike him blind, and Jove, in ambiguous compensation, granted him the prophetic powers which enabled him to foretell the ruin of the house of Laius. The only act of Lucan's Aruns is an elaborate ritual purification of Rome, contaminated by the monstrous portents of the coming civil war. His knowledge of the future emerges unsought from these very rituals, and he fears that revealing it will be itself an impious act (*Phars.* 1.584–638).

---

19. Wilson, "Prophecy by the Dead," 27–28, suggests that Vergil's anger is due to his earlier conjuring by Erichtho, who is markedly absent from Canto 20. Hollander, "Tragedy of the Diviners," 177, suggests that Erichtho is in some sense represented by Manto, also *cruda* and also a necromancer.

20. The "dove rui?" with which Vergil imagines the Thebans taunting Amphiaraus (*Inf.* 20.33) echoes *Theb.* 8.338, where Thiodamas envisions Amphiaraus rushing not to hell but to heaven.

Barchiesi, "Catarsi classica," 78–95, sees Dante's invention here as part of a deliberately reductive treatment of Amphiaraus which would support Vergil's contemptuous view of him. But this identifies Vergil's perspective with Dante's to an extent that the later portions of the canto seem to me to call into question.

That Vergil finds a grim satisfaction in the enigmatic fates of the seers suggests that he feels an unwilling affinity with them. He, too, had both sorrowed at the loss of the primitive Italy represented by figures like Aruns and the Manto of the *Aeneid* and presumed to read the future in claiming a destiny of power and glory for Rome. It is as if he were seeking to exorcise what he now sees as the folly of both attitudes,[21] accepting the inevitability of loss and rebuking the blindness which had revealed itself in his affirmative prophecy.[22] Vergil has learned in spite of himself a lesson of which the Veglio is the emblem, an emblem he had conspicuously declined to interpret earlier. To know the future is to know too little or too much. The punishment of the seers, who now see only what is behind them, is being visited on Vergil as well, in the recognition of how inevitably his role as the prophet of empire resembles in retrospect the actions of those for whose "sin" he expresses such scorn.

Prophecy has a complex and contradictory status in the *Aeneid*. Though Vergil's Troy had lived out the "falsa gaudia" of her last days unmindful of the prophecies of Cassandra and Laocöon, prophecy plays an essential role in the later books of the poem, determining the course of Aeneas and his followers, and justifying their mission as divinely sanctioned. But every prophecy is in some way ambiguous, and while they must somehow be interpreted favorably, most, like that of the Harpy Celaeno recalled in *Inferno* 13, offer forebodings of "futuro danno."[23] The first voice to identify Italy as the Trojans' new home had been that of Cassandra (*Aen.* 3.183–87), and the irony of their belated appreciation of her veracity is pointed out by Juno in her climactic debate with Venus (*Aen.* 10.68), a debate which ends with Jupiter's famous, bewildering declaration of impartiality, leaving the outcome of the war and the fortunes of the Trojans to fate (*Aen.* 10.105–13). Even Anchises' prophecy of the future glory of Rome is charged with ominous sug-

---

21. See Dotti, *Divina Commedia*, 24. I cannot, however, agree with Dotti's further claim that Dante is here letting Vergil affirm a modern, humanistic sense of the value of human reason and human dignity.

22. Hollander, "Tragedy of the Diviners," 169–75, notes that Vergil deliberately misreads Statius' treatment of Amphiaraus and Ovid's of Tiresias.

23. See above, chap. 2, p. 52.

gestion,[24] and Vergil himself assumes the mantle of *vates* only in preparing to tell of "horrida bella" (*Aen.* 7.41). To feel hope or momentary happiness in the *Aeneid* is always to be in the position of Aeneas, "rejoicing in ignorance" as he contemplates the future events inscribed on his shield (*Aen.* 8.730). To know the whole story is to be with Aeneas as he beholds the fall of Troy portrayed on the walls of the temple of Juno in Dido's Carthage and recognizes the universal truth enacted in the city's destruction but feels himself at the same time renewed by the compassion of the tragic artist (*Aen.* 1.450–63).

The Vergil of *Inferno* 20 knows too much, and seems hardly able to acknowledge the truth. The vision of Anchises has been answered by Lucan's cruel parody, a prophecy of the annihilation of Rome and all things meaningfully Roman (*Phars.* 7.385–427),[25] a disaster so complete that he can wish the Roman republic had never existed (*Phars.* 7.440–44). Vergil himself (who is nowhere more nearly a full human being than in *Inf.* 20) has learned, in Limbo and as Dante's guide, the ultimate futility of his hopes and the truth of his forebodings.

Read in this light, Vergil's elaborate revision of the story of Manto and the founding of Mantua can seem virtually an escapist fantasy. The account in the *Aeneid* (7.198–203) had itself departed from the well-established tradition of Manto the seer, daughter of Tiresias. Vergil's Manto had been Italian, and her gift of prophecy had been part of her legacy to Mantua, and so to Vergil himself. The Manto he now recalls is Theban; like Erichtho she is called "cruda," and practices unnamed arts, but these, and a brief reference to the fate of Thebes, are the only hints of her vatic powers. She had come at length to settle in a Mantua that is literally a backwater, cut off from the greater world by a noisome marsh, and its appeal for Manto is its total isolation, "sanza coltura e d'abitanti nuda" (*Inf.* 20.84). The line recalls both the primitive Italy where Vergil's Saturn, like Manto, had sought refuge (*Aen.* 8.319–23) and Lucan's foretelling of the reversion of Rome to the same barren state (*Phars.* 7.391–99).

---

24. On this subject, see esp. Feeney, "History and Revelation"; O'Hara, *Death and the Optimistic Prophecy,* 128–75.

25. See Feeney, "History and Revelation," 8–9, 16–19.

The Manto who had lived in solitude, and whose bones are buried by the city that bears her name (*Inf.* 20.85–93), could hardly be more different from the Vergil who, sprung from Mantua, had come forth to write of Italian civilization on a progressively grander scale. But the rejection of history and civilization by the "vergine cruda" (*Inf.* 20.82) recalls the reluctance with which Vergil had taken on larger poetic tasks. During Augustus' founding of the empire he had written pastoral (*Georg.* 4.559–66), then "come out of the woods" to idealize Italy in the *Georgics,* before finally facing the challenge of epic violence, "horrentia Martis / arma."[26] The new account of Manto is like a tacit abrogation of responsibility, a hint that Vergil may sometimes wish never to have written the *Aeneid.*

The account of Eurypylus which follows has almost the effect of a sardonic joke. The passage in the *Aeneid* that mentions Eurypylus is part of the speech of Sinon (*Aen.* 2.114–19), whose falsehoods persuade the Trojans to draw the wooden horse into the city. It thus refers to an incident which presumably did not occur, and does not identify Eurypylus as an augur, though he is said to have been sent to consult the oracle of Apollo, and his report refers to the Greeks' departure from Aulis. Vergil's account to Dante, though it claims for itself the authority of the *Aeneid* and takes for granted Dante's acceptance of that authority (*Inf.* 20.112–14), seems to show an imperfect recollection of a passage which was in any case sheer invention, on his own part and on Sinon's, as though he had momentarily lost all concern for the authoritative status of his poem.

---

26. The phrases quoted are from the lines supposed to have been prefaced to the earliest editions of the *Aeneid*:

> Ille ego qui quondam gracili modulatus auena
> carmen, et egressus siluis uicina coegi
> ut quamuis auido parerent arua colono,
> gratum opus agricolis, at nunc horrentia Martis
> [Arma uirumque cano . . .]

> [I am he who once played his song on a slender reed pipe; then, coming forth from the forest, I taught the surrounding fields to obey the most demanding husbandman—a work farmers might enjoy. But now, [my song is of] Mars' terrible [arms, and of the man . . .]

The lines summarize Vergil's poetic career, and though they may not be Vergil's, they nicely capture his mixed feelings about his felt responsibility to Rome.

With Eurypylus begins a series of progressively less significant figures that ends, in the words of the admirable Sinclair, with "them that peep and mutter."[27] There is no plausible explanation for Vergil's ability, in this one instance, to identify Michael Scot and the other medieval seers, as there is no accounting for his knowledge of the history of medieval Mantua. As John Kleiner suggests, the problem is perhaps more a matter of genre than of chronology or epistemology;[28] to show the "altissimo poeta" taking an interest in modern affairs is one more way of mocking his claim to a timeless authority.

Vergil's limitations are pointed up in a more dignifying way by his own reference to the *Aeneid* as his "alta tragedìa" (*Inf.* 20.113). Dante's reference in Canto 21 to having talked with Vergil about "things of which my Comedy is not concerned to sing" (*Inf.* 21.2) may seem to relegate Vergil's discourse generally to the Limbo of false knowledge and stunted vision,[29] but the opposition of tragedy and comedy is an important consideration in the later cantos of the *Inferno,* and Dante shows himself learning new and more complex lessons from the Poeti. By the end of the *Inferno* ancient poetry has regained its privileged status, but while it continues to strongly influence Dante's invention, it also serves him in the fuller realization of his unique ambitions.

Trial and Error: Inferno 21–24

After Vergil's display of weakness in Canto 20, one of the more puzzling features of Cantos 21 and 22 is the extent to which his authority reasserts itself. Canto 20 ends with Vergil's warning that time is passing, and the moon is setting—that same moon which, Vergil says, had helped Dante in the dark wood. Given their divinely ordained mission, the passage of natural time can hardly pose a serious problem. But the warning recalls the Sibyl's similar warning to Aeneas as they approach the citadel of Dis

---

27. Sinclair, ed., *Inferno,* 256.

28. Kleiner, *Mismapping the Underworld,* 79–82, 160–61nn31–32.

29. See Barolini, *Dante's Poets,* 214–18; but as she also notes (219–20), Vergil retains the status of an "unwitting prophet, who is unknowingly a carrier of both truth and falsehood."

(*Aen.* 6.539), and the reminiscence, followed by the surprising reference to the opening scene of the *Commedia,* marks a transition. As if to confirm the vatic associations he had rejected in Canto 20, Vergil will now assume for a while the role of his own Sibyl, warding off threatened danger with a minimum of explanatory commentary, and concerned mainly with keeping to the proper path.[30] His recall of the dark wood prepares a new departure, a stage at which Dante must learn new rules and standards, and discover by trial and error how to deploy the new, more powerful voice he had assumed so abruptly in Canto 19.

The disproportion between the amount of space devoted to barratry and the paucity of judgmental commentary is striking. The several references to the Pilgrim's anxiety about threatened torments, from which he must, on reflection, know himself to be providentially immune, suggest a curious uncertainty of purpose. The leaping, diving barrators have the aimless energy and incorrigibility of the characters in an animated cartoon, and such homely comparisons as Aesop's fable of the frog and the mouse, or a dog chasing a rabbit, are an appropriate complement. When Dante finally attempts to achieve moral distance, his all-too-predictable inveighal against the fraternal orders is immediately interrupted, as both he and Vergil react to the shocking image of the crucified Caiaphas (*Inf.* 23.109–26).

Perhaps it is the nature of barratry, a sin so pervasive that no one performing civic duties can fail to feel its effects, which renders Dante so ineffectual in these cantos.[31] That Vergil's concern for the Pilgrim's well-being extends to concealment, and finally flight, suggests that what he seeks to avoid is not just the sin itself, but the risk of contamination that accompanies it, suggested by the repeated references to pitch.[32] But the

---

30. The reduction of Vergil's role is itself Vergilian. As Putnam remarks, "the hero of the *Aeneid,* after his season in the underworld, remains unguided except, finally, by the tugs of his emotions" ("Virgil's Inferno," 110). Barolini, *Dante's Poets,* 222–23, notes how Vergil's deception by Malacoda exposes his limited understanding of the nature and history of lower hell.

31. See Spitzer's famous analysis of these cantos, as a farce in which sinners, guardians, and onlookers are reduced to the same level; "The Farcical Elements," 84–86.

32. On the danger of "metamorphic contagion" in Dante's exposure to certain sins, see Barkan, *Gods Made Flesh,* 147–49.

sudden appearance of Caiaphas restores a note of seriousness, a seriousness that is markedly Vergilian. Vergil is uncharacteristically amazed at Caiaphas' plight, in which he recognizes a new, harsher form of the "eterno essilio" that he himself endures (*Inf.* 23.124–26; cp. *Purg.* 21.18), the doom of an archsinner for whom the underworld of pagan tradition provides no precedent.[33]

In Canto 24, again, much is made of Dante's dependence on Vergil to no clear purpose. Losing heart, he is restored by a "sweet look" which again carries him back to the poem's opening scene (*Inf.* 24.16–21). And again, as in Canto 1, we see Dante laboring on a steep incline, the ruins of the broken bridge. There is something artificial about the way the canto unfolds. The very long opening simile, complex and richly suggestive,[34] nonetheless refers to unexplained anxieties that turn out to be groundless. Dante's long account of the climb over the ruins says nothing of their significance, though like all the ruins in the *Inferno* they are the result of the earthquake that attended the Crucifixion and heralded Christ's descent into hell (*Inf.* 12.31–39), a fact which should provide sufficient reassurance to lighten a labor Dante seems scarcely able to perform. Vergil's heartening words, which hold up earthly fame as the reward of the fulfilled life, seem similarly overdramatic:

> "E però leva sù; vinci l'ambascia
> con l'animo che vince ogne battaglia,
> se col suo grave corpo non s'accascia.
> Più lunga scala convien che si saglia."
> (Inf. 24.52–55)

> [Rise, therefore; conquer your panting with the soul that
> wins every battle, if with the heavy body it sinks not down.
> A longer ladder must be climbed.]

---

33. On Vergil's response to Caiaphas, see Hawkins, *Dante's Testaments,* 116–18.

34. Cioffi, "Anxieties of Ovidian Influence," 78–79, reads Dante's comparison of frost to an artist whose work cannot match that of snow (24.4–6) as showing Dante's anxiety as he anticipates challenging Lucan, and especially Ovid, in Canto 25.

This exhortation aspires to become a spiritual allegory, but the effect of the third line, though it echoes Anchises' discourse on the destiny of the soul (*Aen.* 6.731), is bathetic, and like Dante's flagging spirit the words are further weighed down by their prosaic context. The detailed description of the literal climbing by which the Pilgrim seeks to rise also works against Vergil's attempt at inspiration. Dante, however, claims to have been rendered "strong and fearless" by his words, and urges him forward with an almost jaunty "Va" (*Inf.* 24.60).

The episode explicitly recalls the poem's opening. Dante's "va" and his claim to be "forte e ardito" echo his assertion of "buono ardire" in urging Vergil forward at the end of Canto 2 (*Inf.* 2.130–39). But it is a faint echo, and Dante twice admits to acting more vigorous than he feels (*Inf.* 24.58–59, 64). Though Vergil's reference to the "longer ladder" that still lies ahead recalls the larger purpose of their journey, it is for the moment as if they were going through the motions, observing the conventions of high poetic endeavor without an appropriate theme.[35]

Indeed, from Dante's account of the fifth and sixth Bolgias one might wonder whether the *Inferno* itself has a serious purpose, whether he has learned anything from his time in hell. But a part of what these cantos express, I think, is the disorientation that had followed Dante's first truly significant assumption of authority, his denunciation of papal corruption in Canto 19. As if giddy from so high a flight, he descends into silence in Canto 20, while Vergil critiques and revises the "scritta morta" which is all that remains of the vision of the Poeti. This experience would seem to have clarified his sense at least of what sort of material is inappropriate to his project as the author of a "commedia" (*Inf.* 21.1–2), but what follows is comedy of a very low order. Though it nonetheless holds the Pilgrim's interest over some three hundred lines, what it most suggests is his need to escape for a time from the challenge of finding his true voice by indulging his sheer virtuosity.

As we descend to the seventh Bolgia the sight of a ditch filled with serpents seems to renew Dante's poetic amour propre, and prepares us

---

35. For a different reading of the opening of the canto, see Barolini, *Dante's Poets,* 238–39, who sees Dante here reaffirming his love for Vergil and thereby counterbalancing the "erosion" of Vergil's authority in Cantos 21–23.

for the elaborate display of his skill in the following canto. At this point, however, he is clearly still mustering his resources. We have only his word for the claim that the variety and powers of these serpents far exceed those of Lucan's Libyan desert.[36] When he cites the cyclical life of the Phoenix to describe the burning and reconstitution of Vanni Fucci (106–11), the unaptness of the comparison and the irrelevance of its details suggest a clumsy attempt to add dignity to his account. And the apostrophe to divine power (119–20), while it recalls the "O"s and "Ahi"s of Canto 19, is palpably a compliment to himself.

Dante's only further part in the scene is the revelation—by Vanni's own account as painful to him as the fact of his damnation (*Inf.* 24.133–35)—that he had known Vanni in his earthly life. It is Vergil who questions the sinner, and it is Vanni himself who is finally the dominant presence, fixing on Dante and answering Dante's exploitation of his plight with a devastating prophecy of the violence which will end in the defeat and exile of the Bianchi of Florence, including Dante himself. One of Dante's own weapons has suddenly been turned against him, and the utter haplessness and near-anonymity of his victims in Canto 25 can almost seem intended to protect the Pilgrim from further retaliation of this sort.

From the self-preoccupation of these cantos it may seem a long step to the magnificent invention of Ulysses' speech in Canto 26, but here, too, it is possible to see Dante engaged with the ongoing problems of maintaining artistic and moral control of his material. It is generally accepted that Ulysses' wholly uncanonical and disastrous final voyage constitutes a powerful and damning critique of epic heroism, and there is firm ground for this reading. But no less significant is the manner in which the episode calls into question the possibility of such categorical damnation, and more important still is the test it provides of Dante's ability to adapt this heroic material to the larger theme of the *Inferno* while simultaneously meeting its inherent challenge, and proving his worthiness to be numbered among the Poeti.

---

36. Lucan is not named, but as at *Inf.* 14.14–15, Dante clearly has in mind Book 9 of the *Pharsalia*.

Epic and Tragedy

The Dante we see at the beginning of *Inferno* 26 seems to have learned from his mistakes, and appears acutely aware of the dangers implicit in the pyrotechnics and grotesque transformations of the preceding cantos. His response on beholding a valley filled with flames, each of which envelops the soul of an abuser of language, shows him eager to curb any impulse to virtuoso self-assertion:

> e più lo 'ngegno affreno ch'i' non soglio
> perché non corra che virtù nol guidi;
>   sì che, se stella bona o miglior cosa
>   m'ha dato 'l ben, ch'io stessi nol m'invidi.
>   (*Inf.* 26.21–24)

> [and I curb my genius more than I am wont, lest it run
> where virtue does not guide it; so that, if a kindly star
> or something better has granted me the good, I may not
> grudge myself that gift.]

The poet who speaks these lines is aware of the danger of emulation in the world of the *Inferno,* and aware as well of his good fortune in being guided, not just by the intelligence of Vergil, but by the "miglior cosa" which he will recognize with increasing clarity as the gift of grace and something like the power of prophecy. But the lines also reveal an awareness of his own artistic gift, the "ingegno" which, rightly directed, may gain him the good, not just of salvation, but of poetic fame. For perhaps the first time Dante seems fully aware of both his spiritual and his poetic vocation as he enters a new realm of experience.

But as the lines that follow make clear, Dante's fascination with what he sees and senses, in this place where the power of language is both judged and affirmed, renders his situation precarious. The simile which compares the flames to fireflies expresses this fascination innocently enough, but a second, more ambiguous simile is embedded in the lines that follow, an extended allusion to the ascent of the prophet Elijah, as beheld by his successor, Elisha. The passage is introduced by a brief reference to Elisha's first shocking exercise of his prophetic powers, a curse, uttered "in the name of the Lord," on a group of boys who had mocked him, and who are then attacked by bears.[37] The simile itself compares Elisha's perception of Elijah's ascent to the appearance of the flames which conceal the spirits of false counselors (26.34–42).

It would be hard to imagine a more vivid image for the transmission of vatic and linguistic authority, and the recipient's exercise of his dangerous and unwieldy new resource. The bears who enacted Elisha's curse and avenged the insult to his prophetic dignity recall the linkage of language and punishment in the previous canto, adding the disturbing suggestion that even prophecy can be assessed in terms of sheer power rather than revelatory import. But at the center of the simile is the contrast between Elijah's ascent, borne upward in a whirlwind by a chariot and horses of fire, and Dante's imagining of what Elisha sees, "the flame alone, like a little cloud ascending" (38–39). Dante's substition of a "nuvoletta" for the biblical whirlwind seems intended to suggest how easily the assumption of new powers can lead to a diminished awareness of the authority that sanctions their exercise. The complexity of the simile makes it an appropriate introduction to Dante's encounter with Ulysses, in which the authority of great poetic forebears is both reverently acknowledged and boldly set aside.

Remarkably, Dante discovers an aesthetic fascination in the form taken by the punishment itself in this bolgia. When Vergil points out to him the double flame which holds the spirit of Ulysses, Dante involuntarily "bends toward it with desire," as if eager to imitate its movement and establish a reciprocal relation with the spirit it contains (26.69). So strong is his desire, indeed, that he seems hardly to hear Vergil's explanation of the several sins for which Ulysses is punished, the vast providential design within which his heroic stature is dwarfed, and his famous resourcefulness judged by a new and higher standard. Dante's attitude is plainly one of reverence, a reverence that Vergil reinforces when he intervenes on Dante's behalf and offers his own reverent address to the flame. As Dante defers to Vergil and Vergil in turn bows before the shades of the

---

37. IV Kings, chap. 2, vv. 11 and 24.

two heroes, a hierarchy is asserted, one in which the authority and dignity of Homer are accorded the highest place and providential history is veiled by poetic tradition.[38] Every detail of the scene collaborates in prompting Dante to disregard for the moment his own spiritual situation.

Ulysses' famous speech is presented without comment, and his own matter-of-fact narrative conceals any hint as to his attitude toward the story he tells. There is of course plenty for us to interpret, and ample grounds for the judgment of those critics who have emphasized the deep flaws in Ulysses' character.[39] We are bound to recognize the limited capacity for social feeling in his inventory of the bonds of family: attraction to the "dolcezza" of a little son, an obligation of reverence for an aged parent, a need to express love toward Penelope which is glossed in quasi-Pauline terms as a "debitum" (26.95), all of this radically opposed to the image of familial *pietas* that Vergil's Aeneas presents.

We see that the unconquerable "ardore" which is Ulysses' greatness is now squarely at odds with responsibility, and seeks expression in nothing higher than an unfocused desire for new experiences. The "little oration" in which Ulysses exhorts his now aged companions is exciting in its resonance, but finally empty.

Given his indifference to the well-being even of his loyal companions, it is fitting that Ulysses' desire for experience should lead him finally, not to "virtute e conoscenza," but to a "mondo sanza gente," a world without people. Dante has created a hero whose sense of community, of the function of language, of the value of human life itself—to all of which he applies the demeaning adjective *picciola*—is fundamentally stunted, whose aspirations, if heroic, are also chronically self-indulgent, fatally immature.

---

38. Vergil's reference to "the horse that made the gateway by which the noble seed of the Romans went forth" (*Inf.* 26.59–60) reduces providential history to the theme of the *Aeneid*. Cf. Statius' more complex and knowing reference to a similar paradox at *Purg.* 21.82–84. Barolini, *Dante's Poets,* 228–33, shows clearly how Vergil, by recalling his own "alti versi" (82), encourages Ulysses to "mask his sin" with high rhetoric, whereas the low style of Dante and Guido in Canto 27 produces honesty and truth.

39. On the complex and divisive history of Ulysses in Dante criticism, see Barolini, *undivine Comedy,* 48–54.

How then to account for Dante's reverence, or even Vergil's? The beginning of an answer to this question must lie in the very fact of Dante's having appropriated the story of Ulysses as he has. It is a gesture in comparison to which his earlier attempts to rival Ovid and Lucan are mere bravado. More decisively than at any point in the *Commedia* he is claiming for himself an authority like that of his revered Poeti, for whom the adapting of Homeric themes to their own time and vision had been an essential task. To a poet who revered the Poeti as Dante did, his own presumption in revising the heroic tradition will have seemed hardly less perilous than the reckless "ardore" he attributes to Ulysses. In sending Homer's hero into the uncharted waters beyond the Pillars of Hercules, he is also, as if borne by another Geryon, projecting his own poetic vision into new realms. The wisdom of Vergil and the sustaining power of the classical tradition have pointed the way, but they can no longer guide him. Dante, then, is in a real sense his own Ulysses. The *Commedia* is an artistic voyage such as no previous poet had undertaken. In his exile Dante, like Ulysses, has found a substitute for family and *patria* in the pursuit of a radically personal vision. And in assigning to Ulysses a speech which makes plain the selfish and reckless aspects of the hero's quest, he is tacitly acknowledging the element of presumption, of heroic hubris in his own.[40]

But the identification thus powerfully affirmed has also a positive side. For Ulysses' quest, though governed by the self-centered code of the Homeric hero and fatally circumscribed by the spiritual horizons of paganism, is grounded in the aspiration to knowledge, which Dante celebrates in his *Convivio* as the noblest attribute of human nature, capable of making a man into something godlike. Ulysses, viewed in this aspect, is a humanist manqué, and it is perhaps not just an ironic judgment, but a tacit acknowledgment on Dante's part of the inherent nobility in which Ulysses' reckless "ardore" is grounded, that the Homeric hero's final voyage should have brought him within sight of Purgatory. To the extent that

---

40. This by no means original view is neatly encapsulated by Barolini, "Arachne, Argus, and St. John," 213: Dante's Ulysses is "a lightning rod . . . to attract and defuse the poet's consciousness of the presumption involved in anointing oneself *scriba Dei*."

Ulysses' speech evokes unquestioning admiration for the hero's adventuring spirit, it confirms the mendacious power of the eloquence for which he is forever damned. But a clear-sighted recognition of the bad-faith aspect of Ulysses' rhetoric should not preclude our sympathy with Dante's reverence toward him. In Kenelm Foster's terms, both of the two Dantes are very actively at work in shaping our perspective on Ulysses and the tradition he represents, and for the first time their roles are fully synchronized.

Ulysses' speech by itself does full justice to both the heroic and the culpably selfish aspects of his character and career, and give an added meaning to Vergil's remark that he and Diomede "a la vendetta vanno come a l'ira" (*Inf.* 26.57). The customary gloss on this line reads "ira" as the wrath of God which had punished their earthly actions by condemning them to the "vengeance" that now torments them. But the line itself places "vendetta" and "ira" side by side, simultaneous but distinct, and this is appropriate to what Dante achieves in Ulysses' speech. If we understand in "ira," not divine wrath, but human passion, the self-centered and potentially ruthless "ardore" that goads even so virtuous a hero as Aeneas, we can recognize how completely Dante has integrated his artistic and spiritual purposes. Ulysses' "ira," reinforced by Dante's, is also an agent of "the vendetta," for he is damned out of his own mouth, and damned precisely for being Ulysses,[41] an archetypally human figure who nevertheless can have only a negative relation to the economy of sacred history. It is hard to adequately define the importance for Dante of his complex and profound identification with Ulysses, and I have little to add to the fine studies of Barolini, Boitani, Padoan, Picone, and other Dantisti who have followed the Ulyssean theme through the *Commedia*.[42] Suffice it to say that from Dante's initial comparison of himself with one who has escaped from sea to shore (*Inf.* 1.21) to his final glimpse of the sea, which recalls Ulysses' "folle varco" (*Par.* 27.83), at every new stage in his poetic experience, when the sense of "novità" and the fear of presumption are strong, the shadow of Ulysses is on him.

---

41. The paradox is expressed in the high style of Ulysses' speech which, as Barolini, *undivine Comedy,* 89, notes is "truly and consistently 'great,' limited only and precisely by knowing no limitations, by its greatness."

42. Barolini, *undivine Comedy,* 48–58, 105–16; Boitani, *L'ombra di Ulisse,* 41–60; Padoan, "Ulisse 'fandi fictor,'" 170–99; Picone, "Canto XXVI," 359–73.

In Ugolino Dante encounters a "hero" of a different kind. For if Ugolino is a figure of treachery, and in this sense appropriately contained by his place in hell, he is also a tragic figure whose sense of wrong endows him with a colossal stature, and so adds a new complexity to the problem of punishment. If Ulysses challenges our knowledge of his damnation by the beauty and truth of his "ardore," Ugolino, to the extent that we allow him to complicate our response to his horrible story, can be said to prevail by the sheer power of his presence. The most obvious precedent the *poetae* provide for Dante's invention here is Statius' horrific account of the final cannibalistic agony of Tydeus at Thebes, but Ugolino's exordium to his narrative echoes Aeneas' preface to his account of the fall of Troy (*Inf.* 33.1–6; *Aen.* 2.1–13), and like Aeneas he cannot imagine his hearers failing to be moved by his story. Despite his place in hell, in his own mind he is a tragic victim, and Dante allows him to give full expression to his sense of wrong. But to isolate the tragic Ugolino is no easy matter, for his testimony, if no less powerful than Ulysses', is deeply corrupt, and corrupt in a way that is new to the poem.

A brief essay by Jorge Luis Borges on *Inferno* 33 points to the qualities in Ugolino's story that expose this corruption, which is crucial to our understanding of Dante's purpose in this canto. Borges' primary concern is with what he calls the "false problem" posed by line 75, Ugolino's famous assertion that after days of starvation during which he witnessed the deaths of four sons, "hunger proved more powerful than grief." Borges reviews the history of critical commentary on Ugolino's enigmatic declaration, and concludes that we cannot know whether Ugolino was driven to eat the flesh of the four victims, as many have supposed, or simply died of hunger after withstanding the effects of grief. To attempt to resolve this question, moreover, is to misread Dante's purpose, for the ambiguity is crucial to the effect of the scene: "To deny or affirm Ugolino's monstrous crime," says Borges, "is less horrifying than to be stunned by it."[43]

What Borges' astute argument points up is the difficulty, and perhaps even the irrelevance, of any attempt to pass a definitive judgment on Ugolino. But no less significant is the one complex turn in Borges' generally straightforward argument, his treatment of the earlier lines in which Ugolino's sons offer themselves to their father as food:

---

43. Borges, "El falso problema de Ugolino," 33.

"... tu ne vestisti
queste misere carni, e tu le spoglia."
(*Inf.* 33.62–63)

["... you did clothe us with this wretched flesh; and do you
strip us of it."]

In the face of a hallowed critical tradition, Borges professes to find here "one of the very few falsehoods present in the *Commedia*": Dante, he says, "could not but feel its falseness, which is made more serious, without doubt, by the circumstance of the four children simultaneously toasting the ravenous banquet. Some will insinuate that we are dealing with a lie of Ugolino, concocted to justify (to suggest) the previous crime."[44] We should note that Borges' insistence on the falseness in these lines is based, not just on what he sees as the implausibility of Ugolino's depiction of his children's last hours, but on its quality as art. There is a sense in which this narrative is unworthy of Ugolino—or, better, incommensurate with the tragic power of Dante's conception of him. The "falseness" of Ugolino's story reflects the grim absurdity of his attempt to vindicate himself by exploiting a system of values in the light of which he can scarcely be considered human. But it also suggests the limitations of a code which cannot possibly express or even acknowledge his tragic sense of wrong.

Of all the damned souls in the *Inferno,* only Ugolino is assigned a punishment which consists in the perpetual avenging of the suffering he claims to have undergone. The desire for vengeance that drives him to gnaw endlessly on the neck of Archbishop Ruggiero is of course insatiable, an eternal goad, but he is allowed to believe that he is causing eternal pain to his victim, and it is only in order to inflict the further pain of infamy that he interrupts his labors to tell the story of Ruggiero's treachery. Dante goes so far as to hint at a kind of savage enthusiasm for the endless task when he compares Ugolino to a dog gnawing a bone (78).

It is as if the sheer force of Ugolino's obsession with his wrongs had placed on Dante's sense of justice a claim which could not be denied. Like Farinata, Ulysses, or Guido da Montefeltro, he compels our attention

---

44. Borges, "El falso problema de Ugolino," 32.

in ways to which the sin he stands condemned of seems irrelevant, defying judgment and inviting a kind of uneasy sympathy. On first seeing Ugolino the Pilgrim himself raises the possibility that his rage against Ruggiero may be justified (*Inf.* 32.135–39),[45] and he is permitted to introduce and dominate the following canto, a privilege elsewhere granted only to Justinian and St. Bernard. Though Dante later concedes that Ugolino had been called a traitor (33.85–86), he does not confirm the charge, and the condemnation which follows is directed not against the Count but against his city.

That this condemnation centers on the treatment of the children suggests a tacit sympathy with Ugolino's intense rage, and an unquestioning acceptance of his story—a story which only Dante has heard. But the focus of Dante's sympathy suggests as well the Pilgrim's vulnerability to the appeal of sentimental piety in Ugolino's narrative, an appeal which stands in unresolved contradiction to the colossal force of his pain and rage. As Robin Kirkpatrick suggests, his is the plight of Lear's "unaccommodated man,"[46] tragically at the mercy of his need for food, family, and vindication.

It is this strange, savage power that led Matthew Arnold to discover in Ugolino's colossal self-absorption, as in that of Milton's Satan, something monumental, a kind of heroism.[47] And it is this power also that makes the pathos of his account of his sons' suffering, which for many has proven both deeply moving and spiritually profound, ring false, for Borges, for Dante, and no doubt for Ugolino himself. The elaborate emotionalism of Ugolino's appeal aims at extorting grief and tears from the Pilgrim (40–42), but the experience he relates had left the speaker himself "unmoved," in the sense in which Farinata or Ulysses is unmoved, rendered

---

45. As Barkan, *Gods Made Flesh,* 147–48, observes, Ugolino is unique in being both perpetrator and victim of the same sin, and Dante seems at least as interested in Ruggiero's treachery as in Ugolino's.

46. Kirkpatrick, *Dante's "Inferno,"* 415–27.

47. In "The Study of Poetry," 16–18, Arnold quotes lines 49 and 50, in which Ugolino contrasts his own stony incapacity for grief with the weeping of his children, lines Arnold sees as exhibiting "the very highest poetic quality." It is perhaps worth noting that Arnold considered Vergil "inadequate" to the task of writing a heroic poem.

stable by sheer preoccupation with self. We need not question Ugolino's account of how, being now blind, he had groped over his sons' bodies and called their names (72–74), but we must recognize also his inability to reach out to them while they were still alive.[48] At no point does he express remorse for this failure, and when at last, irredeemably cut off from any possibility of repentance or reparation, he acknowledges their suffering, the manner in which he does so amounts to an exploitation of their pain, an attempt to make of it grounds for his own vindication.

And it is a telling sign of Ugolino's bad faith, and Dante's honesty, that the picture we are shown is bad religious art, a narrative in which the poignancy of the young men's willingness to die, Christlike, to ease their father's pain makes a demand on our sensibilities that is finally outrageous. Not only is the self-centered savagery of Ugolino impossibly distanced from the innocence and charity of the sons with whom he seeks to identify himself: The tale he tells is kitsch, in the serious sense this quality can assume when it appears in a context that is in other respects truly serious. It is kitsch of the sort that most of the world recognized instantly as the defining quality in Mel Gibson's cinematic treatment of the Passion of Christ, which dares us to keep our eyes fixed on its sadistic representation of sacred suffering while at the same time inviting us to indulge a kind of sentimental partisanship better suited to Bambi or Rocky Balboa. It is just this unholy coupling of extreme brutality with sentimental piety that constitutes for Borges the falsehood of the narrative of Ugolino.[49] As Ugolino himself is damned as a traitor, so his story amounts to a betrayal of authentic spiritual values, and the falseness of his art is a telling sign of his guilt.

---

48. Durling and Martinez, *Time and the Crystal,* 220–23, point out that Ugolino repeatedly echoes the *canzone* "Cosi nel mio parlar," but displays only the lady's stony unresponsiveness, and none of the lover's desperate desire to communicate.

49. It is a further sign of Ugolino's palpable design that he takes pains to represent the children in his story as small and helpless, though two were grandsons, and the youngest of these, "little Anselmo," was already in his teens. And as Barolini points out (*undivine Comedy,* 96), the importance of these "children" to the historical Ugolino was largely in the political connections they enabled him to form.

But this is not all there is to say about Ugolino. Dante has in effect reduced him in his religious aspect to a mere grotesque, a character who could not possibly understand his situation in authentic religious terms. But what renders Ugolino's false piety grotesque is not just its falseness but its inadequacy to express his colossal presence and sense of wrong. If we set aside his spiritual status and the putative moral implications of his place in hell, we may see him as simply extraordinary, a psychologically gigantic figure in every sense of the word, horrific, verging on the inhuman, but at the same time somehow magnificent. So viewed Ugolino is also a potentially tragic figure, the emblem of a view of human experience that the Middle Ages could not fully acknowledge, but one that clearly had an absorbing interest for Dante.[50] His seeming inability to judge Ugolino is in part a way of acknowledging a complex interaction of character and situation that defies conventional judgment. Ugolino's sufferings are not the sufferings of Job, but he can remind us of Oedipus in his old age, or Heracles in his final madness, or Ulysses embarking on a new odyssey out of sheer invincible egotism.

But perhaps the only adequate comparison for Ugolino is with the figure on whom his situation in hell is modeled, the Tydeus of Statius' *Thebaid,* who, in his last moments, repudiates honors and funeral rites, and asks only to be given the head of the still-living Melanippus, who had inflicted his death wound (*Theb.* 8.733–40). At first he is content merely to contemplate this trophy, but even as the goddess Pallas is descending to grant him "eternal glory" (759), he is driven by Tisiphone to gnaw at it, covering his jaws and face with living blood. As his companions try vainly to tear the head from his grasp, the goddess turns away in horror.

But for all his savagery Tydeus has been a heroic figure, loved by the gods, admired by Statius for his great-spiritedness ("ingentes animos," 734) in the face of death, and contemptuous of the the frail body which has abandoned his soul ("desertorem animi," 739). Even after his "ardor" has turned to madness and he has earned the hatred of Argives and Thebans alike, he can still elicit a hero's elegy from Polynices, and in the end the Argives valiantly defend his corpse. Ugolino, too, demands of us the

---

50. Ugolino's tragic aspect is noted by Dotti, *Divina Commedia,* 41.

same combination of horror and a kind of admiration. Ugolino can never finally avenge himself, and that is his hell, but revenge is all that concerns him, so that his subjection to the divine "vendetta" seems hardly to affect his situation. His is human rage in its purest form, and it is important to recognize how carefully Dante has framed his speech. Not only do the opening lines of Ugolino's narrative echo Aeneas' exordium to the story of the fall of Troy, but his final words, followed by his renewed attack on the neck of Ruggiero, recall the final lines of the *Aeneid*. There Aeneas, momentarily moved by the helpless Turnus' dying appeal to his *pietas,* is then goaded by the sight of the belt of the young warrior Pallas, whom Turnus had killed, and avenges his friend by killing Turnus in a state of near-madness, "furiis accensus et ira" (*Aen.* 12.946). It is this final emphasis on "ira," as Michael Putnam observes, that gives the *Aeneid* its profoundly ironic "spiritual wholeness," for Aeneas in his final wrath is in effect collaborating with the Juno whose anger has driven the action of the poem.[51] Ugolino, too, is goaded by the memory of the cruel deaths of those he loved; as he tells his story, the grief which had "pressed on his heart" ("'l cor mi preme," 33.5) is revived, and with it his savagery. Aeneas, whose stoic sense of duty has compelled him to suppress the pain of loss ("premit alto corde dolorem," *Aen.* 1.209), is driven in the end by "savage grief" (12.945). However we understand the "hunger" that concludes Ugolino's story, what lives on is the hunger for revenge, which, even in its cannibalistic form, is close to the dehumanizing rage which drives Aeneas beyond the bounds of *pietas*. Both figures have been starved emotionally, thwarted by circumstance and their own rigid characters in their every attempt to express love or passion.

It is appropriate that the *Inferno* reaches its climax in the story of Ugolino; it is a powerful assertion of Dante's feeling for the tragic element in the vision of the *poetae,* and an acknowledgment of his fundamental debt to Vergil, through whom he experienced this tragic vision most profoundly. It is appropriate, too, that the one remaining human encounter in the opening canticle should take the form of a weaker, perhaps deliberately parodic version of the same Vergilian moment. Fra Alberigo's spirit,

---

51. Putnam, "Virgil's *Inferno*," 96.

like that of Turnus in the final line of the *Aeneid,* has descended to the world of the shades leaving his body behind, a fact which Alberigo mentions several times, and which is apparently the point of the episode for Dante himself (*Inf.* 33.155–57). Like Aeneas, Dante is deaf to an appeal to *pietas,* refusing Alberigo's poignant "aprimi li occhi" with the smug reflection that at times to be churlish is to do the decent thing (*Inf.* 33.149–50). In the wake of Ugolino's narrative, we may assume, to dwell on degrees of sinfulness or the aptness of judgment would be beside the point.

I return to Foster and his "two Dantes," one a humanist passionately concerned to teach his countrymen to aim at an excellence consistent with their nature, the other dedicated to the belief that fulfillment comes from beyond ourselves, that our highest excellence is knowing and loving God. The two commitments can coexist, as Foster's wonderful argument makes plain, but pursued far enough they become mutually exclusive. Ugolino is the extreme, the classic example of this irreconcilability, but his story demonstrates, like that of Ulysses and in a far more challenging way, that divine justice and human tragedy can take identical forms.[52]

---

52. As Foster notes, *Two Dantes,* 189, the fates of the great pagans in the *Inferno* suggest that sins committed "in the absence of any counter-attraction by the Christian God" can be considered "mortal." Such a view "is hardly compatible with the doctrine of God's universal will to save," and theologians could only maintain it "as idle speculation, or because of the relatively slow development, in the Church, of concern with the implications of the doctrine of God's will to save all men."

4

Cato's Grotto

Purgatorio 1

Lucan is not a significant presence in the last cantos of the *Inferno,* and it is obvious that he must cease to play a major role once Dante has left the underworld, as befits a poet for whom hope is a delusion and spiritual aspiration virtually unimaginable. In saying this I am aware that Dante's most sustained and striking engagement with Lucan, the encounter with Cato, has not yet taken place. But while Cato is commonly identified as the warden of Purgatory, and so seen as vindicating an isolated religious strain in the *Pharsalia,* I will argue that his role should rather be seen as completing the economy of the *Inferno,* for his outlook and language are governed by Lucan's essentially "infernal" poetics. It is only after Vergil and the Pilgrim have undergone Cato's inquisition and passed on that the Pilgrim's experience of Purgatory can be said to begin.

To appreciate this requires considering first how the encounter with Cato is framed. The *Purgatorio* opens with a passage in which the vocabulary of damnation is used to establish a new perspective. Poetry itself, which had "died" in the oppressive atmosphere of the *Inferno,* now revives, and there is a nicely tempered hint of adventure in the comparison of Dante's "ingegno" to a little boat, now clear of the "cruel" waters of hell. He has emerged from the "dead air" to behold, as at the beginning of the *Inferno,* the beauty of the heavens, made joyous by Venus, and adorned with stars unknown to a northern hemisphere "widowed" since the loss of Paradise. The sense of imaginative renewal could hardly be stronger, and Dante's invocation of the "sante Muse" suggests a new sense of the integration of spiritual and artistic purpose.

Amid all this, Dante invokes Calliope:

> e qui Calïopè alquanto surga,
> seguitando il mio canto con quel suono
>   di cui le Piche misere sentiro
>   lo colpo tal, che disperar perdono.
> (*Purg.* 1.9–12)

[and here let Calliope rise up somewhat, accompanying [or "following"] my song with that strain whose stroke the wretched Pies felt so that they despaired of pardon.]

In the Ovidian episode here recalled, Calliope had "risen up" (*Met.* 5.338) to answer the Pierides' impiously distorted account of the giants' battle against the Olympian gods with the story of Ceres, Proserpina, Pluto, and Triptolemus, in which an act of divine violence is redeemed by incorporation into a productive cycle of death and renewal. Calliope's inspiration would thus seem highly appropriate to the *Purgatorio,* which is in so many ways Dante's song of the earth, imbued with hope for the recovery of the pristine condition of human nature, and so of its proper role in the hierarchy of nature at large. Dante, surprisingly, makes no reference to the substance of Calliope's song, mentioning only its sound or tone ("suono," 10) and its effect on the Pierides. But the lines also bear on Dante's situation as poet at this crucial stage in the evolution of his poem, and in this context their language deserves another look, for it shows him reflecting in a newly significant way on his relation to ancient poetry.

That Calliope is bidden to "follow" Dante's song is a significant indication of this new departure. As Dante and Vergil moved through the underworld, Dante had invariably followed Vergil, his guide, master, and teacher.[1] Though Dante's own "buono ardire" is at times explicitly the motivating force as they proceed, notably at the end of Canto 2, where he responds to the compassion of Beatrice, Vergil is always in the lead. Here at the opening of *Purgatorio*, Calliope, the voice of ancient poetry, is invoked only after Dante has already declared his dedication to the "sante muse." She is apparently a secondary power, one who is bidden to rise up "only so far," and to follow or accompany Dante's song with her own. The apparent shift of emphasis and the fact that the appeal to Calliope is qualified by the oddly prosaic "alquanto"[2] announce a new function for the Poeti, one in which their role will be ancillary to Dante's higher theme, the purification of the human spirit. But ancillary in a complicated way: the "suono" that he summons the epic muse to deliver presumably denotes the continuing influence of ancient poetry, which we are perhaps invited to imagine as a kind of basso continuo in relation to the theme of the *Purgatorio*. But the terms of the summons are oddly out of keeping with the emphasis on renewal in the surrounding lines, for Calliope's song is to have the effect of a "colpo," a rebuke so harsh as to reduce the Pierides to despair. Dante is imputing to Calliope's song the power of the "parole crude" of Charon, assailing the damned spirits on the shores of Acheron. And the imagined wretchedness of the Piche as Dante imagines it reminds us of the plight of many damned spirits in the *Inferno*, where religious discourse conveys an inevitable reminder of damnation, and a compulsive impiety is a common symptom of spiritual death.

---

1. Dante uses the verb more or less interchangeably with *seguire* to denote the Pilgrim's following of the literal footsteps of Vergil, as well as the words and actions of Vergil and other authorities. See, e.g., *Inf.* 1.113; 11.112; 16.91; *Purg.* 1.112; 2.84; 5.2; 12.10; 19.40; 29.9. In *Purg.* 1.10 the likely meaning of *seguitare* is "accompany," "follow," or "adapt oneself to" in a musical sense, but the passage nonetheless presents a unique instance in which ancient poetic authority is conceived as following modern.

2. Clay, "Metamorphosis of Ovid," 71, suggests plausibly that Dante is recalling the "*paulo* maiora canamus" of the opening line of Vergil's prophetic fourth *Eclogue*. The allusion would point forward to Statius' revelation of the redemptive power of Vergil's poem (*Purg.* 22.67–72).

I emphasize the discordant hints of the infernal in Dante's invocation of Calliope because they help to prepare us for the Pilgrim's meeting with Cato, an episode whose function in the *Commedia* seems to me to have been largely misunderstood. This extraordinary figure is of course for most readers the fullest confirmation of the renewal that the opening of *Purgatorio* depicts: Cato's release from Limbo to stand at the threshold of Purgatory is read as an affirmation of the continuity of natural virtue with the virtue attainable through grace. Auerbach is clear and decisive: Cato is a unique individual whose historical commitment to liberty justifies his transposition to "a state of definitive fulfillment, concerned no longer with the earthly works of civic virtue or the law, but with . . . the freedom of the immortal soul in the sight of God."[3] Mazzotta locates in the texts of Lucan and Vergil the concrete details of Cato's experience which seemed to medieval historians and commentators to manifest a Christlike selflessness. He shows how Cato's life can be conformed to the redemptive pattern of Exodus, and concludes that Dante's revisionary treatment of him constitutes "a mimetic representation of the redemptive pattern of history." As further evidence of Cato's personal redemption, clearly implied by Vergil's reference to the radiance his body will emanate at "the great day" (*Purg.* 1.75), Mazzotta cites the four stars which illumine Cato's face, in which he finds an intimation of the restorative *gratia sanans*. When Cato professes himself unmoved by Vergil's appeal to him in the name of his earthly wife, Marcia, the assertion amounts to a "palinode of earthly love," marking Cato's spiritual regeneration and indicating as well that "no reciprocity is possible between the lost and the elect."[4]

The impulse to sanctify Cato is of course well attested also in medieval commentary on the *Pharsalia*,[5] and seems amply supported by the elaborately reverent language Lucan employs to describe him, language which is the source of the oft-cited passages of the *Convivio* where Dante

---

3. Auerbach, *Dante, Poet of the Secular World*, 7.

4. Mazzotta, *Dante, Poet*, 36–37, 48–52, 60–65; see also Barolini, *Dante's Poets*, 35. On the four stars, see also Scott, *Dante's Political Purgatory*, 69, 227n1.

5. de Angelis, "Il testo di Lucano, Dante e Petrarca," 70–76, and ". . . e l'ultimo Lucano," 165–76; Goar, *Legend of Cato*, 77–110.

out-Lucans Lucan, making Cato's "sacro petto" the repository of the cardinal virtues in their noblest form.[6] There can be no denying such varied testimony, as there are scant grounds for doubting that the historical Cato possessed the remarkable strength of character attributed to him by contemporaries so astute as Cicero and Sallust. Nonetheless, if the Cato of the *Purgatorio* is in some sense Dante's "Roman Moses,"[7] he is also one of the great anomalies of the *Commedia*. Dante's Cato has unquestionably freed himself from the constraints and enticements of the world, yet he exhibits no capacity for participation in the dynamic spiritual life of Purgatory.

Virtually every feature of Cato's appearance and conduct is curiously hard to characterize. The light which illumines his face has been taken as a sign of grace, but there is also something hypothetical about it, derived as it is from four stars "never seen before save by the first people" (*Purg.* 1.24). Cato himself vanishes abruptly at the rising of the sun, suggesting that his status differs from that of the *ombre* Dante will later encounter. When Vergil and the Pilgrim resume their journey, Cato's last words suggest his complete dissociation from their subsequent progress (106–9), and as they turn away they seem to Dante "like a man who returns to the road he had lost" (119). In keeping with his anomalous status, the caves in which Cato evidently dwells alone ("le mie grotte," 48) seem to belong neither to hell nor to Purgatory. It would appear, indeed, that Dante has provided the martyr of Roman liberty with a Limbo all his own.[8]

In Purgatory it is once again possible to love, imagine, and aspire, yet Cato exhibits none of these impulses, and so stands in a wholly antipathetic relation to the governing poetics of this portion of the *Commedia*. In a realm where grace is the ruling power, Cato is associated emphatically with old and unalterable laws. The *Purgatorio* opens with rejoicing over the Pilgrim's release from the "aura morta" of the underworld, yet Cato initiates the action by threatening Vergil and Dante with the very laws of hell (*Purg.* 1.40–48). His words are charged with menacing reminders of

---

6. See *Conv.* 4.5.16; 4.6.10; 4.27.3; 4.28.13–19.

7. Franke, *Dante's Interpretive Journey,* 223; also Hollander, *Allegory,* 124–26.

8. Carlo Grabher, in a note to *Purg.* 1.75 in his edition of the *Commedia,* calls Cato's abode "quasi un altro ideale 'nobile castello'" (cp. *Inf.* 4.106), though he suggests that Cato will finally be reunited with his body and ascend to heaven.

the endless imprisonment and deep darkness that impose themselves as law on damned spirits such as he takes Dante and Vergil to be. They have the quality of the inscription over the gates in *Inferno* 3, or Caron's "parole crude," and they offer a veritable lexicon of the idiom of infernal demoralization ("cieco," "pregione," "notte," "nera," "inferna," "abisso," "dannati"). They convey Cato's still-vivid memory of the world from which he has been withdrawn, but offer no hint that he is aware of an alternative world, or any higher purpose in human life. They suggest, moreover, a limited capacity to imagine God. Cato says nothing to confirm or deny the pagan Vergil's apparent assumption that he will be among the saved. But later, when he rebukes the "slothful" pilgrims in Canto 2, momentarily distracted by Casella's song, and bids them rid themselves of "the slough which prevents God from being manifested to you" (2.122–23), the terms of his admonition may hint that he himself has not been granted religious vision and cannot recognize it in others.

At the outset of a journey that will involve the resurgence of poetry, which had become dead in the loveless world of the *Inferno,* Cato appears uniquely hostile to both love and poetry. He is immune to what he views as the mere "lusinghe" of Vergil's eloquence (92),[9] that same "parola ornata" which has mediated to Dante the will of the court of heaven and reawakened the love which sustains him in his journey. Cato acknowledges at second hand the influence of the "donna del ciel" who "moves" Vergil (91), but shows no sign of any comparable motivation, and seemingly fails to recognize that Vergil's courtly words, while they inevitably have much in common with those of a Jason or Ulysses, are also the means by which Vergil is fulfilling his commission. As in the *Pharsalia,* Cato's pride is in his *immovability,* his immunity to "dulcedo animae" (*Phars.* 2.380–82; 9.392–94). He is precisely unmoved by the memory of Marcia (89), and the only motion associated with him is that of his venerable white hair (42).

Yet it is just the ability to be moved, whether by the appeal of the "donna del ciel" or by Cato's moral gravity, that empowers Vergil and Dante. Hence it is appropriate that they leave Cato fixed in the unbending

---

9. Barolini, *Dante's Poets,* 241, offers a positive reading of Cato here, though she also notes Dante's care to reaffirm his reliance on Vergil in *Purg.* 3.5–6.

posture of his earthly self, and descend to kneel on the marshy shore, where Vergil ministers to Dante the quasi-sacrament of binding him with a rush (133). The humble, pliant nature of these plants, whose growth is subject to higher than natural laws, and which lend themselves to a mysterious purpose, anticipates the new law of Purgatory, and at the same time defines the limits of the world of self-assertive natural powers within which Cato remains fixed, neither damned nor redeemed.

Cato in Lucan

Dante was as attentive a reader as Lucan has ever had, and his strange and forbidding Cato is at one with what he recognized as the deeply ambivalent portrayal of Cato in the *Pharsalia*. Such is the egotism of Lucan's Cato that he is virtually incapable of human sympathy. He can be an example, and relishes this role, but he cannot be a friend. The gravity which Dante instantly recognizes in his bearing deserves no less reverence than a son owes his father (*Purg.* 1.32–33), but it is a reverence that does not necessarily involve love.[10] Cato can hardly be loved as a man, and that in itself would perhaps be enough to exclude him from Purgatory. But he can be worshiped as a quasi-deity, and as in the *Purgatorio,* the unique status the Lucanian original claims for himself fairly begs to be assigned a religious significance.[11] One of the most remarkable features of the *Pharsalia*, indeed, is Lucan's elaborate meditation, at once reverent and deeply ironic, on what is godlike in Cato, and what his deification would imply.

---

10. See *Conv.* 4.13.13, on the "debita pietade" of son toward father, and 4.8.11, where "reverenza" is glossed as "confessione di debita subiezione per manifesto segno," emphasizing its formal and quasi-official character. "Debita" in both passages corresponds to "dee" in *Purg.* 1.33, emphasizing something owed, a matter of principle rather than affection, like the "debito amore," with its overtones of the Pauline conjugal *debitum,* which Ulysses grudgingly acknowledges as owed to Penelope (*Inf.* 26.95–96).

11. As Tambling, *Dante and Difference,* 19, observes, Dante's Cato is radically "depersonalized," not so much a text as a cluster of attributes prefabricated, as it were, for allegorization. Cp. Ahl, *Lucan,* 274–78, on Cato as the symbol of *pietas.*

The *Pharsalia* is a poem without a hero. Each of its leading characters is shown failing to fulfill the synecdochic role required of the cental figure of a truly epic poem of Rome.[12] Cato's portrait is accordingly mixed, outwardly idealizing, yet faithful to the perversely inflexible character of the historical man. For it is clear that admirers of the integrity and self-consistency of Cato's conduct as man and politician were at the same time put off by his rigidity. A refusal to compromise, which made Cato the implacable enemy of any waiving of the constitutional prerogatives of the Senate, has been seen as largely responsible for goading Caesar and Pompey into the alliance which eventually undermined the republic. It forced Cato to accept a provincial appointment that amounted to political exile, and it ended in a rivalry between the two great generals that made civil war inevitable. Thus Cato, the champion of liberty and the republic, could be said to have paved the way for Caesar's final triumph and the extension of that triumph to the establishment of the *imperium*.[13]

In one sense, and certainly at first sight, Cato embodies what Lucan considers finest in the Roman character. The *Pharsalia*'s opening image of a powerful nation driven to pierce its own vitals (*Phars.* 1.2–3) overshadows the ensuing narrative with a premonition of Cato's suicide (which Lucan nowhere mentions), suggesting that this act was the truest expression of the tragic fate of the republic. We first encounter Cato himself awake in the dead of night, pondering the precarious state of the nation, "uncaring for his own well-being but fearful for the people" (2.240–41), focused on what he sees as the common good. It is to Cato, as to an oracle, that his nephew Brutus, eager to act at this critical time, comes for counsel.

But as the ensuing dialogue makes plain, Cato's concern for Rome coexists with an egotism which verges at times on the grotesque. For all his public eloquence, Cato's real wish is to be *the* embodiment of loyalty to the republican ideal: he points to his own "fearless virtue," and makes it a measure of the desperateness of Rome's plight that even he ("et me," 2.288) could be drawn into the "summum nefas" of civil war. He is equally

---

12. See Hardie, *Epic Successors*, 3–8.

13. See Scullard, *From the Gracchi to Nero*, 112–17; Syme, *Roman Revolution*, 44–46. For a more positive view of Cato as politician, see Gruen, *Last Generation*, 53–55.

insistent that Roman freedom, the one thing for which he is prepared to fight, is dead. He will twice be hailed as the father of Rome (2.388, 9.601), but he himself sees his paternal duty as that of a father participating in the funeral rites of his sons:

> . . . non ante reuellar
> exanimem quam te complectar, Roma; tuumque
> nomen, Libertas, et inanem prosequar umbram.
>   (*Phars.* 2.301–3)

[. . . never will I be forced to abandon you, O Rome, until I have embraced your lifeless body, and I will follow [to the grave], O Liberty, your name and your empty shade.]

Yet despite the avowed futility of his cause, Cato can imagine offering himself as a sacrifice, atoning with his blood for Rome's guilt, and sparing conquered nations from Roman violence (2.312–15). His argument in support of this wish (which seems to have had no practical consequence) is hard to follow; the rhetoric in which it is cast and the role it defines are little short of Christlike, but what seems most important to Cato is that through such a death he would prove himself the last, the sole true champion of republican values—values which now possess meaning, he declares, only insofar as they are identified with him:

> Me solum inuadite ferro,
> me frustra leges et inania iura tenentem.
> Hic dabit, hic pacem iugulus.
>   (*Phars.* 2.315–17)

[I alone must be pierced by your swords, I who vainly cling to laws and liberties that have no force. It is the cutting of this throat that will bring peace.]

Then, having made this dubious claim, he anticlimactically elects to ally himself with Pompey, who is at least nominally in the service of the state, recognizing as he does so that if they prevail the most Cato can hope to achieve is to dilute Pompey's sense of having conquered entirely for himself (319–23).

In his own way Cato is at least as devoted to self-advertisement as Pompey or Caesar. Nearly all the words Lucan puts into his mouth are about himself.[14] Even his famous encomium on the fallen Pompey ends by setting principled suicide above a death like Pompey's, inflicted by an enemy's hand (9.211–15)—as though Cato were already anticipating a way to assert his superiority to a rival champion in the only area that has meaning for him. All of this lends credibility to Augustine's assertion that Cato's own suicide was provoked by the fear that Caesar would pardon him, and thereby gain glory at his expense.[15] He shows no responsiveness to the devotion of Brutus or Marcia; indeed all merely personal feeling is categorically excluded from his character. As his Dantean counterpart will acknowledge, he is moved by Marcia's plea for the renewal of their marriage vows, but what Marcia asks is marriage in name only ("tantum nomen inane," 2.342), and Cato grants nothing more. In permanent mourning for humankind, he is immune to even legitimate wedded love ("iusto . . . amori," 2.379). His whole life, Lucan asserts, has been unsullied by any concession to natural feeling ("sibi nata uoluptas," 2.390–91), a claim which places him beyond the bounds of even Stoic rigor.[16]

The hero who had foreseen himself as "leading the long funeral procession to the tomb" (2.298–99) is absent during the main action of Lucan's poem,[17] but he reenters the poem in Book 9, leading the last of the republican forces through the African desert in a seemingly endless

---

14. Morford, *Poet Lucan*, 9, is perhaps being unintentionally ironic when he calls Cato's great speech against the power of oracles (*Phars.* 9.566–84) "a worthy summons by the great Stoic to his disciples to share in the proving of his virtue," and notes that Cato's style rises when speaking of himself.

15. *De civitate Dei* 1.22–24.

16. See Johnson, *Momentary Monsters*, 35–40.

17. Lucan does not tell us that Cato, despite his zeal for self-sacrifice, was in Corcyra seeing to the supply of arms and provisions during the battle at Pharsalus. Plutarch, *Cato Minor* 54, says that Pompey, knowing that in the event of victory Cato's devotion to the republic would make him resist Pompey's further ambitions, feared to give him a more powerful command.

march toward death. Like all of Cato's appearances in the poem, the episode occurs in its own removed space. What is significant in the story of the *Pharsalia* has been told: the battle has been lost and Pompey killed. Cato's desert journey can accomplish nothing. Its motive is entirely personal, and it serves mainly to display his exemplary qualities. Throughout, Cato maintains his unfaltering strength of character, refusing any kindness that might suggest vulnerability to need, and daring his soldiers to live up to his example. It is a march which, as Cato tells his men, can offer no hope, no promise of survival:

> At qui sponsore salutis
> miles eget capiturque animae dulcedine, uadat
> ad dominum meliore uia.
>
> (*Phars.* 9.392–94)

[But should any soldier require a guarantee of safety,
or feel the desire to give delight to his spirit, let him take
a more favorable path, and seek [another] master.]

What can these lines mean? The march amounts to no more than a way of proving Cato's loudly proclaimed virtue, and he himself can hope for nothing more, but why should he insist so relentlessly on its futility? "Durum iter ad leges," he had declared a few lines earlier (385): the road to freedom is hard. But the tone of the lines just quoted is almost contemptuous, and in the ensuing narrative we can see Cato using the standard of his inimitable self-discipline as a blunt instrument to humiliate his already miserable troops. The main effect of his austere presence is that loyal soldiers, dying in horrible pain, are ashamed to acknowledge their suffering.

Even the famous speech in which, disdaining oracles, he asserts that the virtuous man has god and truth within himself (9.566–84) is an exercise in sheer self-assertion, meaningless in a world which has been reduced, by his own act of will, to a serpent-infested desert. Traditional religion has proven incapable of granting sure knowledge or sustaining a sense of purpose in life. Yet Cato claims to find vindication in his own conscious virtue, and certitude in the inevitability of death. There is an undeniable sublimity in this speech, but the god it affirms is a projection of Cato's own fanatical sense of rectitude.

Dante was clearly fascinated by this portion of the *Pharsalia*. An allusion to the desert "once trodden by the feet of Cato" (*Inf.* 14.15) introduces the Third Circle and the figure of Capaneus, whose pride in his scornful defiance of the gods, which continues undiminished in hell, is like a parody of Cato's self-centered rigor. And the challenge posed by this same episode provides the impetus for the bravura performance of *Inferno 25*, Dante's own exercise in Catonian cruelty. As in his own later representation of Cato, Dante here is keenly aware of the strongly critical aspect of Lucan's treatment of his republican icon.

It would be wrong to see Lucan as utterly repudiating Cato and his Stoic virtue, though at least equally wrong to see the portrait as wholly idealizing, as so many critics of the *Pharsalia* have found it.[18] Just as recent criticism of the *Aeneid* has emphasized the darker aspects of the poem, so recent readings of Lucan have tended to focus on his pessimism and to stress the contradictions and absurdities in Cato's role and character. Philip Hardie notes Cato's "megalomaniac" altruism, and Ralph Johnson can speak of his "unfailing inhumanity."[19] For Matthew Leigh, the elaborate framing of the desert journey as an allegory of Stoic discipline, punctuated by bursts of fulsome praise and culminating in the wish that a Rome restored to freedom may some day revere Cato as a god, is the foil to a complex act of autosubversion on Lucan's part.[20] Cato's struggles, taken as ethical allegories, show virtue defeated, and his moral instruction has no clear effect.

But even a Cato committed to success rather than failure could make little difference, for the plight of the just man in the *Pharsalia* is literally impossible. Lucan is at pains to ensure that virtuous action can take only a negative form. Already in Book 7, with the decisive battle still to take place, the poet goes so far as to declare his own artistic project a lost cause:

---

18. On the need for a balanced view, see Leigh, *Lucan*, 266–67, and his comments on the readings of Ahl and Masters, 54.

19. Hardie, *Epic Successors*, 11; Johnson, *Momentary Monsters*, 37.

20. *Lucan*, 265–73. On Lucan's palpably allegorical intention in Book 9, see also Morford, *Poet Lucan*, 13–14.

cum bella legentur,
spesque metusque simul perituraque uota mouebunt,
attonitique omnes ueluti uenientia fata,
non transmissa, legent, et adhuc tibi, Magne, fauebunt.

(*Phars.* 7.210–13)

[when the story of these wars is read, they will excite hope
and fear, and still-born prayers. All will be held in suspense as
if by events still to come, rather than a report of what is past.
And even now, Pompey, they will side with you.]

It is an extraordinary declaration. Lucan's readers are condemned to a
useless act of *pietas,* offering empty prayers for a favorable outcome to
disasters long past, as if they were still to happen. Lucan here resembles
his own Cato, who had joined with Pompey fully aware that his doing so
could accomplish nothing.

It is with all of this in mind that we should read the famous lines
which have seemed to represent the apogee of Lucan's devotion to the
memory of Cato:

Ecce parens uerus patriae, dignissimus aris,
Roma, tuis, per quem numquam iurare pudebit,
et quem, si steteris umquam ceruice soluta,
nunc, olim, factura deum es.

(*Phars.* 9.601–4)

[Behold the true father of his country, one supremely worthy
of your veneration, O Rome. It will never be shameful to
swear an oath in his name, and if ever you stand erect, having
cast off the yoke, then at last you will declare Cato a god.]

Moving as we may well find them, the lines harbor a terrible irony: Having declared the futility of his own artistic project, Lucan here makes the
same declaration in different terms. To exalt Cato will be to provide precisely the recognition he longs for, repudiating the anti-Catonian world
of Caesar and empire, but acquiescing in Cato's negativism, accepting that

Fortune rules and that Cato's peculiar blend of dignity and futility is finally all there is to affirm.[21] In this respect Cato is the emblem of Lucan's own endeavor, the endeavor of a poetry activated by the self-destructive impulse of the world it describes. The context of deep pessimism and the savagery of Lucan's skepticism about the reality or efficacy of the gods are sufficient to make the recovery of Roman liberty a harmless fantasy, and reduce the deification of Cato to a sort of taunt, a last stand against the overwhelming defeat of virtue and patriotism.

There is finally a strong complementarity between Lucan's Cato and his Erichtho. If Cato is an epic hero manqué, an embodiment of virtue and spirituality in a world where neither has meaning, Erichtho is in effect Lucan's Muse. She is the poem's link to traditional epic, with its controlling deities and patterns of fate and destiny, for it is only through her manic energy that the action of the *Pharsalia* is informed with any purpose other than that represented by Fortune. Though her motives are abhorrent, and her conjurations finally pointless, she cares passionately about history, and in her frenzied assault on fate and its laws the dark inspiration of the *Pharsalia,* Lucan's bitter anger at the destruction of Roman freedom, finds its most forceful expression.

But Cato and Erichtho are deliberately relegated to the margins of the history Lucan records. They pursue their peculiar ends in an isolation defined by their own obsessions (in Cato's case his virtue, in Erichtho's her wickedness), and a strenuous refusal to venerate the gods. It is Erichtho's pride that her wicked designs sway the gods more forcefully than the *pietas* of others (6.443–44, 523–28), and Cato's one acknowledgment of the heavenly powers is the wish that they might join with the gods of hell in condemning him to die in atonement for the evil of the times (2.306–7). Both figures are engaged with history in a way that is at once intense and futile. Cato's peculiar purposes depend on the certain knowledge that the cause he is joining is lost. And however seriously we choose to take the magic Erichtho practices, her powers are equally limited. The prophecy

---

21. In *Phars.* 7.454–59, the climax of a long meditation on the evil effects of the impending battle, Lucan anticipates a time when men will be worshiped as gods. This is surely a thrust at the cult of the Caesars, but deifying Cato would amount to a comparable abandonment of true religion.

she elicits, conveyed obliquely through the conflicting emotions of the shades of heroes and villains of the Roman past as they contemplate the coming battle, emphasizes the foregone conclusion of the war and the emptiness of the republican cause. The only suspense it creates is over the question of where each general will meet his death ("ducibus tantum de funere pugna est," 6.811). And as Erichtho portentously weighs the fates of men already dead,[22] and affirms her power to grant or withhold the release of final death, the futility of her manic energy anticipates the similarly futile self-assertions of Cato in Libya, mocking his men with his superior ability to endure pointless suffering while holding in reserve only the power to destroy himself, the sole means of endowing his life with the significance he craves for it.

The End of Pagan Virtue

Why Cato? The answer, I think, is that Cato, like Ulysses or Ugolino, confronts us with a profound contradiction. Ulysses' "orazion" expresses both the glorious will to realize life's possibilities to the full and a profound immaturity; Ugolino is at once tragically grand and appallingly selfish. In both a stunted humanity betrays an authentically heroic *virtus.* In Cato *virtus* itself is defined by a similar contradiction. Dante's purpose is less obvious than Lucan's manipulation of the clichés of Stoic ethics, in that we are at least initially bound to view his Cato as indeed a "santo petto," recalling as we must the eulogizing passages of the *Convivio* and the contemporary judgments of Cato that Dante echoes in his encomium there.[23] But in the *Purgatorio* Dante views Cato's exemplary role in the light of a more searching reading of Lucan, and discovers a self-serving and aggressive virtue which is as committed to the acquisition of glory as that of Pompey or Caesar. Cato's strength of character and that of his republican forebears may show them to have been divinely inspired, as the *Convivio*

---

22. *Phars.* 6.632–33: "fata peremptorum pendent iam multa virorum, / quem superis revocasse velit." At other times Erichtho seems keenly aware of the finitude of the powers she invokes; see esp. 6.730–49.

23. For these, see Scott, *Dante's Political Purgatory,* 70–78, 228–31.

suggests, or demonstrate, as argued in the *Monarchia,* that the ascendency of Rome was due to the just manner in which she exercised her power. In either case they are wholly defined by their role in a larger plan, providential and political, and their exemplary value is correspondingly limited, a public heroism that is not the expression of an inner humanity or spirituality. The goal and reward of their virtue was the "onrata nominanza" which, in Vergil's mistaken view, gained for Brutus, Lucretia, and Cato's Marcia a place in Limbo (*Inf.* 4.76–78, 127–28).

If Erichtho represents the perilous temptations of artistic freedom, Cato embodies the dangers of political and ethical individualism, the danger that always threatens one who, in regard to these things, is of no church. Dante himself, forced to renounce "ogne cosa diletta" and dwell in exile among hostile and brutish men as a party of one (*Par.* 17.55–69), might well see in Cato a version of his own lonely integrity, all the more admirable for its superiority to bodily desire. But he was too honest not to see as well the pride and self-righteousness which threaten a man so isolated and so radically devoted to the cultivation of private virtue.

How then to reconcile this critical view with the idealized Cato of the *Convivio,* the Cato who in the *Monarchia* embodies a "blessedness in this life" which represents the fulfillment of the virtue that is ours by nature?[24] This blessed state is figured by the Earthly Paradise, and it is by figural reading of the same order that the *Convivio* makes Lucan's account of the remarriage of Marcia to Cato in old age (*Phars.* 2.326–49) a representation of the noble soul returning to God in the final phase of life (*Conv.* 4.28.13–19). No human being could better signify God than Cato, Dante declares, for in his life nobility reached its fullest expression, dedicated in maturity to the good of mankind, and in old age providing repose to virtuous souls (*Conv.* 4.27.3, 28.15). The *Convivio* is silent about Cato's suicide, but the *Monarchia* cites it as an act undertaken to teach the value of freedom (*Mon.* 2.5.15). When Dante declares that Cato's sacrifice cannot be expressed in words, he perhaps alludes to the fact that Lucan says nothing of Cato's death, but he also expresses an idea which recurs twice in the *Convivio:* so admirable is Cato that one hardly dares speak of him (*Conv.* 4.5.16; 4.6.10).

---

24. *Mon.* 3.16.7. See also Foster, *Two Dantes,* 192–201.

The image of Cato that emerges from the prose works would doubt-less have given satisfaction to the Cato of the *Pharsalia*. He is a historical figure, an authentic champion of republican liberty, but at the same time a saint, Christlike in the exemplary quality of his every word and gesture. Finally he is sui generis: his virtue approaches the divine, yet can only be expressed in relative terms ("what earthly man was more worthy to sig-nify God ?"), or by recourse to the formulas of ineffability.

But the very indefinability of Cato's virtue provides a significant link between the idealized Cato of the *Convivio* and the gruff and self-centered warden of Purgatory. It is of a piece with the uncertain significance of the imagery which surrounds this harsher Cato at his first appearance, and his indeterminate placement in an isolated realm between hell and Pur-gatory. And it links him as well with the paradoxical significance of Cato in the *Pharsalia*, a Cato whose virtue is finally ungrounded. For all his force of character, even the public life of Lucan's Cato must be seen as a fail-ure, devoid of positive political consequence, and the rigor of his personal character is his one weapon. He is the statesman without a living, truly public cause; the leader whose sense of private integrity matters more to him than the well-being of his followers or the political well-being of Rome; the ascetic who has made a religion of his own austerity.

In the hybrid world of *Convivio* 4, where Dante is concerned to grant the fullest possible scope to natural virtue, and reduces Lucan's portrait of Cato to a series of icons, we are not likely to notice these limitations. In the *Purgatorio* they emerge more plainly. If the reward of human virtue is happiness, the "something divine and blessed" which for Aristotle is its final end, Cato's total dedication to an abstraction which has lost all rela-tion to reality, the "nomen inane" of freedom, is something else. His ex-ample is at once positive and negative, perfect self-mastery uninformed by any trace of aspiration, impervious to base desires, but impervious as well to love. By repudiating the hopes and fears of traditional religion, and electing to live by the standard of a freedom which is finally only the ability to determine his own fate, he has immunized himself against the demoralization of those who still languish in the suspense of Limbo. His capacity for renunciation is the sole example he presents to spirits newly arrived on the shores of Purgatory. He can assist their forward progress only in negative ways, making them fearful of the beguilements of language and song, or demanding that they rid themselves of the grime and scurf of earthly attachments.

Spiritually, too, Cato exists more or less in vacuo; only in his isolation can he be clearly differentiated from the inhabitants of Limbo. These spirits, as Vergil will tell Sordello, are deficient only in having lacked the three "holy virtues" (*Purg.* 7.34–36). The tragic expression of this defect and its consequences is the role in the *Commedia* of Vergil himself, keenly aware of the true God whom he had not known in life, and profound in his compassion for those who share his suffering, yet irrevocably doomed to an eternity "sanza speme." In contrast, the Cato of *Purgatorio* 1 can be said to represent the consequences of a virtual immunity to the appeal of the holy virtues. The religion he acknowledges consists entirely in conformity to law. His ultimate salvation is seemingly affirmed, but it is worth noting that the assurance is provided by Vergil (*Purg.* 1.75). It is Vergil, too, whose reverence toward Cato recalls the *Convivio*,[25] and we should note also the firmness with which he imposes a reverential posture on the Pilgrim (49–51). One may ask whether Vergil, who died when the empire was still young and the horrors of Lucan's lifetime had not eroded all confidence in Roman ideals, is buying into the myth of a saintly Cato in a way that Lucan himself could not, reading Lucan's language before the fact and so failing to recognize its ironies. So he will later confess having found in the *Thebaid* only the horrors of war, and none of the spiritual intuitions that hint at Statius' conversion (*Purg.* 22.55–63).

As the *Convivio* correlates the story of Troy and Rome set forth in the *Aeneid* with the narrative of the Old Testament (*Conv.* 4.4–5), Dante's treatment of the Poeti in the *Commedia* reflects an acute sense of how literary tradition can be interpreted in the light of sacred history. History controls our sense of the irredeemable spiritual situation of Vergil, deeply religious, yet in crucial respects a prisoner within the confines of pagan belief. The anomalous status of Cato expresses Dante's sense of Lucan's lonely plight at the beginning of the Christian era, utterly disillusioned with traditional religious culture, yet too embittered by the encroachments of *imperium* to be responsive to new spiritual currents. In this respect Lucan is indeed, as when we see him in Limbo, "l'ultimo," the last

---

25. For Vergil Cato is a "santo petto" (*Purg.* 1.80; cf. *Conv.* 4.5.16).

voice of a pagan culture which has no spiritual center, and no larger goal than the acquisition of earthly power.

In the same sense Cato is the last voice of pagan virtue, the reductio ad absurdum of an ethics in which self-discipline and perhaps virtue in general are finally forms of self-assertion. He is both the saint of the *Convivio* and Lucan's archegotist, assigned by Dante to a role which invites us to consider both aspects of his character. We must take seriously the fact that Dante has freed him from the underworld, that there is a sense in which he is free of the taint of sin. But in his obsession with self-discipline he is psychologically crippled, immunized in advance against the impulses his stoicism claims to have overcome, and in his death reduced to a futile demonstration of his stunted devotion to freedom.

Cato Redeemed?

Vergil and Lucan represent for Dante the poetic vision of the ancient world, and the conclusion of *Purgatorio* 1 comments, quietly but tellingly, on the relation between the *Aeneid* and the *Pharsalia* as Dante read them. As the travelers, departing from Cato, return to their proper path (119), Dante emphasizes the spiritual communion between them. Vergil assumes a priestly role, first washing Dante's cheeks with dew, to restore the natural color which the atmosphere of hell had obscured (121–29), then ministering to him the quasi-sacrament of the rushes (133).

A complicated transition is taking place in this little scene. As Dante, correctly interpreting Vergil's "art" (126), presents his tear-stained face to his guide, we recall their initial encounter at the opening of the *Inferno*. There Vergil had at first appeared distant, bemused by Dante's plight. Here his art is in intuitive sympathy with the Pilgrim's desire, reminding us of the qualities in his poetry which enable him to mediate to Dante the will of heaven, and perhaps reconfirming the authority which had been called into question by the anxious confrontation on the threshold of Dis.[26]

---

26. The ritual cleansing Vergil here performs for Dante corresponds to Aeneas' lustration before entering Elysium (*Aen.* 6.635–36). Here for perhaps the first time allusion to *Aen.* 6 assumes a positive significance.

But the episode is also a valediction to Lucan, in the person of Cato, markedly and surprisingly sympathetic. Here, if anywhere, one can see Dante defining a quasi-spiritual role for Cato. On the one hand virtually every detail of the scene contributes to our sense that only now, having withdrawn from the presence of Cato, is Dante truly embarking on his second journey. Yet the ritual which initiates this new departure has been prescribed, and carefully defined, by Cato himself, in recognition of what he apparently recognizes as the sacred nature of Vergil's commission (91–105). Cato's long second speech, which begins with an acknowledgment of his former love of Marcia, and a hint of regret at the law which has now made it impossible for him to be moved by her memory (*Purg.* 2.85–90), suggests another way of viewing Cato's seeming lack of feeling, even as it reaffirms his austerity. That he had, after all, known love— Lucan himself acknowledges that Cato's rigidity was softened by Marcia's return to him (*Phars.* 2.350)—is perhaps what enables him to recognize a significance in the heavenly lady whose commission Vergil bears (91–93).[27] We must also take note of his recognition of the importance of purification (95–99), and his intuition of the nature of the pliant rushes with which Dante must be crowned (100–105). All this seems at odds with his rigorously self-directed behavior hitherto, and suggests an emotional and spiritual potential that in different historical circumstances might have come to fruition.

Cato's abrupt disappearance leaves us with only the most tentative hint of a possibility of transformation. As Dante is no Aeneas, so he does not elect to make a god of Cato. But if the impasse in which Dante leaves this figure recalls the barren virtue of Lucan's Cato, his placement at the very threshold of the dynamic world of Purgatory not only invites us to complicate our view of his role but suggests as well that Dante has detected in the fierce energy of Lucan's own anger evidence of a spiritual capacity to which history had denied expression. Such is the crucial and paradoxical role of the *poetae* in defining the trajectory of the *Commedia*.

---

27. See Paratore, *Antico e nuovo*, 204–10, who notes the grouping of Lucan's Marcia, Julia, and Cornelia with Lucretia in Limbo (*Inf.* 4.128) and suggests that Dante recognized in Lucan's heroines a capacity for "portata universale, sotto il velo . . . di un'allegoria legata ai soli valori della classicità pagana."

5

Ovid and Vergil in Purgatory

Typically Dantisti treat the relationship of Ovid and Dante as the medieval schools approached the *Metamorphoses,* by a process of segmentation, dealing separately with Dante's reworkings of particular myths without attempting to characterize his response to the larger movement, the "flumen" which gives continuity to Ovid's poem as a whole. An exception is Warren Ginsberg, who, by way of a careful and astute reading of *Inferno* 25, provides what amounts to a theory of Dantean metamorphosis. It is first and last a process of "unbecoming," a "failure of form" whereby the rational soul is displaced as the ordering principle, reducing human subjects to creatures "who lack inner depth, creatures devoid of an animating essence."[1] It appropriates the structure of Ovidian metamorphosis but differs fundamentally in that the changes Dante effects are meaningful within a coherent moral and spiritual order, whereas Ovid's are mere "facts," meaningful only insofar as we accept his invitation to see them as pathetic, tragic, or poetically just.

---

1. Ginsberg, *Dante's Aesthetics,* 116.

Ginsberg's distinction between Dante's transformations and Ovid's is a powerful tool for interpretation. It rightly credits Dante with a transformation of Ovid's poetics that grants metamorphosis a truly allegorical function, as distinct from the superficial and arbitrary allegorizings of Ovid in the compendia of the grammarians.[2] But Ginsberg's argument, while sophisticated and persuasive, retains something of the character of the schoolroom Ovid. Concerned entirely with the limitations of Ovid's use of the theme of metamorphosis, it requires a reading *in malo* of the *Metamorphoses* as a whole. Ovidian metamorphosis as he describes it is a phenomenon proper only to the world of the *Inferno,* a function of the justice that "moved" the creator of hell (*Inf.* 3.4), and so has always already taken place before we see sinners in their infernal condition.

Even the elaborate metamorphoses that Dante engineers in *Inferno* 25, undertaken as they are in emulation of the art of poets whose transformations amount to mere "poetizing" ("poetando," *Inf.* 25.99), are significant, so to speak, in spite of themselves. Insofar as they reflect an imaginative re-creation of the form justice has taken in punishing a particular sin, they embody a uniquely Christian poetics, and point to radical, substantial transformations "beyond the power of any pagan writer to imagine."[3] For Ovid, on the other hand, transformation alters only external forms. Hence the imagery of Ovidian metamorphosis can never be more than a source of metaphor, a vehicle for the superficial representation of the changes Dante's poem describes, and will come closest to reality when describing the negative, deforming effects of sin and judgment.

There is abundant evidence that medieval theologians, as well as grammarians, viewed the very idea of metamorphosis in these terms.[4] And many of the myths of the *Metamorphoses* undeniably express, for Dante as for Ovid, the reality of a world where human interaction is all too rarely controlled or tender, where *pietas* and the institutions it cherishes are mocked and defiled, and something like charity seems an impossi-

---

2. *Dante's Aesthetics,* 117. Robson, "Dante's Use . . . of the Medieval Allegories on Ovid," argues for Dante's use of such material; but see Hollander, *Allegory,* 202–14.

3. On this, see Ginsberg's careful reading of *Inf.* 25 in the light of the spiritual embriology of *Purg.* 25 (*Dante's Aesthetics,* 118–37).

4. See Barkan, *Gods Made Flesh,* 140–44.

bility. But however accurate as a characterization of the infernal Ovid, whose value for the Dante of the *Inferno* consists largely in his descriptions of the victimization of more or less helpless subjects by more or less inexorable forces, a reading such as Ginsberg's omits important aspects of the *Metamorphoses* themselves, and does not address the unobtrusive but pervasive presence in the *Commedia* of an Ovid whose most significant quality is his humanity. As the pairing of Ovid and Lucan in *Inferno* 25 suggests, Dante recognized that Ovid's cynicism often anticipates the bitter irony of the *Pharsalia*, and expresses a similar detestation of corrupt and abusive power. But he recognized as well that in both poets mockery veils a deep sadness, and a strong desire for renewal. And just as he manages to harness Lucan's savage energy for the purposes of the *Inferno*, so in the *Purgatorio* he can be seen discovering a function for Ovid that does justice both to Ovid the creator of exquisite torments and to the humanity that flows beneath the surface of Ovid's text. He acknowledges as well the ways in which this humanity emerges to inform the transformations of Ovidian subjects, expressing a desire for peace, freedom, and even transcendence.

Though in the *Purgatorio* Dante's allusions to specific Ovidian stories are relatively few, Ovid's poetics, and the spirit of metamorphosis in its positive aspect, are continually present. "Only now," says Dante's Statius, newly released from penance, "my soul felt free volition for a better threshold" (*Purg.* 21.68–69); to ascend the mountain of Purgatory is to undergo a prolonged metamorphosis. And the role of Ovidian paradigms and imagery in Dante's representations of positive spiritual change involves more than the provision of metaphor. Several of Dante's stories of transformation can best be understood as rereadings of Ovid which, while they may involve modern characters and contexts, fulfill the desire implicit in their Ovidian models.

The Shadow of Ovid

If *Inferno* 3 belongs to Vergil, as Padoan suggests,[5] perhaps *Purgatorio* 5, though it makes no explicit allusion to Ovid's poetry, is the "canto ovidiano

---

5. See above, chap. 2, p. 25, n. 1.

per eccellenza." The reading of Ovid implicit in this canto is impossibly distanced from the bravado of *Inferno* 25, a challenge which had in view only the surface of Ovid's poetry and the cruel brilliance of his transformations. There Dante's uncertain command of his artistic resources had resulted in a temporary loss of moral control, so that his representation of change, for all its intricate artistry, was pointlessly grotesque. In the *Purgatorio* poetry is being tested in preparation for higher tasks, and a very different reading of Ovidian metamorphosis provides a uniquely effective foil to this new departure.

By Canto 5 both Dante and Vergil have learned from their experiences since leaving the domain of Cato, but their learning has taken very different forms. Vergil, apparently ashamed at having been diverted by the song of Casella and so having incurred Cato's rebuke, is concerned chiefly with time, and the need to keep moving forward. He gives elaborate answers to Dante's questions, and at one point seems almost to attain a Christian perspective on the phenomena of Purgatory (*Purg.* 3.31–39), but the basis of his explanations of these phenomena is entirely cosmological. Like all spirits he casts no shadow (3.25–30), but his understanding is still shadowed by the limitations of the temporal world, and though his counsel can seem uncanny in its anticipation of the experiences Dante will undergo, his authority perceptibly diminishes as Dante ascends.

Dante, on the other hand, has been liberated to the point at which he can reciprocate the abiding love of Casella; voice no anxiety at the sudden intervention of Cato,[6] which stirs compunction in the penitent spirits and shames Vergil; and smile (!) tolerantly at the sloth that continues to dog Belacqua in the afterlife. He has seen his own poetry vindicated as something more than the "amoroso canto" which Francesca had echoed so deceptively in the underworld. Freed from the deadening gravity of hell, he can hear Casella's rendering of the noblest of his *canzoni* with a full appreciation of its sweet style, untroubled by any question as to its appropriateness in this new context, until the scene is dis-

---

6. Both Dante and Vergil move on abruptly at Cato's words (2.133), but the "fretta" is Vergil's, and Dante notes the uncharacteristic loss of dignity (3.10–11).

rupted by the ambiguous intervention of Cato. And in the course of his upward movement, in marked contrast to Vergil, he has rediscovered in his soul the *virtù* that experiences pleasure, "dilettanze" so absorbing that they cause him to lose contact with that other "potenza" within him which keeps track of the passage of time (4.1–9). Reflecting, he compares the two faculties:

> ch'altra potenza è quella che l'ascolta,
> e altra è quella c'ha l'anima intera:
> questa è quasi legata e quella è sciolta.
> (*Purg.* 4.10–12)

[for one faculty is that which notes [time], and another that which possesses the entire soul [through pleasure or pain]. The latter is, as it were, bound, and the former is free.]

This summarial conclusion to a rather elementary exercise in faculty psychology seems straightforward enough, but in the context of the *Purgatorio* the status of natural law is equivocal. As the opening cantos have indicated, here it is Dante's capacity to give himself wholly to his experience that is liberating: if his spirit is "bound" he is also undergoing change, though a full appreciation of this will come to him only gradually. Vergil's concern with time, on the other hand, is a symptom of his alienation, and he is free only in being uninvolved with the dynamic life of Purgatory. As the travelers move upward, the paradoxical relation of bondage and freedom will be important to our understanding of the changing relations of Dante and Vergil.

We can see this plainly in the contrasting concerns of the two poets in the opening lines of Canto 5. Dante's palpably physical presence in Purgatory immediately evokes the frank amazement of the shades, and their awe is mirrored in his own realization that it is he who so astounds them. His musing, beautifully expressed in the "pur me, pur me" of line 9, shows him wholly bound by this interaction, and it is immediately interrupted by a strong rebuke from Vergil, who urges him to free himself from his "entanglement." For Vergil the penitents are only "le genti," and he exhorts Dante in Cato's voice to be a "torre ferma" in the face of all such distractions (13–14). His curt response to the shades who run to meet Dante has the same aloofness, and ends with the wholly inappropriate suggestion that they would do well to honor the Pilgrim (36).[7] It is in implicit resistance to Vergil's command that Dante stays his steps, and yields to his natural sympathy with the moving "o"s and "deh"s of those who repented at the final hour (53).

A great deal of meaning is compressed in Jacopo del Cassero's brief description of the setting of his assassination:

> "Corsi al palude, e le cannucce e 'l braco
> m'impigliar sì, ch' i' caddi; e lì vid' io
> de le mie vene farsi in terra laco."
>
> (*Purg.* 5.82–84)

["I ran to the marsh, and the reeds and the mire so entangled me that I fell, and there I saw form on the ground a pool from my veins."]

The uncommon verb *impigliare* which describes Jacopo's entanglement had been used earlier in the canto by Vergil, indignant at Dante's allowing his mind to be "entangled" ("s'impiglia," 10) by his awareness of the souls who marvel at his presence. In fact Dante's involvement with these souls is a crucial part of his experience here, and Jacopo's entanglement at Oriaco was similarly crucial to his. It reduced him to helplessly watching the pooling of his blood on the ground, and it is while contemplating this pool that he was at once captured and freed.

---

7. For Singleton, Vergil's words mean that Dante will ask those dear to the penitents to pray for them. But Vergil shows no real interest in these shades, and little sense of their condition. While he may be thinking of prayer, his tone suggests something more like the vaguely defined "praise" that Beatrice had promised to him (*Inf.* 2.73–74), or the honor he had seen as rightly shown him by his fellow poets in Limbo. His offer would seem in any case to be discredited by Jacopo's words to Dante in 64–66. See also Kleiner, "On Failing One's Teachers," 69–70, who notes Singleton's reluctance to make the obvious connection between Vergil and the losing gambler of *Purg.* 6.1–3.

The details of Jacopo's fragmentary narrative are minimal, but we are given enough to enable us to recognize in the circumstances of his death a spiritual reenactment of the transformation of Narcissus. We are not told that Jacopo saw his own reflection in the pool of blood, but he has experienced something more profound in gazing at this "laco," in effect a benign version of the fearful "lago del cor" of *Inferno* 1. He has realized his own mortality, and this moment of solitary contemplation has brought him to repentance rather than the despair of Narcissus on coming to know himself (*Met.* 3.346–48).

Jacopo's vision is untroubled by the obstacle of self: his brief story is delivered anonymously, and he mentions his origins only as a means of soliciting prayers. His physical exhaustion, the impossibility of escape, and the encroaching vegetation, all of which suggest the first stages of entrapment in an Ovidian metamorphosis,[8] have become for him a means to spiritual liberation. In this respect the story may serve as an emblem of the way in which metamorphosis will operate in the *Purgatorio*: Ovidian narrative patterns are adapted to stories in which the unresolvable crises of the Ovidian characters are rewritten in spiritual terms and their impossible longings fulfilled. No explicit allusion signals the correspondence, but to recognize it is to see both the manner in which poetic tradition supports the project of the *Purgatorio* and the larger possibilities Dante discovers in traditional motifs.

Similar but still more oblique and complex in its evocation of Ovid is Buonconte da Montefeltro's account of how, fleeing the field of Campaldino and bleeding from a wound in his throat, he had fallen and died on the bank of the river Archiano. Having called on Mary with his last breath, his penitent spirit was received by an angel, and the devil, denied possession of his "eternal part," took revenge on his body, creating a storm

---

8. Cestaro, *Dante and the Grammar*, 122–24, in a fascinating materialist reading of *Purg.* 5, notes that Dante makes this scene "entirely personal, between Jacopo and the elements," like any number of Ovidian transformations. On the other hand I cannot understand Cestaro's emphasis on the "confusion" of Jacopo and Buonconte, their "blindness to the fragility of corporeal borders" (8, 32–33). It is true that both died after running for their lives, but their posthumous narratives are notably objective, calm, and clearly focused.

which undid the cross his arms had formed on his breast as he died, and swept the corpse downstream to the Arno, where it became buried in debris (*Purg.* 5.88–129).

At first sight the story seems quite un-Ovidian in character. The efficacy of Buonconte's last-second salvific prayer might seem to show even more clearly than that of Jacopo the irrelevance, if not the meaninglessness, of the sort of victimization Ovidian metamorphosis commonly involves. Like the devil's punishment and rough burial of the body which Buonconte's spirit has abandoned, Ovid's transformations tend to alter only the physical world, while the true identities of Dante's penitents lie deeper and are finally inviolable. There is in any case no obvious Ovidian pattern here, and I am aware of perhaps having invented one. But the thwarting of violence by *pietas* in Buonconte's salvation suggests an Ovidian subtext which, whether or not by Dante's devising, provides an effective foil to Buonconte's experience: it is the passage which climaxes Ovid's account of the rape of Philomela, in which the central figure is not Philomela herself but her tongue, at the moment of its severing by Tereus:

> ille indignantem et nomen patris usque vocantem
> luctantemque loqui conprensam forcipe linguam
> abstulit ense fero; radix micat ultima linguae,
> ipsa iacet terraeque tremens inmurmurat atrae,
> utque salire solet mutilatae cauda colubrae,
> palpitat et moriens dominae vestigia quaerit.
> hoc quoque post facinus (vix ausim credere) fertur
> saepe sua lacerum repetisse libidine corpus.
>
> (*Met.* 6.555–62)

[Seizing her tongue with tongs, as it protested and struggled to speak, barely pronouncing the name of her father, [Tereus] cut it away with the cruel sword. The root of the tongue remaining quivers/gleams; the tongue itself lies trembling and murmuring on the dark earth. And just as the severed tail of a snake is apt to twitch, so the tongue trembles, and as it dies seeks the feet of its mistress. And even after such cruelty it is said (I hardly dare believe it) that [Tereus] kept repeating his act of lust on her wounded body.]

At first this passage would seem only to confirm the view of those who see Ovid's representation of pain as sadistic. Feminist critics have understandably found it pornographic, and sensed a disturbing continuity between the act of the rapist and that of the poet who records his action.[9] Only such an Ovid, it seems, would invite us to observe the flashing vibration of the bloody stump remaining in Philomela's throat, or deploy for the quivering tongue the clinical comparison of a snake's severed tail. After such description the further violence of Tereus is almost anticlimactic, and the Ovidian narrator's parenthetical "vix ausim credere" sounds smug and cynical.

Philomela's tongue utters the name of her cruelly deceived father in vain,[10] and yearns to be reunited with a "domina" who, dispossessed of her own body, has thereby lost all claim to autonomy. Her life has been irreparably damaged, and her embroidered record of her loss will only goad her sister Procne, and what survives of Philomela herself, to further violence. The murder of Itys is the almost inevitable answer to the violation of Philomela in a world from whose horrible symmetry the fantasy of metamorphosis is the only release.

The warrior Buonconte, whose wounded throat utters a last appeal that is heard and answered, is thereby exempted from violation, uplifted beyond the world of cruelty and change, where "the cross he had made of himself" as he died (126–27), like the virtue which is the essence of Philomela's sense of identity, is desecrated. As in Philomela's case so in Buonconte's it is the victim's enduring piety that provokes the climactic violation, and the human form itself that is violated. But Philomela's virgin body is crucial to her identity, her sense of her integrity as a human being,[11]

---

9. See Richlin, "Reading Ovid's Rapes," 162–66; Marder, "Disarticulated Voices," 156–62; Enterline, *Rhetoric of the Body*, 152–55.

10. The phrase "nomen patris usque" (555) underscores the futility of her prayer.

11. Philomela fears that as a consequence of her violation her shade, too, will bear the marks of her defilement (6.540–41).

whereas when Buonconte's spirit has once been claimed by the angel, his body, as he himself points out, ceases to be human—"e rimase la mia carne sola" (102).[12]

The contrast of the two stories is carried forward in the brief speech of La Pia. Imprisoned and violated like Philomela, and perhaps driven by despair to turn away from God, she has now been released into a world where her violation, still a clear and painful memory as she speaks (134–36), can be seen as providential. The very name by which she asks to be remembered is the emblem of a faith which has survived and undone the transformative effects of her violation. Philomela's world offered no grounds for such faith, and she was freed from it only to become, through her metamorphosis, an emblem of sublimated pain and artistic fantasy. But the *disiecta membra* of her story will linger in Dante's mind as he ascends through Purgatory, attesting how deeply its cruel power had impressed itself on his imagination.

Ovid's surface response of grim fascination, in the face of a suffering which his imagination seems to have penetrated to the heart, will always invite accusations of gratuitous cruelty, or a failure of taste or judgment. While great poetry hath, or ought to have, a privilege, there is probably no way to refute this charge. But such cruel details are necessary means to Ovid's depiction of the deeper, larger cruelty of power itself, and we should also see in his treatment of Philomela's mutilation an acknowledgment of what Elaine Scarry has identified as the problem of pain— that it is impossible for the victim to fully express, or for a witness to adequately compassionate, extreme suffering.[13] The agonized gestures of Philomela's tongue—gestures which had traditionally been reserved for descriptions of death in battle[14]—are a sign of how utterly Ovid repudiates the heroic world, present here only in distorted form in the person

---

12. The distinction between the animate, and therefore human, body and the mere flesh which survives the departure of the soul is important to Dante. Cp. *Inf.* 9.25; *Vita nuova* 8.1.

13. Scarry, *Body in Pain,* 3–11.

14. Lines 555–60 clearly echo *Aen.* 10.395–96; cp. Homer, *Il.* 10.457; Ennius, fr. 472. Here the struggles of the tongue reenact the appeal to love and *pietas* in the painful final speech of Philomela's father, Pandion (*Met.* 6.496–503).

of Tereus. His actions, like those of the anonymous and unseen murderers of Jacopo and Buonconte, are meaningless, though they will continue to haunt the *Purgatorio.*[15]

It is important to note how selectively Dante deals with the Ovidian myths he deploys. The reference to the song of Calliope at the opening of Canto 1 seems to point to various ways of integrating Ovidian world history into the project of the *Purgatorio.* On the one hand the allusion to the punishment of the impious Pierides seems to nicely define the negative relation of Ovidian change to the profounder and more illuminating transformations to which Dante is led by the "sante muse." And Calliope's song tells of an angry Ceres, who curses the land from which Proserpina has been stolen. But her recovery of her daughter reaffirms the innocence of nature, and she restores fertility to the world; her consecration of Triptolemus as the apostle of agriculture and her intervention to save him from imminent death at the hands of Lyncus suggest a new, providential relation between the goddess and humanity (*Met.* 5.471–661). It is easy enough to see the typological potential in such a story, which takes us from the paradise of Enna to the underworld and partway back again, but Dante chooses not to develop this theme, as he will consistently avoid the sort of facile correlation of myth and sacred history which had become canonical in the schoolroom through the mythographers and works like the "Eclogue of Theodulus." When Triptolemus is obliquely recalled later in the *Purgatorio,* it will be from the unique perspective of Statius,[16] and Dante's evocation of Proserpina is reserved for the Earthly Paradise (*Purg.* 28.49–51).

Ovidian norms and such sustaining continuity as his worldview allows would thus seem to have little or no positive significance for Dante. The experience of Jacopo is radically private, immunized against the denaturing pride that had doomed Narcissus and impervious to psychological analysis; the pool he contemplates harbors no curse but represents in the most intimate possible way his mortality, and in recognizing this he turns to God. Buonconte's narrative shows the utter irrelevance of his

---

15. See, for example, the little cluster of penitents whom Dante encounters at the beginning of *Purg.* 6 (13–18), and whose fates so resemble those of Jacopo and Buonconte as to seem like a kind of aftershock.

16. See below, chap. 6, pp. 180–81.

physical plight to his spiritual destiny. By his prayer to Mary he is separated from the world as utterly as Philomela's tongue from her body, and
to the extent that the Ovidian legend informs his story it can be seen as
an emblem of the freedom with which Dante exploits and transforms
his Ovidian material.

But there is also a sense in which Dante's appropriations consecrate
the Ovidian moments they recall. While his allusions to Narcissus and
Philomela undeniably imply by contrast the deeper level at which the
crises of Jacopo, Buonconte, or La Pia are resolved, their full meaning depends on our recognizing that they acknowledge in Ovid's own reading
of his myths a depth and humanity that "touch the mind," and in relation to which the barbarism of a Tereus becomes something trivial. Ovid
has always been preeminently a poets' poet, and an indispensible resource
for artists of all kinds. This is due in large part to their sense that while
his frequent sentimentality, cruelty, and grotesquerie are indeed superficial responses to the changes he depicts, their inadequacy is calculated,
and they invite a more probing and humane reading precisely by the challenge they offer to our basic humanity.

O imaginativa . . .

Ovid's stories of change possess another quality, too, harder to define but
fundamentally important to the work of the *Purgatorio*. From the moment at which Ovid is named in *Inferno* 25, he is identified with the sheer
power of poetic imagination, and metamorphosis comes to represent the
imaginative process itself. The greatest challenge the *Metamorphoses* present to Dante, though its full implications will become clear only in the
Paradiso, is Ovid's ability to give free rein to his imaginings while preserving his orientation and sense of purpose. The recklessness of Dante's
own challenge to Ovid (*Inf.* 25.97), together with his carefully placed
allusions to Ovidian overreachers like Arachne, Phaethon, or Marsyas,
makes it clear that he recognizes the potential dangers of such imaginative boldness. For as Ovid himself well knew, it was his willingness to
seemingly abandon his senses and *ingenium* to the power of mythic imagery that caused him, even in his own time, to be judged irresponsible

and inhumane.[17] But the associative freedom of Ovid's imaginings and the fluency of his imagery, which could obscure his essential humanity but never compromise it, were the qualities that in Dante's eyes established Ovid as one of the Poeti. If Vergil taught Dante to fully understand the vision of paganism, and the tragic character of that vision, if he learned from Lucan the power and limitations of sheer human passion as a source of poetic energy, Ovid and his poetics of transformation taught him to recognize, indulge, and finally trust his imaginative response to his experience. In itself Ovid's influence remains, no doubt, ambiguous and potentially dangerous. But the versatility and humanity of his descriptions of change make the *Metamorphoses* a uniquely valuable model for the *Purgatorio,* and he thereby played an important role in preparing Dante to become what Vergil will finally declare him, master over himself.

Dante's recourse to Ovidian paradigms in imagining the deaths of Jacopo and Buonconte is disciplined by the necessary emphasis on their intense awareness of God as they die. Hence it gives only a hint of the complexity with which the workings of imagination will soon begin to present themselves, and the ways in which metamorphosis will function. But Canto 9 begins with a cluster of images that show Dante giving freer rein to metamorphic imaginings:

> La concubina di Titone antico
>> già s'imbiancava al balco d'orïente,
>> fuor de le braccia del suo dolce amico;
> di gemme la sua fronte era lucente,
>> poste in figura del freddo animale
>> che con la coda percuote la gente;
> e la notte, de' passi con che sale,
>> fatti avea due nel loco ov' eravamo,
>> e 'l terzo già chinava in giuso l'ale.
>> (Purg. 9.1–9)

---

17. For Roman judgments on Ovid, see Hopkins, "Dryden and Ovid," 167–68; Dewar, *"Siquid habent ueri uatum praesagia,"* 383–412.

[The concubine of old Tithonus was now showing white on
the balcony of the East, forth from her sweet lover's arms; her
forehead was glittering with gems, set in the form of the cold
animal that strikes men with its tail. And in the place where we
were night had already taken two of the steps with which she
climbs, and already the third was bending down its wings.]

The much-discussed opening tercet is fraught with ambiguity. It would
seem to herald the coming of dawn, but it may refer to the lunar Aurora
which precedes the rising of the moon.[18] "Concubina" and "dolce amico"
distract us from the "antico" of line 1, which recalls Tithonus' decline into
withered old age after being claimed by Aurora. The erotic diction, the
addition of the balcony, and the elaborate imagery of jewelry invite us to
focus on the pale lady herself rather than her cosmological role. When the
jewels are revealed as stars, and finally form the sign of the deadly scor-
pion (4–6), the image is set off still more vividly, as if by an ominous but
protective barrier. These opening lines seem to announce a new departure, but one that is tentative and ambiguous, and marked by signs of reluctance and potential danger.

In the beautiful image that follows the hours of the night are, first,
the stairs by which night ascends the sky, or perhaps her ascending footsteps ("passi," 7), then instantaneously transformed into living beings who,
one by one, fold their wings as the night passes (9). Balancing the opening lines, the transformation suggests the wholly divine order by which
time is governed in Purgatory, and the irrelevance of natural law to its
workings. If there is a specific source for this strange but compelling motif,
it is perhaps an Ovidian myth that is almost equally strange. In a corner
of the cloth woven by Ovid's Pallas in her contest with Arachne, there
appears Cinyras, weeping as he embraces marble steps which were once
his daughters (*Met.* 6.98–100). If Dante recalled this myth (known to us
only from this moment in Ovid), his "hours" would represent an undo-
ing of Ovidian transformation, as well as a transcendence of the Ovidian

18. For differing views on the time of Dante's falling asleep, see Singleton's
long notes on lines 1–9, 4–6, 7–9; also Spillenger, *"Purgatorio* IX," 128–35.

world itself. Again the effect would be to counter the opening lines of the canto: they seem to portend a significant metamorphosis, but its enactment is continually deferred, as the original image is elaborated in a series of merely imagistic transformations.

On the threshold of Purgatory proper, Dante's mind remains beset by old preoccupations. The opening dawn image is sheer poetry, beautiful and allusive, but to no clear purpose. The hours of night, by contrast, are transformed in a way that is wholly unprecedented in the *Commedia,* and suggest the lines along which Dante's poetics must evolve.[19] But the image remains remote, barely articulated, and it is as if it were the effort of such imaginings that causes him in the lines that follow to "fall away," yield to the Adam in himself, and succumb to sleep. A final allusion to metamorphosis identifies the time of Dante's dream by the song of the swallow, "perhaps recalling her former woes" (15), woes that are presumably those of her human existence as Philomela. The reference to Ovidian tragedy extends the sequence of image and counterimage, balancing the quasi-avian transformation of the steps of night and drawing us back into the sphere of traditional poetic imagination.

Dante's private experience in the canto begins with a radical separation of body and spirit. As the Adam in him lies sleeping, his mind, Eve-like, departs, passing from waking "pensier" into a realm where thought is controlled by dream (*Purg.* 9.10–12, 16–18, 25). From this point forward Dante's experience will take place on two distinct levels, one defined by more or less deliberate allusions to myth, the other involving him unawares in the sacramental workings of Purgatory. As the eagle of the dream circles above him, his recollection of Ganymede provokes a vague sense of being in a special situation (25–27), but he is then aware only of being seized and borne upward to the sublunar circle of fire and wakes in terror.

Everything in this account serves to make it plain that Dante's imagination is doubly circumscribed: by the limits of the physical universe and

---

19. Picone, "Dante e i miti," 25–27, usefully distinguishes the eschatological orientation of Dante's images of transformation from the etiological character of Ovid's.

by the resources of ancient poetry. Like the Tithonus of the opening lines, like Ganymede, he feels himself possessed by a divine force, which, however, effects no meaningful transformation in his condition. As the burning sphere within which the dream experience is contained is formed by the natural love which causes fire to adhere to the inner surface of the lunar heaven,[20] so Dante's imagery is governed by purely natural forces. The influence of this dream world continues to define his thoughts on awakening, as he compares himself to the boy Achilles borne into hiding by his mother, Thetis, whose divine powers proved unable to prevent him from pursuing his native bent as a warrior. The complex allusion suggests by contrast the enduring efficacy of the divine powers that oversee Dante's journey, and also the paradoxically inhibiting effect of his dependence on the guidance of the Poeti, whose influence resists his need to realize to the full the spiritual capacities of his own imagination. The allusions to boys menaced or driven by ineluctable forces suggest a helplessness that is really a spiritual immaturity, an inability at this stage to collaborate actively in his experience of Purgatory. The extreme contrast between these imaginings of possession and Vergil's account of the intervention of Lucy, the enemy of all cruelty (*Inf.* 2.100),[21] shows Dante still bound to a world where, as he reminds us, Philomela's transformation leaves her haunted by her human fate, where change is inseparable from a more or less violent loss of autonomy. His dream experience is in synchrony with his spiritual progress—Lucy and sleep depart, as they had apparently come, "ad una" (63)—but it is clear that unlike Sordello and the other "gentil forme" who are able to ascend on their own (58), he is not yet ready to experience spiritual transformation directly. It is only after Vergil's full account of what has taken place, and in full dependence on his guide,[22] that he is able to proceed.

---

20. See *Conv.* 3.3.2; *Par.* 1.115.

21. Here as generally in the *Purgatorio*, the verb *togliere*, used of Lucy's lifting of Dante's body (59), no longer carries the suggestion of dispossession that had marked its use in the *Inferno*.

22. Dante's dependence is made clear by the "si mosse" of 9.69 (cf. above, chap. 2, p. 42, n. 27). Since a moment of enthusiasm at 3.12–15, he has been wholly submissive to Vergil.

How far Dante's state of mind falls short of spiritual preparedness is further suggested by the change he undergoes ("mi cambia' io," 67) in response to Vergil's reassuring words. The narrative calls attention to the significance of the moment as they finally move on (70–72); but the change is superficial, and Vergil must still draw him forward (107). Dante's first real contribution to their progress is his humble plea to the keeper of the gate of Purgatory (109–11). Even as the gate opens, he recalls the brief and quickly compromised stand of Lucan's Metellus against Caesar's looting of the temple of Saturn (*Phars.* 3.114–68), a final image of submission to superior force, before undergoing his first truly metamorphic experience. The creaking of the metal doors arrests him, becoming a "tuono" which intermittently reveals itself as the "dolce suono" of the Te Deum (133–45)—an effect as mysterious as the transformation of the hours of night.

Moving beyond Vergil

In the next few cantos metamorphosis of this new, mysterious kind is an important concern, and Dante's adaptation to its demands begins with a fundamental alteration in the role of his senses. Canto 10 begins with an account of the climb to the next terrace which makes it clear that Dante and Vergil, however different their experiences of Purgatory, are virtually in lockstep at this point. Aside from a few rather redundant words of Vergil's, and Dante's fatigue, everything is conveyed in the first person plural, and when they emerge onto the terrace they are alone together, both equally uncertain of how to proceed (19–21). But already things are changing around them. The sharp turnings of the rocky path through the cleft in the mountain wall by which the travelers ascend are described in terms of movement ("si moveva," 8), and somehow resemble the ebb and flow of a wave (9). On emerging Dante is subjected immediately to the synaesthetic power of the reliefs on the marble wall, in which figures seem perpetually on the point of coming to life, conveying the effects of speech, motion, and sequential action in a way beyond the power of human art. Interwoven with the Pilgrim's experience of these representations are several curiously precise indications of his physical relation to Vergil, and the deliberateness with which he passes from one relief to another. As Dante ponders the Annunciation, Vergil, "'l dolce maestro" (47), who has Dante on his left "where people have their heart," and who has apparently reconsidered his stern rebuke to Dante at the beginning of Canto 5 (16–18), urges him not to focus too much on one panel. As Dante "moves" his eyes "beyond Mary" Vergil "moves" him forward (49–51). The Pilgrim then "passes" Vergil, and moves himself close to the next panel, "that it might be displayed before my eyes" (54). The prosaic diction and cumbersome syntax of the passage reduce the relationship of Vergil and Dante to mechanical terms, while Dante's own imagination is becoming subject to new, transformative forces.

Dante's experience here clearly recalls the opening book of the *Aeneid*, where Aeneas and Achates are confronted with a similarly vivid and mysterious representation of the war they have just survived, panoramically displayed on the walls of Juno's temple at Carthage. The tragic realization Aeneas comes to in beholding the depiction of all he has lost is at the same time strangely restorative, renewing hope and confidence as preparation for his own epic labor (*Aen.* 1.450–52). But it is also a profound statement about the limited power of even the greatest artistry, a reminder that all human art can do is record the truth of human experience. The scene in Purgatory is similar in many respects. Vergil is here the Achates to Dante's Aeneas, contributing little more than "heart," the reassuring fact of his faithful presence, as the Pilgrim follows the sequence of carvings. And as the definitive representation of the tragic history of his people releases Aeneas into a new realm of experience, so Dante, suddenly empowered to perceive sacred history with a new clarity, is being conditioned to respond to a higher destiny.

Of course the two scenes differ significantly. Dante's new awareness amounts to a prophetic gift, an ability to apprehend the true, sacramental meaning of a work of art, but his response to what he sees is described almost entirely in conventional aesthetic terms. What delights him is its vividly realistic quality, and he candidly acknowledges his excitement in the presence of so much "novelty" (103–4). The reminders he provides of the religious significance of the tableaux function like the prose of the *Vita nuova* to enhance retrospectively the meaning of experiences which, as Pilgrim, he had only partly understood. But it is clear that an important transition is taking place. On the one hand the passage affirms the necessary role of art as the vehicle of Dante's enlightenment. But it is clear at the same time that art as such is incapable of adequately representing this new reality. It is this that accounts for the crudely allegorical charting of his relation to Vergil, who can here be said to stand for poetic tradition, orientative and inspiring, but in itself essentially static. Vergil moves Dante while apparently remaining in one place. Dante meanwhile, moved by Vergil, is also learning to move for himself first his eyes, then his feet in response to what he sees (49, 70).

Dante is here deliberately expressing the relation of art to spiritual experience in the plainest possible terms, and any hint of the depth and beauty of the bond between the two poets would obscure his meaning. But the stark precision of his description of their relationship at this moment has an additional significance. By presenting an aesthetic experience which plainly evokes one of the most profound moments in the *Aeneid*, while at the same time reducing Vergil to the role of a mere spectator, Dante is indeed "moving past" Vergil. The verb *varcai* (53), which describes his movement as he stations himself before the tableau of the Ark and the dancing king, always in the *Purgatorio* denotes a liminal experience, the crossing of a barrier or the removal of an obstacle.[23]

Dante has ascended to a new level of perception, visionary in a way which is explicitly defined in terms of a distancing of himself from Vergil, and Vergil's authority will be perceptibly reduced as the two continue upward. The Pilgrim's new independence is still uncertain, and he is not yet capable of disciplining his newly enhanced faculties. Hence his instant response to a prompt from Vergil (whose voice has for the moment been reduced to a murmur by Dante's absorption in the art of the supreme "fabbro"), and his oddly ingenuous explanation that his eyes were eager, as always, to behold novelties (100–105). But the scenes which draw him beyond Vergil are preparing him for a new and complex poetic role, one which will require both the perfect and perfectly articulated submissiveness of Mary and the more-than-Ovidian, ecstatic (but humble) recklessness of David dancing before the ark.

---

23. See *Purg.* 7.54; 12.4; 19.43.

Very quietly, the depiction of the Annunciation suggests a new relationship between language and meaning. It is not just the masterly carving but the truthfulness of the representation of the angel that makes his "Ave" perceptible—this and the presence of Mary, whose answering words appear in her image "propriamente," not in the form of explicit letters, as in Simone Martini's wonderful Uffizi Annunciation, but as an inherent property of her perfectly submissive nature.[24] The absolute purity of this communication is of course unique, but having taken in this proclamation of a new order, Dante is able to move his eyes "beyond Mary" (50), and the image of David leading the procession of the Ark of the Covenant speaks to him in more personal terms. The oblique reference to the destruction of Uzzah, who had presumed to touch the Ark (57), recalls the stigmatizing of Dante himself as an "Uzzah" for his boldness in prescribing the duties of the Church.[25] Here the reference shows his awareness of the office he is now preparing to assume, that of an authentically Christian poet. In similar fashion the face of Michal, scornful of the immodesty of David girt up to dance (67–69), suggests a foreboding of the moment when Dante must face the scrutiny of Beatrice. But it is David, more than king in his divinely sanctioned role, less than king in the recklessness of his self-abandonment, who implicates Dante most directly. Both have assumed a role that cannot be legitimized in the conventional terms of political or spiritual authority. Each has a unique vocation which enables him to speak to his people, and on behalf of his people, in uniquely personal terms. The world of the Poeti could imagine no such role.[26]

As if to confirm this new relationship between Dante and Vergil, the final panel announces a new role for empire. If Rome had the dual mission, in Vergil's classic formula, of succoring weakness and bringing down

---

24. "Propriamente" occurs only here in the *Commedia*, but its significance can be gauged by its relation to the use of *proprio,* especially in the *Paradiso,* where it often refers to the divinely ordained, fundamentally natural properties or status of its referent. See *Par.* 1.57, 92; 5.125; 26.87; 32.14.

25. *Epist.* 11.9, 12.

26. As Barolini, *Dante's Poets,* 276, notes, "Dante's *poema sacro,* his *comedia,* is both more and less than the king of poems, the *tragedia;* as David's humility makes him more glorious, so the *comedia*'s lowly standing makes it more sublime."

the proud (*Aen.* 6.853), Trajan's response to the widow's appeal gives a new prominence to the first of these duties, and it is appropriately followed by the appearance of the heavily burdened penitents, a powerful but wholly unmartial representation of the humbling of pride which provokes Dante's reflection that if we would become "angelic butterflies," we must recognize that we begin as worms (124–29).

Ovidian Art

It is appropriate, too, that Dante's reaction to the ordeal of the prideful should be expressed in terms of an image of metamorphosis, for if Vergil remains the touchstone against which Dante's progress must ultimately be gauged, the new poetics which is gradually emerging can best be defined in relation to Ovid and the *Metamorphoses*. The "visibile parlare" (95) here rendered in marble is the fulfillment of the classic Ovidian fantasy of a work of art so fully realized as to be virtually alive, so perfect that it seems to rival nature. Metamorphosis itself is frequently described by Ovid in terms that make plain how closely it is connected in his mind with artistic creation.[27] It is again and again sculpture, particularly sculpture in marble, that provides the imagery for Ovid's pursuit of this theme, and his criterion of beauty and dignity. Postdiluvian civilization begins with the transformation of stones into human beings, in the process reaching a point of semiformation at which, it seems, they could evolve into either men or statues (*Met.* 1.404–6), achieve formal perfection or take the divergent path of human mutability. Narcissus, stunned by the discovery of his reflected image, resembles an image in marble (3.419), and it is only her tears and the stirring of her hair by a breeze that persuades Perseus that Andromeda is not a marble statue (4.673–75). Ovid alone reports Perseus' use of Medusa's gaze to transform two hundred unruly wedding guests into statues (*Met.* 5.177–209).

All this is conventional enough: even Vergil's Anchises concedes to the Greeks the power to cause bronze to breathe, and draw living faces

---

27. See Solodow, *World*, 203–14, a discussion to which I am much indebted.

from marble (*Aen.* 6.847–48). But while many of Ovid's graceful equivocations about the interplay of art and nature seem merely ingenious, they are underlain by a serious concern that emerges most clearly in the surprising frequency with which he refers to works of art, not simply as rivaling nature, but as setting a kind of standard for nature to aspire to. Here again the relation of metamorphosis and artistic creation comes into play. When they create figures exemplary of good and evil, endow particular images with a classic or monumental status, or do no more than establish interesting configurations, both art and metamorphosis perform a clarifying function, defining the objects that engage our thoughts and passions, helping us to view the world with greater understanding and appreciation.

In this respect Ovid's graven images assume something like the function of Dante's. Aristotle had used sculpture to illustrate his argument that excellence in art is a form of wisdom,[28] and as Solodow observes, art as Ovid conceives it can create meaning as well as beauty.[29] Hecuba in her prime had been the "image," at once emblem and embodiment, of the pride of Asia (13.484). Pygmalion's statue is surpassingly beautiful, but also virtuous: you would think it was modesty, rather than the fact of being made of ivory, that prevented her from expressing desire (10.250–51). Here we are on the verge of something like Dante's "visibile parlare," but Ovid carries the suggestion no further. His poem fulfills its purpose insofar as it asserts the humane and civilizing power of art.

In a sense, then, Canto 10, by so vividly evoking the aesthetics of Vergil and Ovid, and setting them in significant contrast even as it transcends them, is relegating both poets to the status of "mere" art, the art whose reward, as Oderisi will soon observe, is a renown that is "nought but a breath of wind" (*Purg.* 11.100–101).[30] But if the communicative power of the scenes of the terrace is beyond the reach of the Poeti, its clear allusion to their poetry and poetics is what enables us to gauge the differ-

---

28. *Eth. Nicom.* 6.7, 1141a, cited by Singleton (together with the commentary of Thomas) as the likely source for Dante's reference to "Policleto" (10.32).

29. Solodow, *World*, 213–14.

30. Oderisi's words of course also implicate Dante, as Petrarch recognized. See the discussion of his sonnet "Padre del ciel" (*Rime sparse* 62) in Kennedy, *Authorizing Petrarch*, 19–20.

ence, and reminds us that the presence of Vergil and Ovid is a constant in Dante's experience.

Determining his relation to classical artistry, in particular the kind of realism that fascinates Ovid, continues to be a problem as Dante proceeds. The lines which praise the realism of the figured pavement of Canto 12 are markedly Ovidian in tone (67–69), and seem to continue the pattern of evoking and transcending classical art that characterizes Canto 10. But the canto also shows us the incomplete metamorphosis of a hapless Arachne, suspended from the threads of her ruined embroidery (43–45), arrested in her attempt at suicide, and half-transformed into a spider, as if in parody of the "angelica farfalla" of Canto 10. The image obviously expresses the folly of Arachne's presumption in competing with Pallas and the inevitability of her punishment, and to that extent can be taken *in malo.* But in a canto where realism is the criterion of artistic excellence, it is hard to forget that Arachne's terrible fate was a consequence of her brilliant success in the realistic rendering of scenes which, like those on Dante's pavement, have a world-historical significance. The tapestry of Pallas, which shows the gods solemnly founding Athens, is, as Rachel Jacoff observes, a "simplistic moralized allegory of divine power,"[31] which denies historical truth by suppressing any hint of the conflict which arose among the gods over the naming of the city—a conflict which will later be presented to Dante as an emblem of wrath (15. 98).[32] Arachne's answering tableau shows the gods as they really are, shaping human history by the pursuit of their ruthless desires. The rape of Europa will lead to the founding of Thebes; Leda will give birth to the story of the fall of Troy; a version of history is given definitive expression which is in perfect continuity with Ovid's own, and its truth is perversely confirmed by Pallas' fierce retaliation.

How to judge an artist whose creations are blasphemous but perfectly true to life? Ovid describes Arachne's transformation in remorseless detail but points to the survival of her deep-seated will to create (*Met.* 6.140–45), and his ironic suggestion that it was pity which caused Pallas to prevent

---

31. "The Rape/Rapture of Europa: *Paradiso* 27," 236.

32. The focus of the scene in Canto 15 is on the vengeful anger of the wife of Pisistratus, but this is underscored by her reference to conflict among the gods.

her from hanging herself (135) offers a tragic perspective on her fate. His irony clearly recalls the similarly ironic pity of Juno for Vergil's Dido, whom Juno herself had effectively destroyed. Seeing Dido in agony, the goddess dispatches Iris, bearing the rainbow to which Arachne's weaving will be compared (*Met.* 6.61–64), to cut the vital thread and free Dido from a life she can no longer endure (*Aen.* 4.693–705). Pallas, more cruelly, allows Arachne to live, but ensures that she will forever hang ("pende tamen," 136) bound by the threads she herself creates, the prisoner of an artistry which is doomed to be perpetually at odds with power.

Dante seems to explicitly condemn Arachne, but his tone is hard to read:

> O folle Aragne, sì vedea io te
>   già mezza ragna, trista in su li stracci
>   de l'opera che mal per te si fé.
>   (*Purg.* 12.43–45)

> [O mad Arachne, so did I see you already half spider,
> wretched in the shreds of the work which to your own
> hurt was wrought by you!]

The horror-film quality of Arachne's incomplete metamorphosis, the harshness of "stracci," which describes the ruined tapestry,[33] and the *versi tronchi* by which the image of Arachne herself is framed (43, 45) all recall the harsh cruelty of Pallas' reaction to her success. Her entrapment in the ugly deformity of "mezza ragna" is also Pallaslike, calculated to obliterate any reminder of the beauty Arachne's ill-judged artistry had produced. But Arachne remains "trista," an object of human pity, and her ambiguous position suggests Dante's reluctance to wholly destroy her human self. The odd syntax of line 45 can be read as diverting the blame for her fate from Arachne herself to the work created by or through her ("per te"), a work which gives consummate expression to the truth of Ovid's vision of human existence.

---

33. The word appears only here. "Stracciando" describes the tearing of human flesh at *Inf.* 22.72.

The beauty of Arachne's depiction of the gods' desires is perverse, and the same perversity is present in the surging rhythm of the lines that introduce the panorama in which she appears, an account of the lightning-like fall of Lucifer, "nobil creato / più ch'altra creatura" (25–26). These lines introduce an orthodox world-historical vision, and by offering Lucifer as the archetypal model of Arachne's fatal presumption, they define it as sin. But the very lines that condemn Lucifer have a majestic beauty that will be echoed in St. Bernard's great prayer to Mary at the summit of Paradise.

Artistic imagination, then, is hard to reduce to moral terms. Perhaps in his treatment of Arachne Dante is exorcising the descriptive virtuosity which had presented itself as a temptation in the *Inferno,* the power which had produced a Ulysses too hungry for life and an Ugolino too colossal in his misery to be wholly subsumed to the ethical system of hell. The new artistic role for which Dante is being prepared will endow him with all the power of Ovid, but a power defined and disciplined by responsibilities unprecedented in poetic tradition.

The Limitations of Vergil

As if announcing a new beginning, Canto 13 begins with Dante and Vergil emerging onto a terrace wholly devoid of imagery. As in Canto 10, Dante emphasizes the placement of the travelers: Vergil carefully aligns his body before addressing the sun (14–15). He places himself between Dante and the outer edge of the terrace as they proceed (79–81), and hence Dante must turn away from him to address the shades of the envious, whose punishment no living man could behold without pity (52–54), though Vergil merely points them out. Dante carefully turns to Vergil before addressing these spirits but then ignores Vergil's characteristic command that he be "breve e arguto" (78), prefacing his one-line question with seven lines that amount to a theological *captatio benevolentiae* (85–91). At the end of the canto, for the first time in the *Purgatorio,* Dante, in explaining his presence to Sapia, refers to Vergil as his guide but identifies him only as "he who utters no word" (141).

Vergil will continue to play an important role, but the details I have noted indicate that this role has changed as he and Dante have ascended.

The encounter with Statius will briefly restore the poet of the *Aeneid* to his position as "the glory and light of other poets," but in the meantime he will be primarily a source of doctrine. His invocation of the sun, whose generous diffusion of light and warmth is itself a lesson against envy, is a sign of how his natural wisdom will guide the Pilgrim, but it also suggests its limitations. Far more meaningful here is the situation of the temporarily blinded penitents, who, though "heaven's light denies them its bounty" (13.69), nonetheless move ahead. Repeatedly Vergil will use images of light, the sun, and the movement and influence of the spheres to illustrate the proper orientation of human desire. His insights seem at times on the point of transcending the classical universe and entering the realm of theology, as when he speaks of the "infinito ed ineffabil bene" whose diffusion of love is continually increasing in response to the charity it discovers in human souls (*Purg.* 15.67–75). But here as always his vision is circumscribed: he cites the empyrean, the "spera suprema," as the proper goal of human aspiration (52), and his explanation of the principle of the *bonum diffusivum sui*, though fully consonant with Christian theology, is based on the analogy of bodies that give off and absorb light (69).

The inadequacy of such thinking is suggested in various ways. The image which opens Canto 15 has a precise mathematical meaning, but its more significant point is the comparison of the shifting of the ecliptic to a child's game, which sets this sort of precise knowledge in contrast to the eccentric forms in which knowledge will increasingly present itself to Dante's imagination. The point is made again in a more elaborate way by the geometrical image which follows, and which is again set in perspective by the blinding light which finally dominates it. And when Dante is on the point of expressing satisfaction with Vergil's explanation of charity, he is abruptly drawn into an "ecstatic vision" (15.85–86) which carries him far beyond the reach of Vergil's understanding, and challenges Dante to come to an understanding of charity on his own.

The "atto dolce" of Mary, dismissing her anxiety and accepting in her son an independence she cannot understand, and Pisistratus' benign assumption of good intentions in the boy who had publicly kissed his daughter clearly illustrate the importance of tolerance, but it is important to recognize their personal significance for the self-driven, passionate Dante, to whom they speak of the need for gentleness, not just toward others, but toward oneself. An angry spirit, it is suggested, cannot evolve. Wrath sees only its object. Like the scornful Michal, for whom David's ecstatic dancing is merely contemptible, it threatens to destroy the conditions in which love and understanding can come to fruition, until, as shown in the murderous anger of those stoning Stephen, one can lose the capacity for *pietà* itself. His conditioning in humility has liberated Dante to the point at which he can acknowledge the dangers for himself implied by all three examples, but the shock of confronting the "non falsi errori" of which he has been guilty (117) has left him disoriented. Vergil, who understands the lesson implicit in Dante's vision but not its profound effect on the Pilgrim, can only urge him to be vigilant and move on. It is appropriate that both travelers end the canto in darkness.

It is perhaps caviling to place so much emphasis on Vergil's inadequacy, or to seek a precedent in natural science for his every doctrinal utterance, for Dante in the *Purgatorio* is clearly allowing him a range of understanding he had not previously demonstrated. And certainly it would be hard to deny the biblical quality of his injunction to Dante to open his heart to "the waters of peace," poured forth from the "etterno fonte" (15.131–32). But even in these beautiful lines the diffusion of the waters is a matter of gravity; they lack the vivid energy of the fountain which, in the Gospel, "gushes forth to eternal life" (John 4:14). Vergil understands the practical workings, but not the dynamics, of Purgatory. He recognizes that Dante is destined to know a profound pleasure, but cites nature, rather than supervenient grace, as its source (15.31–33). Like Boethius' Philosophy, he offers rational understanding, but cannot intuit the psychological challenges that for Dante make rational understanding difficult, or the imaginative and spiritual conditioning that will render it finally irrelevant.

The three central cantos of the *Purgatorio* offer three separate versions of the rational view of the human condition which has characterized Vergil's discourse. They have the important function of defining the issues that most concern Dante at this stage in his journey, but in each case the argument is fundamentally flawed, and the three cantos finally make clear the inadequacy of philosophy as a guide for Dante from this point forward.

First Marco Lombardo explains that human beings, innately capable of distinguishing good and evil and possessed of free will, are thus equipped to withstand the influence of the material universe, free to subject themselves to a higher power, the "better nature" which has endowed us with mind, the intellective soul (16.73–81). We are at once free and subject ("liberi soggiacete," 80), Marco declares, and we are therefore responsible if the world strays from the path of right (82). This seems theologically sound up to a point, but the status and power of the "miglior natura" which enables us to withstand the powers of the planetary spheres remains uncertain, and the uncertainty inheres in the phrase itself. It is borrowed from Ovid's account of the ordering of the primordial chaos (*Met.* 1.21–25), where a "melior natura" collaborates with divine power ("deus") to produce a coherent universe which will nonetheless undergo the endless change which for Ovid is the central fact of life.

The uncertain function of this guiding principle becomes a critical problem when Marco goes on to describe the newborn human soul, to which God joyfully gives life, and which runs childlike from one earthly pleasure to another, so that it must be guided or restrained (85–93). For the "guida o fren" to which Marco refers is not a power of the soul but the institutional authority of king and Church, and it is the corruption of these powers, not a flaw in individual human nature, that has resulted in a wicked world (94–105). This abrupt leap from psychology to politics leaves a great deal unexplained. Marco goes on to develop the political theme which is his real concern, and makes no attempt to resolve the apparent contradiction between his earlier assertion that responsibility for the world's evil rests with the individual (82–83) and his claim that corrupt institutions must bear the blame. His dialogue with Dante ends, not with further reflections on these matters, but with a rather uninformative eulogy of the "good" Gherardo, and an equivocal reference to Gherardo's daughter which leaves open the possibility that despite his exemplary life (moral? political? knightly?), the influence of his "miglior natura" may not have been lasting.

The absence of a unifying principle in Marco's discourse is surely implicated in the strange passage which opens Canto 17. The first word, "Ricorditi," anticipates an important theme of the canto, but the memory it evokes is curiously undefined, and the brusque opening imperative seems to have no real purpose. A description of the sun as viewed through mountain mist is said to resemble Dante's view of the sun as he emerges from the fog in which he and Marco had moved together (1–12). The passage has the structure of a simile, but simply identifies the two experiences, rather than compare them, and the added reference to the mole (whom Dante may have supposed to be totally blind) tends to further obscure rather than clarify its meaning. When the narrative resumes it exhibits a similar lack of resonance. Dante has deliberately matched his steps to Vergil's (10–11), and for the moment there is nothing dialectically significant in play between them, no clear purpose in Dante's adherence to the "passi fidi" of his master. The passage ends by noting that he emerged to see "rays which were already dead on the low shores" (12), a line which might almost have been taken from the inscription over the gate of hell.

It is as if in following Vergil Dante were moving in the wrong direction. Their emergence from the fog deliberately recalls the escape of Aeneas and his family through the smoky darkness of fallen Troy (*Aen.* 2.721–25), but the allusion, like the opening nonsimile, merely points up the emptiness of the moment. For Aeneas and his family the departure was both an ending and a new beginning. The familiar image of "parvus Iulus," too small to match his father's strides ("non passibus aequis," 724), suggests a destiny that he must grow and mature in order to realize, while the spiritually immature Dante, faithfully marching to Vergil's cadence, is in effect retreating into the past.

What these flat and somber lines express is the exhaustion of the physical universe as a model, and of natural philosophy as a vehicle, for the presentation of the doctrine pertinent to Dante's progress. Vergil will expound the nature of love as an experience of the individual soul, with no recourse to cosmological metaphor, and with a poetic energy resonant with echoes of Dante's own poetry. Though his discourse does not lead to genuine religious insight, he provides a more coherent, detailed, and encouraging version of the psychology imperfectly sketched by Marco. Yet this canto and the next will show Dante distracted by imaginings wholly beyond Vergil's power to comprehend, which have already jolted him out of his submissive acceptance of the authority of his mentors even before Vergil's teaching has begun. And his only clear response to Vergil's teaching will be a drowsiness which preludes his dream of the Siren.

If the bleak and anticlimactic introduction to Canto 17 has no other purpose, it at least makes all the more startling the apostrophe to "imaginativa" which immediately follows, announcing a new series of three visions that amount to an inventory of the resources of Dante's poetic imagination. Each of the three tableaux has its own definition. Procne's murder of Itys, her son, and her transformation into a singing bird are "imprinted" on Dante's *imagine,* imagination in the broadest sense, the faculty which deals in imagery. The crucifixion of Haman "rains down within a high fantasy," suggesting that the knowledge of sacred history is a dispensation that engages the highest capacities of the imaginative faculty. Finally Lavinia "arises" before his vision, emerging unbidden from the storehouse of memory, and suggesting how completely Dante has assimilated the *Aeneid* into his vision of world history.

We can perhaps define the three visions more specifically. The story of Procne's action and her metamorphosis is self-contained, a mythological unit ready-made for adaptation to poetry. Once conjured up, Procne draws Dante's mind away from external reality to focus on his own imaginative activity, effectively neutralizing the passion and violence the figure of Procne evokes,[34] and making her transformation an image of poetic creation itself. The wholly involuntary reception of a vision such as that of the crucified Haman, charged with typological significance, suggests the relation of imagination to prophecy, and despite the vividness of the central image Dante is able to acknowledge also the faithful Mordecai, an emblem of the sacred history of which the story is a part. Lavinia, conspicuously silent in the *Aeneid,* here speaks to proclaim the historical transition her world is undergoing, and in the process defines her own role as a symbol of that change, a placatory offering to ensure that the traditions of defeated Italy will survive the triumph of Troy and Rome. Through her Dante asserts his ability to appropriate and reshape poetic tradition by adapting the themes and images of classical poetry to new contexts.

Dante says nothing to Vergil of his vision, or of the new, speaking Lavinia he has imagined. To do so would be to invite Vergil to see in Dante's vision what it in fact strongly suggests—that Amata, the mother of Lavinia, hanging herself in despair at the false report of Turnus' death, expresses in the starkest way the situation of Vergil, burdened with the tragic sense of life and denied the vision of sacred history. He has been a vital resource of Dante's own poetry, but one whose guiding vision can no longer sustain him and who will soon disappear from the poem.

---

34. See Mazzotta, *Dante's Vision,* 130.

We must then ask why Vergil should be assigned the role he assumes in this canto and the next, as the philosopher of human love. To understand this it is necessary to recognize that Vergil's discourses are not intended by Dante as a definitive exposition of the nature of love but rather as confirming the inherent capacities of the human mind, and complementing his teaching with vivid reminders of the pervasive and crucial role of imagination. In the process they define the limits that Dante will transgress imaginatively as he ascends.[35] Like Marco, Vergil is vague about the love which is "d'animo" (17.93), whose proper function is to orient our loving in conformity with the will of the Creator. Instinctively drawn to pursue the good, and incapable of hating self or Creator, the mind can nonetheless fail in its duty through ignorance or intemperance, and allow its attraction to lesser goods to become dominant. Vergil seems to echo the Philosophy of Boethius when he notes that all are capable of apprehending the good "confusamente" (17.127),[36] and like Philosophy he seems unaware of the psychological difficulties that prevent us from seeing clearly the "buona essenza" from which all true goods originate and toward the realization of which they naturally tend.

Recognizing that Dante's desire for knowledge remains unsatisfied, Vergil in Canto 18 offers a more vivid and psychologically probing account of how sense and imagination collaborate to create an impression capable of attracting the mind:

> E se, rivolto, inver' di lei si piega,
>   quel piegare è amor, quell' è natura
>   che per piacer di novo in voi si lega.
> Poi, come 'l foco movesi in altura
>   per la sua forma ch'è nata a salire
>   là dove più in sua matera dura,
> così l'animo preso entra in disire,
>   ch'è moto spiritale, e mai non posa
>   fin che la cosa amata il fa gioire.
>   (*Purg.* 18.25–33)

---

35. See Mazzotta, *Dante's Vision*, 116–34.
36. See esp. the opening lines of *Cons.* 3, Pr. 3.

[And if, thus turned, the mind inclines toward it, that inclination
is love, that inclination is nature, which is bound in you anew by
pleasure. Then even as fire moves upward by reason of its form,
being born to ascend thither where it lasts longest in its matter,
so the captive mind enters into desire, which is a spiritual movement, and never rests until the thing loved makes it rejoice.]

Notable here are the more or less total absence of any concern for the
rational aspect of the experience of love and the abundance of *stilnovo*
diction. What Vergil is describing, at the very center of the *Commedia,* is
apparently nothing more or less than the experience of the "alma presa"
of Dante's earliest lyrics, as true as fire in its fundamental orientation,
but easily contaminated and confused by passion.

But Vergil evidently feels that he has shown Dante more than this.
Now, he suggests, you may see that not all loves are equally commendable,
even though the wax in which the desired object is imprinted is good in
itself (34–39). This is fully consonant with his warning in the previous
canto of the threat posed by ignorance and intemperance to natural, instinctive love; but his attempt to extract a more positive lesson from the
lines quoted is harder to understand. He distinguishes between our initial,
merely natural desire and the more clearly defined desire that we experience "di novo" (27) when our mind has apprehended a particular object,[37]
and he seems to describe an inclination which is spiritual, and produces a
kind of ecstasy. But though this inclination tends naturally toward the
object that will yield the highest pleasure,[38] it seems in itself to be neither
good nor bad, whatever the object that captures it.

There is, moreover, a strong suggestion of necessity in Vergil's words.
Troubled by this, Dante asks how a love which we experience involuntarily
can have merit. Vergil's long attempt to deal with this problem (49–75)
centers on identifying will and knowledge at the most fundamental level
of human consciousness, where the "prime notizie," or primary ideas,
about being/existence provide us with the basis for focusing on the "primi

---

37. See Singleton's note on lines 26–27.

38. See Singleton's note on line 30, which cites Albertus' assertion (*De coelo
et mundo* 4.ii.1) that the "place" to which an object tends is its perfection.

appetibili," the primary objects of desire (55–57). Vergil is aware of these primary realities, though he claims that their source is beyond human knowing (56). It is on the basis of the "prime notizie" that man naturally desires the good, and it is in the light of them that one makes morally significant choices between possible loving actions (64–66). Vergil stops here, leaving further clarification of the nature of free will to Beatrice (73–75). But he acknowledges in passing that every love we experience does indeed arise in us by necessity (70–71). In so doing he seems to quietly acknowledge the problem that Dante had raised, though he goes on to declare again that we have the power to distinguish and control our loving impulses (72).

Here as throughout the *Commedia* the reach of Vergil's argument is limited by its dependence on ancient notions of spiritual experience. His intuition of the "prime notizie" and his understanding of concepts like place and spiritual movement do not provide him with a clear basis for distinguishing good love from bad. Marco's discourse had leaped from personal to political governance without assigning a regulatory principle to the individual soul, and Vergil, too, fails to discover the higher faculty that would enable an authentically spiritual love. His answers to Dante's questions are "clear and plain" (85), but they leave Dante's mind "wandering drowsily" (87), still aware only "confusamente" of what he seeks to understand.[39]

The elaborate image which follows is a telling comment on Vergil's discourse:

> La luna, quasi a mezza notte tarda,
>   facea le stelle a noi parer più rade,
>   fatta com' un secchion che tuttor arda;
> e correa contra 'l ciel per quelle strade
>   che 'l sole infiamma allor che quel da Roma
>   tra 'Sardi e' Corsi il vede quando cade.
>   (*Purg.* 18.76–81)

---

39. Dante's condition here is close to that described by Boethius, *Cons.* 3, Pr. 3, where Philosophy speaks of how the natural impulse to know the good is confused by "multiplex error."

[The moon, retarded almost to midnight, shaped like a bucket
that continues to glow, made the stars appear scarcer to us,
and her course against the heavens was on those paths which
the sun inflames, when they in Rome see it between the
Sardinians and the Corsicans at its setting.]

Like the bucket in this curious image pattern, Vergil is a vessel, from which
a finite quantity of knowledge has been poured, and which continues to
glow with reflected light. The orientation of Vergil's discourse is sound:
it travels the same path as the sun; but he cannot see the end which his argument, fully realized, would attain, as the Roman cannot see Sardinia or
Corsica. The passage recalls the conclusion of Vergil's long, sad speech in
Inferno 20, where he notes that the full moon is "touching the wave" below
Seville (20.124–26). Both passages suggest a trajectory that might lead outward, like the "folle volo" of Ulysses, beyond the Pillars of Hercules and
into uncharted waters. Certainly the geographic range of the present passage makes the ensuing reference to "Pietola" (83; "lesser *pietà?*") seem
all the more diminutive, reducing the renown it derives from its connection with Vergil to something pathetic, like Vergil's own futile attempt to
rewrite the history of Mantua in the circle of the diviners. It is Dante who
has here "burdened" Vergil (84) with the responsibility of offering seemingly authoritative doctrine as a foil to the deeper and richer understanding he is destined to attain, and now, having discharged his duty and laid
down his burden, Vergil is for the moment very much an "ombra" (82).

Vergil and the Siren

As Dante falls asleep at the end of Canto 18 he has in his ears the once-
slothful spirits' reminder of the end of *Aeneid* 5, where Aeneas leaves in
Sicily the women among his followers, as well as others who are "not
eager for the great fame" that has been foretold for those who carry on
(*Aen.* 5.750–51).[40] It is a critical stage in Aeneas' journey, marked by debate among the gods and an anxiety sufficient to make Aeneas consider

---

40. The connection is suggested by Picone, "Canto XIX," 291–92.

abandoning his mission (700–703). He is clearly unprepared for the ordeal that awaits him in Italy, and he resolves to persevere only after a visitation from the shade of his father, Anchises.

Venus persuades Neptune to favor the voyage, and the god himself appears in his chariot, attended by a baroque assemblage of minor sea gods and aquatic creatures, to affirm his goodwill (779–826). Renewed in spirit, Aeneas urges his companions to hasten their preparations for departure. But his state of mind here is uncharacteristic. What motivates him is not just his mission but pervasive, unaccountable thoughts of "sweet joys."[41] For the moment the sense of duty that normally governs his actions has given way to something like the thrill of adventure, the "ardor" that impelled Ulysses to embark on his final mad voyage.

Once on the open sea, Aeneas' helmsman, Palinurus, is visited by the god of sleep, who overcomes his firm resolve and casts him into the water. Aeneas meanwhile continues to enjoy the empowering sense of divine favor:

> currit iter tutum non setius aequore classis
> promissisque patris Neptuni interrita fertur.
> iamque adeo scopulos Sirenum aduecta subibat,
> difficilis quondam multorumque ossibus albos
> (tum rauca adsiduo longe sale saxa sonabant).
>
> (*Aen.* 5.862–66)

> [The fleet speeds on a safe course, unhindered, over the sea,
> and is borne along freed from fear by the promises of father
> Neptune. Now they were sailing by the rocks of the Sirens,
> once a place of danger, and white with the bones of many men.
> From far off the rough rocks resound with the relentless surf.]

Though Aeneas and his comrades, their helmsman gone, are in fact drifting at this point, they do not yet know it, and the sense of a new freedom is very strong. The "quondam" of line 865 implies that the forces which

---

41. *Aen.* 5.827–28: "His patris Aeneae suspensam blanda vicissim / gaudia pertemptant mentem."

sought to ensnare Ulysses no longer threaten:[42] the only sound that emanates from the island of the Sirens is the pounding of the surf. But in the *Aeneid* such exhilaration can only portend disaster. Immediately Aeneas discovers that Palinurus is lost, and the book ends in weeping and lamentation.

Michael Putnam has stated well the significance of this episode for Aeneas, the stage in his experience that it defines:

> Thus far Aeneas' knowledge has resulted only in negation. He has learned what he must not do. . . . There has been no deep spiritual understanding of the meaning of life and the involvements of existence.
>
> Hence at the very end of this world the Sirens appear. They are the ultimate trial, and the ships drift inevitably toward them, for they seem to offer, in the form of the white bones, an example of those who . . . were tempted to cling too closely to an existence false to reality.[43]

With very few alterations this description could be applied to Dante as he transmutes his wandering thoughts into dreams at the end of Canto 18. His schooling has come chiefly from Vergil, and like that of Aeneas it has fallen short of yielding authentically spiritual knowledge. His imagination, the medium through which higher understanding will come to him, remains incompletely disciplined, vividly alive and increasingly responsive to spiritual promptings but still an unwieldy resource. It possesses the poet's power of metamorphosis, but its instinct to idealize the objects of its transformations is, as we will see, at the mercy of a confusion which goes back to his earliest essays in poetry, always liable to generate what Putnam calls "an existence false to reality."

---

42. It is not clear from Vergil's account whether he intends the Sirens to be seen as an existing threat to Aeneas. Putnam takes this for granted; Picone, "Canto XIX," 292, assumes that they no longer exist. Vergil certainly knew the tradition, later made canonical by Fulgentius and the mythographers, that the Sirens would die if a man succeeded in resisting their enticement, as Ulysses did. See Fulgentius, *Mithol.* 2.8; *Scriptores rerum mythicarum*, vol. 1, 15, 108, 233–34.

43. *Poetry of the Aeneid,* 103.

Dante's dream of the Siren, which opens Canto 19, occurs at the hour of the chill before dawn, when the lingering warmth of the sun has wholly vanished from the atmosphere,[44] the hour when geomancers practice their strange, debased form of astrology. We are in a "selva oscura." The vital powers of nature have been temporarily suspended, and the order of the universe is mocked by a pseudoscience which depends (as Dante reminds us in line 6) on darkness, and bears no relation to the heavens that speak of God. As at the beginning of the poem, "il sol tace."

In this setting Dante's dream stages, in the most basic terms, the transformative working of poetic imagination, stimulated by a stunted form of idealizing, and in that sense courtly, love. Dante gazes at the malformed, stammering woman he has conjured,

> e come 'l sol conforta
> le fredde membre che la notte aggrava,
> così lo sguardo mio le facea scorta
> la lingua, e poscia tutta la drizzava
> in poco d'ora, e lo smarrito volto,
> com' amor vuol, così le colorava.
>
> (*Purg.* 19.10–15)

[and even as the sun revives cold limbs benumbed by night, so my look made ready her tongue, and then in but little time set her full straight, and colored her pallid face even as love requires.]

The simile evokes the orderly procession of the natural order, passing from the chilly darkness of the canto's opening lines to the revivifying reappearance of the sun, but its referent reveals something very different. Dante's imagination displaces nature, imparting an illusory vitality to the Siren by a process which has the mechanics, but none of the affective

---

44. At the corresponding moment in *Aen.* 5, "fere mediam Nox umida metam / contigerat" (835–36).

power, of Ovidian metamorphosis.[45] To create a Siren, as Dante has done, a creature who offers no promise of knowledge but is rather the embodiment of erotic temptation,[46] can be a poetic act, but the poetry it generates is the narcissistic fantasy of the pornographer, for whom nothing exists that is not a projection of his desire. The beauty of the "dolce stil" itself has been reduced to an instrument of momentary gratification, as alien from the true order of things as the castings of the geomancers.[47]

The lady who in Canto 9 bore Dante unawares to the threshold of Purgatory, had identified herself to Vergil as Lucy. Here, in Dante's dream, an unnamed "donna" causes Vergil to unveil the Siren's ugliness. That it is Vergil who acts here and that the lady remains anonymous are signs of the very different purpose of this second dream. In Canto 9 we saw Dante's poetic imagination, conditioned by long study of the *poetae,* transposing a spiritual experience into poetic terms. Here what we see is a kind of poetic exorcism. Dante's dream is a remarkably candid acknowledgment of how radically a poetry written "as love desires" can diverge from the ideal of a poetry directed in full awareness to a lady "holy and alert"— the poetry Dante has spent his artistic life learning to create. Though the desire expressed by the dream takes a far cruder form, this dream recalls the eroticism of the dream that had inspired the opening sonnet of the *Vita nuova,* in which Beatrice had appeared "naked but lightly wrapped in a crimson cloth."[48] The erotic detail remains suppressed in the sonnet itself, but the prose commentary makes plain that sexual desire informs the idealizing impulse that generated it. Love ruled the young Dante "by the power which my imagination gave him,"[49] a power which is a sublimated form of the desire his imagination continues to turn into poetry.

---

45. As Picone, "Canto XIX," 303–4, shows, the terms in which the transformation and exposure of the Siren are described resemble most closely the parody of Ovidian metamorphosis in the pseudo-Ovidian thirteenth-century *De vetula.*

46. We cannot know whether Dante, like Homer, associated the Sirens with knowledge. For the mythographers and Dante's early commentators they represent only carnal desire. Macrobius and Augustine read them allegorically as offering the promise of knowledge and the secret of cosmic harmony. See Mazzotta, *Dante's Vision,* 141–45.

47. See Mazzotta, *Dante's Vision,* 146–47.

48. *Vita nuova* 3.3–11.

49. *Vita nuova* 2.7.

In the present scene Dante's imagination does not simply serve "Love," but creates an object of desire that shows it at the mercy of his lower nature. Like Aeneas, Dante has given way to thoughts of "blanda gaudia," so seductive that they wholly displace the ideal lady of his pure imaginings, who then reappears in a recognizably holy but anonymous form, defined only as fundamentally opposed to the Siren. The tableau suggests an abrupt reenactment of the original commissioning of Vergil by Beatrice, but here there is no clear acknowledgment of the "donna" on Vergil's part, and no appeal to his "parlare onesto" on hers. He is simply rebuked and made to act in a way which abruptly reintroduces the standards of serious poetry, and exposes once and for all the peril that constantly attends the transformative workings of the poetic imagination.

Though Vergil at this point is Dante's Palinurus, he is only partly aware of the extent to which Dante's imagination, like Aeneas at the end of *Aeneid* 5, is drifting. Vergil's position can be contrasted to that of Palinurus himself, as he responds to the god Somnus, who, in the likeness of his shipmate Phorbas, offers to relieve him at the helm:

"mene salis placidi uultum fluctusque quietos
ignorare iubes? Mene huic confidere monstro?
Aenean credam (quid enim?) fallacibus auris
et caeli totiens deceptus fraude sereni?"
talia dicta dabat, clauumque adfixus et haerens
nusquam amittebat, oculosque sub astra tenebat.

(*Aen.* 5.848–53)

["Do you bid me cease to study the face of the calm water
and the quiet waves? Do you ask me to put trust in this
monstrous thing, the sea? Shall I entrust Aeneas to the
treacherous winds, I who have so often been deceived by
the false promise of a clear sky? What might happen?"
Such were his words, and he stood firm, never loosing
his grasp of the tiller, and kept his eyes on the stars.]

Palinurus' steadfastness mirrors the characteristic *virtus* of the master he serves, as Vergil's exposure of the Siren's foulness appeals to the high sense of purpose and resolve he has sought to instil in the Pilgrim. But the power of both figures is limited. Vergil's gesture is a distillation of the psychological teaching he had put forth in the preceding cantos, teaching whose limitations Vergil cannot realize, but which has proven incapable of governing Dante's drifting mind. Similarly Palinurus cannot know that the sense of duty and destiny which is the essence of Aeneas' *pietas* has for the moment been lulled into a trustful dependence on the "fallacibus auris" of the willful gods. The fate of Palinurus, in effect an allegory of this momentary lapse, shocks Aeneas into a renewed sense of responsibility, but the episode ends ambiguously. As Dante in his dream lets the "donna" make Vergil bear responsibility for his fantasizing, so Aeneas accuses Palinurus, rather than himself, of having trusted too much in the sky and the calm sea (870). Aeneas, Vergil tells us, now steers the boat in darkness (868),[50] but the irony is clear, for we know that Palinurus, faithful to the last, had taken the tiller with him as he fell (858–59). It is destiny, rather than seamanship, that enables the fleet to touch down safely at Cumae (*Aen.* 6.1–5).

Vergil, unlike Palinurus, remains present to Dante, but like Palinurus he has ceased to direct Dante's course in a meaningful way. He has played an important role in the realization of Dante's higher destiny,[51] but now, as for the drifting Aeneas, a higher power has replaced him. Nonetheless Dante's sense of dependence remains focused on Vergil. He reacts viscerally, rather than with understanding, to the exposure of the Siren, and his first waking action is to turn to his "buon maestro." Even then he is still ensnared by his dream, unable to "depart" from it as if it were itself the Siren. When Vergil uses the imagery of falconry in bidding Dante to acknowledge the summons of "the Eternal King" (63), Dante's response

---

50. Though Vergil's language throughout the episode has implied a fleet of substantial ships manned by a skilled crew, he now employs the term *ratem*, commonly used of a small, rudely fashioned or improvised vessel.

51. Vergil speaks of having "sent ["messe"] three voices" to the sleeping Dante (33–34); the curious phrase may imply his role as transmitter of divine prompting. His "Surgi e vieni" suggests a divine command, perhaps the commissioning of a prophet. In line 35 he employs the second person singular ("tu entre"), rather than the first plural, as previously, to urge Dante forward, again suggesting the uniqueness of Dante's situation and his own ancillary status.

is to simply adapt himself to Vergil's metaphor, and his description of his ascent to the next terrace is purely circumstantial. There, faced with the "dignity" of the nobly born but avaricious Pope Adrian, he kneels, still thinking in terms of earthly hierarchy, as Vergil might well have urged, only to receive the pope's gentle and un-Vergilian rebuke. It is Adrian who bids him move on here, and Vergil from this point forward offers little substantive teaching.

But as Vergil the guide withdraws, Vergil the poet will assume a renewed prominence. Though bathed in an increasingly elegiac light, he will receive as much honor as can be shown to an unsaved soul, as Dante, Statius, and finally Purgatory itself collaborate in confirming his status as "altissimo poeta."

6

Statius

The long speech of Hugh Capet in Canto 20 brings to a climax the *Purga-torio*'s concern with history and politics. The major themes will reemerge in the powerful symbolism of the pageant at the summit of the mountain, but in the meantime Dante will shift his attention to questions of individual virtue, and to the role of his vocation as poet and his various poetic discipleships in the scheme of the *Commedia*. Between the sudden intrusion of Statius and the appearance of Beatrice Dante will probe not only the significance of his relation to the Poeti but also the distancing effect of his commitment to the vernacular "parlar materno," the language which will give expression to his gradual realization of the meaning of Beatrice.

This chapter considers some obvious questions: what the figure of Statius meant to Dante; why he plays the role he plays in the *Commedia*; why Dante puts into his mouth the religious autobiography he narrates, a story almost entirely fictional, but as detailed as that of any character in the poem save Dante himself; and finally, why Statius should have been assigned the long discourse on the formation of the human embryo and the creation of the soul which he delivers in *Purgatorio* 25. Obvious questions indeed. But I propose to consider them primarily in terms of

Statius' own poetry, and this at least is something new. My working assumptions are that Dante took Statius' poetry seriously and saw him as a major figure in the great tradition of the Poeti and that the role Statius plays in the *Commedia* is based primarily, if not entirely, on what Statius himself had written.

These assumptions, too, might seem obvious enough, but critics of Dante have shown a strange reluctance to make them. Fortunately not all would take so casual a view of the matter as the senior Dantista who once assured me that Lucan would have done just as well as Statius, that Dante had more or less flipped a coin between them. But another learned friend put the problem almost as well. When I told him that I was trying to puzzle out why Statius had been so important to Dante, he was sympathetic but concerned; the medieval commentaries on Statius, he suggested, wouldn't help me much, and I would probably have to look for information in the text itself. The advice was well meant, and turned out to be perfectly correct, but the way in which he offered it made "going to the text" of a poet so strange seem like a last resort, a desperate measure, and this reluctance has been the rule among Dantisti.

Even those who have written specifically on the problem of Statius' role have had a hard time approaching it directly. Such excellent scholars as André Pézard and Roger Dragonetti have gone to great lengths to explain Statius' role in the light of Dante's supposed knowledge of the *Silvae,* the one work of Statius that he never mentions.[1] Others have made what they could out of the rather sketchy medieval tradition of allegorical interpretation of the *Thebaid*. But none of the critics who have attempted to account for Dante's Statius by these various means has seriously considered the possible relevance of Statius' actual poetry, beyond the selective allegorizing of a few motifs noted by medieval commentators: the terrible thirst of the Argives as they approach Thebes; the Altar of Clementia; Theseus' intervention in the war.[2]

---

1. Pézard, "Rencontres," 115–33; Dragonetti, *Dante, pèlerin,* 255–71.

2. In the brief twelfth-century commentary *Super Thebaidem* once attributed to Fulgentius, the Argives thirst for "the fountain of faith"; the acts of Theseus and the altar of Clementia manifest divine mercy. Later commentators identify the altar of Clementia with the altar "to the unknown God" of *Acts* 17; see Padoan, "Teseo 'figura Redemptoris,'" 126–28.

In this respect we have progressed scarcely at all since C. S. Lewis' excellent little essay on Dante's Statius appeared more than seventy years ago.[3] This was mainly an inventory of passages from the *Thebaid* whose religious and moral outlook might have appeared to Dante to be in harmony with his own Christian point of view. Lewis made little attempt to establish specific connections between Statius' poetry and Dante's, but his essay remains the one piece of criticism known to me that approaches the problems posed by Statius' presence in the *Purgatorio* directly, on the basis of a careful reading of Statius' poetry. I propose to take my cue from Lewis, and assume that Dante intends us to view his Christian Statius primarily in relation to Statius' own poems, and that for Dante Statius is first and foremost the author of the *Thebaid*.

Statius and the Thebaid

Dante's Statius is consistently identified with his epic. When he announces his name he adds, as if by way of gloss, "cantai di Tebe" (21.92), and Vergil knows of him as the poet who had sung of the cruel warfare of "Jocasta's twofold sorrow," the fatal enmity of her twin sons (*Purg.* 22.55–56). At other points Statius' new situation is defined by the contrast it presents to the world of the *Thebaid*. When he overtakes Vergil and Dante on the fifth terrace of Purgatory, his first words are "O frati miei, Dio vi dea pace" (21.13). The blessing confirms his release from the very different concerns announced in the opening words of his own poem, which speak of brothers driven to mortal combat over the rule of the city of Thebes:

> Fraternas acies, alternaque regna profanis
> decertata odiis sontisque evolvere Thebas
> Pierius menti calor incidit.
>
> (*Theb.* 1.1–3)

> [The Pierian fire arouses my mind to tell of fraternal strife, and alternate reigns contested in impious hostility, and the guilt of Thebes.]

---

3. "Dante's Statius."

Vergil replies to Statius' greeting by invoking for him the favor of the heavenly court which has condemned Vergil himself to "eternal exile," and explains that Dante, too, will one day be among the blessed (16–18, 22–24). Here again, in the vision of a community where the elect will dwell in peace and brotherhood, there is no trace of the world of the *Thebaid,* and the exiling of Polynices, which generates the tragic conflict of Statius' poem, is occluded by the greater tragedy of Vergil's eternal banishment from the true kingdom.

The Statius of Dante's poem has indeed been liberated, from Theban conflict and from the process of his own purification, and he confirms his new freedom by giving a serene account of the natural tranquillity of upper Purgatory. This place, free from all change, its calm disturbed only by the clamorous joy of the penitents whenever one of their number completes his purgation, is again in marked opposition to the world of Statius' poem. For while nature is continually present in the *Thebaid,* and treated with great sensitivity, human life in the poem is chronically at odds with itself and with the order of nature, and joy is virtually unknown.

The dominant theme of the *Thebaid* is conflict. At its center is of course the deadly rivalry of the sons of Oedipus, over which the world of the poem is divided, but at a broader level conflict of one sort or another defines the human condition as Statius presents it. Statius acknowledges the gods, and assigns them a prominent role, but they often appear to be in collaboration with, if not at the mercy of, the forces of "furor" and "nefas." The poem's world is burdened by doubt and a virtually Lucanian cynicism as to their efficacy and benevolence, yet cursed as well by a history of seemingly inescapable guilt, in atonement for which the gods demand the continual sacrifice of innocence, youth, and virtue. In the *Thebaid* a pity like that of Vergil for the youthful victims of the Italian war, "la vergine Cammilla, / Eurialo e Turno e Niso" (*Inf.* 1.107–8), is visited on a world where all are in some sense victims, doomed by a fate they can recognize but not avoid. Statius, a near-contemporary of Lucan,[4] greatly admired the *Pharsalia,* and the *Thebaid* echoes Lucan's despair at the destruction of

_____

4. In *Silvae* 2.7, a commemorative ode addressed to Lucan's widow, Polla, Statius imagines "the *Aeneid* itself" doing homage to Lucan (79–80).

liberty and the social bond by ambition and tyranny. But in the *Pharsalia* human folly and love of power create their own disasters, whereas the disasters of the *Thebaid,* and even human culpability itself, seem to be imposed by higher forces.[5] Set against the powers of fate are allegories, Virtus, Pietas, and finally Clementia,[6] ethical concepts which are brought to life and assume the function of gods. While the traditional gods as Statius presents them act almost exclusively in hostile and destructive ways, the divinized virtues are nonviolent, act only in sympathetic response to human misery, and so emerge only after violence has done its work.

To see Statius primarily as the poet of the *Thebaid* thus raises troubling questions, which are tactfully posed by Vergil. Having evidently read the poem carefully—I like to think of his having somehow received a complimentary copy—he finds in its violent story no evidence at all of the religious conversion Statius claims to have undergone:

> "Or quando tu cantasti le crude armi
> de la doppia trestizia di Giocasta,"
> disse 'l cantor de' buccolici carmi,
> "per quello che Clïò teco lì tasta,
> non par che ti facesse ancor fedele
> la fede, sanza qual ben far non basta.
> Se così è, qual sole o quai candele
> ti stenebraron sì, che tu drizzasti
> poscia di retro al pescator le vele?"
> (*Purg.* 22.55–63)

["Now, when you sang of the cruel strife of Jocasta's twofold sorrow," said the singer of the Bucolic songs, "it does not appear, from that which Clio touches with you there, that the faith, without which good works suffice not, had yet made you faithful. If that is so, then what sun or what candles

---

5. See Franchet d'Espèrey, *Conflit, violence et non-violence,* 407–10.

6. In this chapter the "new" virtues Pietas, Virtus, and Clementia that emerge in the poem's later stages are capitalized and printed in Roman rather than italics to distinguish them from *virtus* and *pietas* in their traditional senses.

dispelled your darkness, so that thereafter you set your
sails to follow the Fisherman?"]

The lines recall the opening of the *Purgatorio,* where Dante shows his own
poem sailing before favorable winds:

> Per correr miglior acque alza le vele
>   omai la navicella del mio ingegno,
>   che lascia dietro a sé mar sí crudele;
> e canterò di quel secondo regno.
>
> *(Purg.* 1.1–4)

[To course over better waters the little bark of my genius
now hoists her sails, leaving behind her a sea so cruel; and
I will sing of that second realm where the human spirit is
purged and becomes fit to ascend to Heaven.]

Dante is here celebrating the release of his imagination from the deadly
burden of dealing with the sins and torments of lower hell, horrors which
he had described repeatedly by reference to the Thebes of Statius' poem.
The Statius who could make such horrors his theme would seem to constitute the antithesis of Dante's new sense of dedication, and his poetry,
haunted from beginning to end by Tisiphone, can easily be read as "scritta
morta" of an unprecedented grimness. Dante's vessel has emerged from
the cruel sea of the *Inferno,* and moves toward a "secondo regno" governed
by love,[7] sustained by an impulse which corresponds to the aspiration toward spiritual purification which is his theme. Statius repeatedly compares the confusion and helplessness of Eteocles and Polynices, driven by
the Fury, to a boat buffeted by storm-tossed waters,[8] and the image might
serve as an emblem for the view of history and human nature that dominates the *Thebaid.*

---

7. The phrase perhaps recalls such phrases as "alterna regna" and "regem
secundum" (*Theb.* 1.1, 143), which define the central crisis of the *Thebaid.*

8. *Theb.* 1.370–75 (Polynices); 2.105–8 (Eteocles); 3.23–30 (Eteocles);
6.450–53 (Polynices). In 1.193–96 Thebes itself is compared to a vessel caught
between conflicting winds.

Dante's Statius frankly acknowledges the absence of Christian traces in the *Thebaid*. Living as he did in the time of Domitian's persecutions, fear made him a "chiuso cristian" (22.90), continuing after his conversion to conduct himself outwardly as a pagan. Whatever spiritual significance lurks in his poetry must be similarly disguised, and Vergil discreetly suggests this as well, referring to the subject of the *Thebaid* as "that which Clio touches with you."

It is appropriate that Vergil names Clio as having inspired a poem he now finds deeply puzzling, for her significance is enigmatic. Statius is unique among Dante's Poeti in calling on this Muse, who traditionally presides over history and thus might seem an unlikely choice to play an informing role in his poem. He first calls on Clio for aid in recounting the deaths of the five Argive heroes who fell at Thebes (1.41–45). The invocation occurs immediately after a hyperbolic imagining of the epic on the reign of Domitian that the Pierides will one day inspire him to sing (1.17–33) and a lurid summary of the preternatural horrors of the Theban campaign (33–40). The choice of Clio evidently expresses Statius' desire to place himself in a neutral relation to the themes of his poem, perhaps an inability to define its inspiration in a more specific way. For in telling of the deaths of the Argives he is bearing witness, not to human *virtus,* but to the overriding power of fate and the hostile gods.

If the *Pharsalia* is a poem without a hero, the *Thebaid* presents an array of heroes, each heroic in his own way but all deviating in one way or another from the heroic model provided by traditional epic, and none sufficiently autonomous to exercise the defining influence that distinguishes Aeneas, or even Lucan's Caesar, Pompey, and Cato. Each is assigned the conventional epic *aristeia* as his final moment approaches, but their deaths differ so radically, and involve human agency to so limited a degree, that none of the traditional Muses of poetry could preside over all of them. Amphiaraus' visionary awareness of the divine and cosmic forces that conspire to destroy him, the savagery of the dying Tydeus, and the Lucifer-like fall of Capaneus seem to belong to different worlds, and require modes of poetry for which epic tradition offers no clear precedent. Under Clio's patronage Statius is perhaps free to record their fates without subsuming them, or committing himself, to an overarching epic design.

A second appeal to Clio introduces what is perhaps the most spiritually significant moment in the poem, the transformation, death, and apotheosis of Menoeceus (*Theb.* 10.628–31), the son of Creon whose ritual suicide is inspired by the prophecy that this alone will save Thebes from destruction. Here epic tradition is not so much confounded as transcended. The Virtus who inspires Menoeceus' act and receives his lifeless body (10.780–81) belongs to a new order of values, and bears no relation to the uncontainable *virtus*, the sheer martial force, of Capaneus or Tydeus. In this case the invoking of Clio seems to represent a disavowal of vatic authority. In recording Menoeceus' death Statius claims to be presenting simply history, "digesta vetustas" (10.631), what the ancient annals preserve, Clio's proper sphere. The invocation defines Menoeceus' situation in ambiguous terms which could easily suggest a tragic hero: Virtus evokes his reverence for the traditional gods to induce in him a state of mind which makes death appear glorious (662–77; cp. 628–30). But what follows is wholly without precedent in ancient tradition, a transcendent experience which culminates with the ascent of Menoeceus' spirit to stand before the seat of Jove. It is here that the presence of Clio becomes significant; Menoeceus' preparation for death and the act itself are portentously described, but with Clio as Statius' Muse the authority of epic tradition is neutralized, and we are invited to make what we can of the hero's death.

The problematic relation of the poem to epic tradition is raised in a different way when Statius summons all the Muses to aid him in describing the destruction of Capaneus. Of all the Argive heroes, Capaneus is the one whose fate most obdurately refuses to yield a coherent reading in traditional terms:

> mecum omnes audete, deae! sive ille profunda
> missus nocte furor, Capaneaque signa secutae
> arma Iovem contra Stygiae rapuere sorores,
> seu virtus egressa modum, seu gloria praeceps,
> seu magnae data fata neci, seu laeta malorum
> principia et blandae superum mortalibus irae.
>> (*Theb.* 10.831–36)

[Dare to join with me, all ye goddesses! Whether his madness was sent from deepest darkness, and the Stygian sisters pursued his banners, forcing him to make war on Jove; or *virtus*, or a reckless desire for glory, drove him to excess; or he was fated

for such destruction; or disaster begins with success, and
mortals are seduced into incurring the wrath of the gods.]

Statius is fully capable of rising to the epic occasion in the conventional
way: he invokes Calliope to recount the mustering of the Argive host
(4.34–35), and again at the renewal of warfare after the death of Amphiaraus (4.35, 8.374). Here, however, the summoning of all the Muses, like
the earlier invocation of Clio, expresses the inadequacy of epic convention to a world as dominated by fate and divine malevolence as that of the
Thebaid. But whereas Clio stands for an abrogation of the role of epic poet,
here the Muses are challenged in epic terms, dared to perform their traditional role, and the invocation expresses a lingering desire to do justice to
human heroism in the face of the dark forces that will inevitably destroy it.
Capaneus, traditionally regarded as the embodiment of titanic impiety
and ruthlessness,[9] is here presented as a heroic figure victimized by fate.
Such is his situation that valor and the desire for glory, the traditional motives for epic heroism, are intensified by his hatred of the degradation
implied by the subservience to arbitrary powers that traditional religion
demands. Statius provides ample grounds for Capaneus' scorning of the
gods, and hints at a grudging admiration for his refusal to obey the re-
straints of traditional cult, but recognizes that his courage will inevitably
prove self-destructive, for reasons that wholly elude a satisfactory ethical
or religious explanation, or the insight any single Muse might grant.

The unique complexity of his inspiration is thus one of the most
striking features of Statius' poem, and I have discussed it at such length
in order to suggest the freedom it affords Dante for reading the *Thebaid*
in his own terms. As Vergil implies, Statius' poetry is finally the only basis
we have for evaluating the words Dante puts into his mouth, and Statius'
evident uncertainty as to the forces that have generated his poem suggests it is poetry of a new kind. In the poem, too, Statius' characters are
repeatedly moved to express insights which cannot be accounted for in
traditional religious terms, and at the end it is the spirit of the new goddess

---

9. Statius elsewhere acknowledges this tradition but prefaces even Capaneus' crudely impious mocking of Amphiaraus (*Theb.* 3.607–69) with assertions
of his nobility and largeness of heart, and a hint that his contempt for the gods is
a function of his superiority (600–603).

Clementia that governs the action. Dante's Statius suggests that new powers have determined his course, emphasizing the connection between his
spiritual history and his vocation as a poet. Vergil is of course the great
influence on both: "Per te poeta fui," Statius tells him, "per te cristiano"
(22.73). And he links the two callings again when he dates his baptism by
reference to the stage he had reached in composing the *Thebaid,* the arrival
of the Argive host at "the rivers of Thebes" (22.88–89), a moment marked
by events of mysterious religious import, and by the appearance of the
exiled princess Hypsipyle, for Dante perhaps the most important figure
in the poem.

But whatever Statius' experience or intention in writing it, the poem
we have begins under a curse and ends in universal mourning. Clearly
we cannot deal with Dante's Statius until we have addressed Vergil's question about the remarkable disjunction between Statius the Christian and
the Statius whose struggle with the dark forces that haunt his poetic world
seems chronically unresolved.

The *Thebaid* itself is structured in a way that seems to anticipate this
disjunction. One of the poem's most distinctive and disconcerting features
is the continual tension between the remorseless forward movement of
its narrative of historical disaster and the various means by which Statius
seeks to arrest or transcend this movement. Equivocal in his treatment
of heroic virtue, he repeatedly isolates for special attention figures and
events whose inconsequence in the poem's larger action is offset by their
embodiment of ethical or spiritual values, qualities which Statius sees as
in some sense heroic, and which he seeks to affirm in the face of the prevailing emphasis on the forces of destruction.

At the same time Statius seems to do his utmost to emphasize the
controlling influence of these malign powers in shaping his poem. The action is inaugurated and overseen by the Fury Tisiphone, whom Oedipus
invokes at the outset in his desperate need to avenge himself on his two
sons (1.46–87), and who remains an ominous presence throughout the
poem. As Chaucer was to recognize, she is in effect Statius' Muse,[10] and

---

10. The opening line of the *Troilus and Criseyde* of Geoffrey Chaucer speaks
of the "double sorrow" of Troilus, echoing Vergil's encapsulation of the theme
of the *Thebaid* (*Purg.* 22.55–56), and the opening stanza ends with the narrator's
appeal to Tisiphone for help in composing his "woeful verse."

imposes on the poet, and the suffering humanity of his poem, a collective vision of life as a living hell.

The seemingly endless chain of disastrous events that constitute Theban history gives rise to a cynicism and bitterness about the workings of divine and human justice which recalls the damned souls in Dante's *Inferno,* and which Statius, like Dante, pursues imaginatively beyond the grave. When the shade of Laius is summoned up by Mercury to goad his grandson Eteocles into preparing for war, his departure from Hades elicits a puzzlingly elaborate comment from an unnamed fellow shade. The shade's words bear no relation to the plot of the poem, and their tone seems to waver between poignancy and sarcasm, but they give full expression to the disillusionment of the spirits of the dead:

> "vade," ait, "o felix, quoscumque vocaris in usus,
> seu Iovis imperio, seu maior adegit Erinys
> ire diem contra, seu te furiata sacerdos
> Thessalis arcano iubet emigrare sepulcro,
> heu dulcis visure polos solemque relictum
> et virides terras et puros fontibus amnes,
> tristior has iterum tamen intrature tenebras."
>
> (*Theb.* 2.19–25)

> ["Go," he said, "o happy one, for whatever purpose you are
> summoned, whether it is at the command of Jove, or whether
> a great Fury compels you to go forth into daylight, or a raging
> Thessalian priestess bids you emerge from the secret tomb:
> alas, though you will see the sweet heavens and the sun you left
> behind, green lands, and rivers issuing pure from their springs,
> yet all the more sadly will you return to these shades."]

The lines anticipate both the sometimes bitter irony with which Dante will endow the "eterno essilio" of Vergil and the yearning his condemned spirits express for the sweet light and free-flowing rivers of the world they have lost. The demoralization they reveal appears in a number of Statius' own reflections on the world of his poem.

Statius is keenly responsive to the evocative power of "green lands, and rivers issuing pure from their springs," and the prevailing gloom of the *Thebaid* is repeatedly broken by his impulse to make contact with the purer world they suggest.[11] The Argives' mourning for Amphiaraus concludes with the priest Thiodamas' beautiful hymn to the Earth, self-sustaining and generous. "Omne homini natale solum," he declares (8.320), the earth is the birthright of humanity, governed, not by the powerful gods (312–13), but by Nature, who has taken Amphiaraus lovingly to her bosom (329–31). But as Statius moves on to invoke Calliope and resume the story of the war, he sees the human world as owed to death, so utterly in the grip of the Furies as to have lost, not just love of family and homeland, but the very "amor lucis," the most enduring love of all (8.383–87).

The voice of the unnamed shade evokes the first of these worlds, then gives way to the demoralizing reality of the second, suggesting the futility of all aspiration, or any hope of happiness. The Furies and necromancers who harass the dead mirror the power of fate and the forces of cruelty over the living. Lurking beneath the words of the shade is the dark suggestion that Statius' attempts to affirm a transcendent reality are mere escapism and that the counterimpulse to record the pain of human suffering owes less to compassion than to an Oedipus-like despair, an involuntary collaboration with the demonic power of the Fury.

We can see clear signs of this inner conflict in Statius' preoccupation with youth, innocence, and purity. The daughters of Adrastus possess charms capable of making devoted husbands of Polynices and even Tydeus, but their modesty, recalled by Dante in the *Convivio*,[12] is such that to be in the presence of a man is a source of shame ("pudor," 1.536–37), and the thought of the marriage bed gives rise to the untranslatable "primae modestia culpae" (2.232–34). Statius dwells at length on the Arcadian boy-warrior Parthenopaeus, a fairy-tale figure whose life is cut off before he has attained true heroism, and whose prominence cannot be explained by any contribution he makes to the action of the poem. So beautiful is he that his warlike behavior only charms those he attacks, and the Thebans, reminded of their own sons, are reluctant to harm him (*Theb.* 9.706–8). His death is treated in operatic style (9.570–907), and at

---

11. See Dragonetti, *Dante, pèlerin,* 171–82.
12. *Conv.* 4.25.7–9.

the mass funeral which concludes the poem both Argives and Thebans mourn his loss (12.804–6). Even Statius' generally unfriendly treatment of the gods is balanced by imaginings of the infancy of Jupiter, as fearful and needy as any human child, of the innocently playful babyhood of Mars and Apollo, and of Juno as a maiden, not yet embittered by her husband's infidelities (4.782–85, 794–96; 10.61–64). But more often the evocation of youth and purity is occasioned by their destruction. Laments and ceremonies for the dead occur again and again in the course of the poem,[13] and the dead are invariably the young and virtuous. Infanticide is a recurrent theme, and assumes a disturbing and enigmatic prominence in the poem's longest and strangest interlude, the episode of Hypsipyle and Opheltes.

In the course of their march toward Thebes, at a moment when a drought created by Bacchus has afflicted them with a terrible thirst (4.680–745), the Argive army encounters the exiled Lemnian princess Hypsipyle, now a slave in the household of King Lycurgus of Nemea and nurse to his infant son, Opheltes. She guides them to the still strongly flowing river Langia, and then, on the eve of the war, the action of the poem is brought to a standstill. Hypsipyle tells the fascinated Argives the story of how the women of her native Lemnos had slaughtered the men of the island, of the coming of the Argonauts and her own bearing of twin sons fathered by Jason, of the Lemnian women's discovery that she had spared and concealed her father, and of her exile and enslavement (5.28–498). While she speaks, the infant Opheltes, whom she had left playing on the grass, is accidentally killed by a giant serpent. The rest of the interlude describes his death and the elaborate funeral and games held in his honor (5.499–6.946).

In itself the story of Hypsipyle has real dignity and pathos, and Statius clearly invites us to imagine her as the heroine of a yet unwritten epic of a new kind,[14] but it is hard to interpret her role in the plot of the *Thebaid,* and harder still to understand the weight attached to the death

---

13. As Martinez shows, "Lament and Lamentations," 58–69, this aspect of the *Thebaid* complements the theme of mourning that runs through the *Purgatorio.*

14. See Frings, "Hypsipyle und Aeneas."

of Opheltes, the forebodings of doom which herald his appearance in the poem (4.718–19, 742), and the strange intensity with which Statius focuses on him. When Hypsipyle sets down her charge on the grass in preparation to lead the Argives to the river, the poet insists on the significance of the simple action:

> a! miserum vicino caespite alumnum—
> sic Parcae volvere—locat ponique negantis
> floribus adgestis et amico murmure dulces
> solatur lacrimas.
>
> *(Theb.* 4.786–89)

[Alas! she places her unhappy charge on the grass close by—so the Fates ordained—and assuages with clusters of flowers and loving murmur the sweet tears that protest his being set down.]

The disproportion between the helplessness and incomprehension of the child and the burden of significance imposed on him is never explained. At his death Opheltes immediately receives a new name, Archemorus (Beginner of Doom), and becomes the focus of a cult, but the evident need to find a meaning in his death cannot prevent a sense of incongruity from intruding on the poet's response to the event:

> quis tibi, parve, deus tam magni pondera fati
> sorte dedit? tune hoc vix prima ad limina vitae
> hoste iaces? an ut inde sacer per saecula Grais
> gentibus et tanto dignus morerere sepulcro?
>
> *(Theb.* 5.534–37)

[What god allotted to thee, little one, the burden of such a fate? Do you fall to this enemy while still on the threshold of life? Was it in order that you might thus become sacred to the peoples of Greece, and in death be honored with such a funeral?]

Though these questions remain conspicuously unanswered, there is perhaps a sense in which Opheltes' death serves a necessary function. The funeral and athletic contests which occupy the sixth book of the *Thebaid* are a precious interlude, a final affirmation of traditional social and religious order, though the games are tainted by a barbarism which heralds the inevitable joining of the chaotic war in which nearly all the Argive leaders will die. But such suggestions are not sufficient to explain the prominence of this episode in the design of the poem. The deification of Opheltes/Archemorus remains an enigma, and we must assume that in placing such a burden of meaning on the relatively minor event of the infant's death, Statius seeks to convey something that he cannot or will not express directly. We are made to feel the spiritual needs of a tormented world which can no longer trust its gods, and for which the existence of youth and innocence, vulnerable though they are, provides at least a tenuous means of sustaining a sense that virtue is meaningful and a better life not impossible.

Statius is capable also of affirming more active forms of virtue, and one of the striking features of the *Thebaid* is the recurring suggestion that virtuous action can attain a spiritual reward. The most extraordinary of such moments, and the most elaborately dramatized, is the ritual suicide of Menoeceus, but his heroism is anticipated by that of the augur Maeon, sole survivor of an abortive Theban attempt to ambush Tydeus as he returned from an embassy to Thebes (2.527–703). Confronting Eteocles with the disastrous result of the king's treasonous stratagem, he foretells the curse that will be visited on his attempt to rule unlawfully (3.59–77), then commits suicide. Statius hails this act as a heroic assertion of freedom, earning Maeon a new life in Elysium (3.99–102, 108–11). The virtue of Amphiaraus, too, persuades Pluto to spare him the pains of hell (8.124–26), and the Argives, even as they mourn his loss, look forward to worshiping him as a god, and gaining sure knowledge at his shrine (8.206–7).

These exemplary figures assume their full significance only when seen in the context of Statius' profound awareness of the different forms that Virtus and Pietas can assume and his recurring emphasis on the contrast between the human qualities he associates with these virtues and the often arbitrary and inhumane values of the cult of the gods with which they are traditionally associated. There is a definite shift in the course of the poem from isolated and tentative protest against needless suffering, as represented most prominently by the death of Opheltes and the terrible grief of Hypsipyle, to a vision of such suffering as the basic human condition. And as this vision evolves, compassion and community in

suffering, as well as the more active forms of spiritual courage, emerge
in steadily stronger terms as the fundamental virtues, wholly displacing
the religious and political values of heroic tradition.

The first serious challenge to the power of the gods occurs in Book 1,
where the Argive ruler Adrastus explains the origin of a local festival by
telling the story of how Apollo, in revenge for the accidental death of his
infant son Linus, sent a monster to devour all the newborn of Argos.
The monster is slain by the youth Coroebus, who, when Apollo retaliates
again by inflicting a plague on Argos, presents himself at the shrine of the
god to claim full responsibility for his act. Refusing to supplicate Apollo,
Coroebus challenges the god in the name of "piety and conscious virtue"
(1.644), accusing him of a love of slaughter and an indifference to human
life. Though he offers repeatedly to give up his life in return for the removal of the plague, Apollo, "awed" ("stupefacti," 665), allows him to depart unharmed, and removes his curse from the city. Adrastus concludes:

> inde haec stata sacra quotannis
> sollemnes recolunt epulae, Phoebeaque placat
> templa novatus honos.
>
> (*Theb.* 1.666–68)

[Hence each year ceremonial feasting renews the established
rites, and new honor propitiates the shrine of Phoebus.]

The ceremonial purpose of the story is fundamentally at odds with its
moral emphasis. Coroebus shows himself ethically superior to Apollo,
and his challenge to the god, motivated by *pietas* and "conscious virtue"
(1.644–45), exposes with unmistakable clarity the element of inhumanity
in traditional religion. But Adrastus complacently regards the episode as
only a reason to further honor the arbitrarily ruthless god rather than acknowledge the heroism of Coroebus' actions, which have twice averted
Apollo's wrath. Unlike the Argives' commemoration of the death of
Opheltes/Archemorus, the events which stem from the death of Linus
produce only a placatory ritual, meaningless save as an expression of fear,
as if to confirm the assertion of the fiercely atheistic Capaneus that such
fear is the only real motive for honoring the gods (3.661). Coroebus meanwhile is left in a position not unlike that of Lucan's Cato. Disillusioned as

to the value of honoring the gods, he remains bound by an enduring need to affirm *pietas* in some way, and by a "conscia virtus" which compels him to offer his life as a sacrifice to the god whose pointless cruelty he has exposed.

But Coroebus' heroism is dedicated, not to the abstract ideal of a lost liberty that inspires Cato, but to the liberation of actual human beings enslaved by fear and misguided reverence. As such it has no equivalent in the traditional heroic code, as is indicated ironically by the inability of Adrastus and his people to see its true value. In this respect Coroebus' role anticipates the achieved self-sacrifice of Menoeceus, an even more radical departure from heroic tradition.[15]

Though a fierce warrior, Menoeceus is also presented as an austere and unworldly figure. His suicide is declared the sole means of saving his city from destruction (10.604–20), but it is for him more a means to spiritual fulfillment than an act of patriotism. He is inspired by the goddess Virtus, who appears in the form of the priestess Manto to fill his mind with the vision of a heavenly destiny (10.632–65). As he stands on the city wall preparing to die, he already appears divine, and at the instant of his death his spirit ascends unfalteringly to the presence of Jove (10.756–59, 781–82).

But while the treatment of Menoeceus constitutes Statius' strongest assertion that virtue can attain a divine reward, its importance to the action of the poem as a whole, like that of the other noble deaths Statius relates, is negligible. His suicide preserves the city only to subject it to the rule of Creon, and he himself is all but forgotten as the war grinds to its inevitable conclusion. Like Coroebus he demonstrates a commitment to virtue for which his culture offers no precedent, and as with Coroebus the full significance of his heroism remains unacknowledged.[16]

A similar complexity appears in Statius' representation of Amphiaraus, in many ways the poem's central figure until his disappearance in Book 7. From the beginning the priest of Apollo embodies in an extreme

---

15. See Franchet d'Espèrey, *Conflit, violence et non-violence*, 376–82.

16. Though Menoeceus receives a grand funeral, it is dominated by Creon's bitterness. He accepts that his son now dwells among the gods but offers human sacrifices to his memory; and it is in Menoeceus' name that he refuses burial to the fallen Argives (12.60–104).

form the conflict between spiritual awareness and inescapable violence that pervades the *Thebaid*. In intimate contact with his patron divinity and deeply versed in augury, he knows from the beginning that the Argive cause is doomed, and tries to persuade his countrymen to abandon their campaign. Shouted down by Capaneus, and laboring under the curse asssociated with the necklace of Harmonia (2.265–305; 4.193–213), he nonetheless joins the host and fights heroically at Thebes until fate intervenes: the earth opens beneath his chariot, and he is drawn down to the underworld.

Amphiaraus' spirituality is unquestionably to be taken seriously. Perhaps the most beautiful passage in the poem, and a striking instance of the impulse to transcendence in his piety, is his meditation on the significance of augury, as he prepares to seek omens of the outcome of the impending war:

> mirum unde, sed olim
> hic honor alitibus, superae seu conditor aulae
> sic dedit effusum chaos in nova semina texens,
> seu quia mutatae nostraque ab origine versis
> corporibus subiere notos, seu purior axis
> amotumque nefas et rarum insistere terris
> vera docent . . .
>
> (*Theb.* 3.482–88)

[The cause is mysterious, but this honor has long belonged to the birds, whether the creator of heaven so decreed as he wrought vast chaos into the seeds of new life; or because they have come to soar upon the wind through a transformation, their bodies altered from an original state like our own; or because the purer air of heaven, and the remoteness of evil, and the rarity of their descents to the earth enable them to know truth . . .]

Amphiaraus' *pietas* clearly involves more than ritual service to Apollo. As they mourn his death, the Greeks look forward to a time when the deceiving oracles will be silenced, and Amphiaraus duly recognized as a god in his own right (8.195–207). Deprived of his guidance, they lose for a time all desire to pursue the war. And even as they mourn the priest himself is giving point to their devotion, asserting his blameless character and persuading Pluto to grudgingly spare him the torments of Dis (8.90–126).

Virtually all the complex issues engaged in the *Thebaid* come together in the situation of Amphiaraus. He displays a moral courage like that of Coroebus, the spiritual dedication of a Menoeceus; and the memory of his virtues arouses the Argives to imagine him becoming, like Opheltes, the object of a new, purer religious devotion. But he is at the same time inescapably one of the Seven against Thebes, bound to act in accordance with the values of his culture, and his deep awareness of his consecrated role rests in unresolved contradiction to a hero's desire for war. We see this clearly on the battlefield, as he begins his final *aristeia:* the conflict between his religious and warlike impulses comes to a head, and sacred knowledge gives way to savagery:

> medios aufertur in hostes,
> certus et ipse necis, vires fiducia leti
> suggerit; inde viro maioraque membra diesque
> laetior et numquam tanta experientia caeli,
> si vacet: avertit morti contermina Virtus.
> . . .
> innumeram ferro plebem, ceu letifer annus
> aut iubar adversi grave sideris, immolat umbris
> ipse suis.
>
> (*Theb.* 7.698–702, 709–11)

[he is borne into the midst of the enemy, sure that he
himself will die, and the certainty of death gives him
strength. His limbs seem stronger, the day more auspicious,
and never has he been more capable of reading the sky,
were he free to do so. But a death-seeking Virtue draws
him away, . . . Like a season of plague, or the baleful light
of an unfriendly star, his sword offers unnumbered bodies
as sacrifices to his shade.]

Later his fellow prophet Thiodamas will incite the Argives to a bloody night raid on the Theban camp, declaring that Amphiaraus has risen from the underworld to order the massacre (10.198–211).

Such contradictory motivation is not unique to Amphiaraus. Menoeceus, too, has the warrior's love of slaughter; when Virtus descends to summon him to his destiny she finds him surrounded by heaps of Argive corpses, so caught up in the lust of battle that the Sphinx who adorns his helmet appears infected with his mad desire for blood (10.655–60). Coroebus' salvific slaying of Apollo's monster is also motivated largely by a warrior's need to affirm his valor and win fame; in facing down the god he is inspired not only by virtue but also by "sacred rage" (1.605–8, 641–42). Even the savior Theseus, to whom the Argive widows appeal in the name of humanity and "sovereign Nature" (12.555–61), is motivated largely by revenge in his campaign against Thebes, and laughs, terrible in his pride and wrath, as he inflicts Creon's death wound (12.769–82).

The cult of Archemorus, too, is tainted by the lingering influence of the violent world of traditional epic. Amphiaraus displays a partial awareness that devotion to the infant god offers an alternative to the religious institutions of the past. It is he who affirms Archimorus' enigmatic merit and the destiny that has led to his deification, and he ventures the desperate wish that Apollo, in the spirit of Archemorus, might defer the war forever (5.733–52). But in the event Amphiaraus himself is the first of the Argives to be seized by the *furor* that leads the epic warrior to his highest displays of courage, a grim *virtus* wholly remote from the spirit of his extolling of the new god. And for Adrastus and the other Argive heroes Archemorus remains the focus of a traditional cult, a power who may be induced by the promise of a grand temple to favor the Greeks in the coming war (7.100–104).[17] The compromising effect of traditional values is further indicated by Statius' treatment of the fate of the serpent who had unknowingly caused the death of Opheltes. His slaying by Capaneus provides an icon of traditional heroism in its classic form, but Statius emphasizes only the hubristic savagery of the act, set off by the poignant response of nature to the creature's death. Nymphs and Fauns, and the fields and groves they inhabit, mourn the blameless serpent as if he were

---

17. Cf. Adrastus' similar prayer and promise to Hypsipyle (4.759–64).

Daphnis or Orpheus, in terms which resemble Statius' account of the end of Opheltes himself.[18]

Moreover, while the Argive's instantaneous affirmation of the cult of Archemorus seems to manifest a dimly sensed desire to break away from the tradition of heroic violence, the grounds for this new departure are uncertain. The imputing of a higher purpose to the life and death of the infant, however necessary this affirmation may be, remains arbitrary. As such it stands in sharp contrast to the genuinely heroic story of Hypsipyle, whose history has been a pre-Christian Life of Constance, a tragic romance, and whose steadfastness is finally rewarded by reunion with her twin sons. In Hypsipyle a generosity like that of Dido, schooled by hardship to minister to the sufferings of others, is combined with a *pietas* that in various ways evokes the character of Aeneas.[19] Though Statius gives no clear sign of his attitude toward Hypsipyle, and she disappears almost unnoticed from the poem, the episode as a whole has the effect of balancing the lingering influence of the traditional order against the fidelity and humanity exemplified by Hypsipyle's conduct in the face of the harshness of fortune and mankind.

In the final book of the *Thebaid,* where the grief of the survivors of the war dominates the narrative, these new values are finally brought to the fore. The women of Argos, widows and sisters of the soldiers who lie unburied at Thebes, come in a throng to Athens, and are discovered by Theseus clustered at the altar of the goddess Clementia. In the Argive women's appeal to Theseus on behalf of their unburied dead ("hominum, indite Theseu, / sanguis erant, homines," 12.555–56), as later in the prolongation of the poem's narrative by Statius' involvement in the final scene of mourning, we see emerging a new compassion of which Clementia is the symbol, and which becomes the dominant element of the moral and spiritual atmosphere in which the poem concludes.

Clementia is a divinity wholly distinct from the "powerful gods" (12.481–82), indifferent to any consideration except the need to respond to human suffering. The new order she represents is heralded by the scene that immediately precedes the arrival of the grieving widows at

---

18. With 5.579–82 cp. 4.779–82, 786–94.
19. See Frings, "Hypsipyle und Aeneas."

Clementia's shrine: Argia, the Argive bride of Polynices, and Antigone, his Theban sister, discover for a moment the "sacred communion of mourning" as they conspire to prepare his funeral pyre in defiance of Creon's interdict (12.392). In the cult of Clementia this bond is affirmed as the one power capable of sustaining the mass of mankind in a fundamentally hostile world.[20] Theseus' final crusadelike campaign against Creon is at least in part a response to this deep need, and the effect of his victory, after an initial "pious tumult" of communal joy and grieving (12.782–83), is to establish in Thebes itself the atmosphere of Clementia. Hostility gives way to hospitality, and the sharing by Argives and Thebans of the "widowed sorrow" of a common bereavement merges with the poet's own retrospective mourning, a grief which embraces the least together with the greatest: "so many pyres, of common warriors and chiefs alike" (798).

Clementia, like the Pietas whom Statius represents as driven from the field by Tisiphone (11.482–96), is a passive quality. Unlike Virtus, who can inspire Menoeceus to heroic action, Clementia exists only to draw a sorrowing humanity together through love and compassion. Her identification is always with the defeated, and she herself is in one sense powerless in the face of evil or cruelty. Her only "victories" are passive ones: a refusal of conflict; a refusal to judge the victims she compassionates; a refusal to accept any tribute save tears. Under her influence, as Silvie Franchet d'Espèrey observes, the old *pietas* of ritual gives place to a Pietas of the heart; compassion and consolation are all she asks of humanity, and all she offers her suppliants.[21]

Statius' account of the worship of Clementia suggests a new and rapidly growing movement: "now already countless peoples know her altars" (12.506). At the heart of her cult, moreover, is the sense of a new dispensation such as no other divinity can offer, the reaffirmation of a divine benevolence long forgotten, a gift which the poet in a beautifully evocative passage compares to the gods' ancient bestowal upon Athens, and through the Athenians upon the world, of the gifts of law and agriculture:

---

20. Emphasizing the unique value of Clementia, Statius finds it "worthy of belief" that *regnum,* as well as fortune, wrath, and violence, is banned from her altar (12.504–5).

21. Franchet d'Espèrey, *Conflit, violence et non-violence,* 281–85.

> Ipsos nam credere dignum
> caelicolas, tellus quibus hospita semper Athenae,
> ceu leges hominemque novum ritusque sacrorum
> seminaque in vacuas hinc descendentia terras,
> sic sacrasse loco commune animantibus aegris
> confugium.
>
> (*Theb.* 12.499–504)

[It is right to believe that the heavenly ones, to whom Athens was always hospitable, just as they had once given laws, and a new man, and sacred rites, and seeds descending into the empty earth, so now consecrated in this place a common refuge for souls in pain.]

Here for a moment we are allowed a truly inspiring vision, the reinstitution of a stable, functional relationship among man, nature, and the gods, as well as a vision of history and a hint of the possibility of social renewal which have no precedent in the poem. It is an intuition which must have spoken to the deepest longings of Statius' audience in the Rome of Domitian. But all is left in the somewhat equivocal area of that which is "worthy of belief " ("credere dignum," 12.499), and it is with a sense of loss, rather than hope, that the poem ends.

Dante's Statius

In considering what Dante might have made of all of this, I would like to note some fairly straightforward connections between the *Thebaid* and the *Commedia,* and suggest that Dante, too, saw in Statius' poem the qualities I have emphasized. Dante's Statius begins his autobiography by placing himself historically in the time of "the good Titus," who avenged the Jews' killing of Christ by destroying Jerusalem (*Purg.* 21.82–84). The reference suggests the typological significance assigned by commentators to Theseus' role in the *Thebaid,* but Statius' account of Titus' action also points to the contradiction implicit in the notion of avenging Christ's redemptive sacrifice—avenging, as he says, "the wounds whence issued the blood sold by Judas" (21.84). In relation to the spiritual significance of the original bloodshed, Titus's action is futile, the pointless extension of a chain of violence, as the violent action of the *Thebaid* and even the concluding intervention of Theseus are finally meaningless in comparison with the prevailing emphasis on loss and compassion, and the implied destinies of virtuous individuals like Amphiaraus and Menoeceus. It is for a moment as if the vision of Dante's Statius were still controlled by the historical vision of epic poetry.[22]

More strongly evocative of the deeper meaning lurking in the *Thebaid* is Statius' account of his first exposure to Christianity:

> Già era 'l mondo tutto quanto pregno
> de la vera credenza, seminata
> per li messaggi de l'etterno regno.
> (*Purg.* 22.76–78)

> [Already the whole world was big with the true faith,
> sown by the messengers of the eternal realm.]

Statius claims to have found the gospel message strikingly consonant with the opening lines of Vergil's Fourth Eclogue (*Purg.* 22.79–81), but in the lines just quoted he is, as he says, giving "color" to the "disegno" implied by his paraphrase of Vergil's announcement of a renewal of the world (70–72, 74–75). "Color" suggests rhetorical enhancement, restating an idea in a more pointed way. And in fact the image of a world made pregnant with truth by the sowing of the Word reflects two stages of coloring, for between Vergil's lines and Dante's we can hear Statius' own, clearly echoéd by Dante, which link the new dispensation represented by the cult of Clementia with the gods' ancient gift of Triptolemus, the "new man," new mysteries, and "seeds descending on the empty earth" (*Theb.* 12.499–502). Dante evidently has this passage in mind, for as Statius goes

---

22. The paradoxical character of Titus' *vendetta* closely parallels Vergil's reference to the Trojan horse, which, at the instigation of Ulysses and Diomede, breached the walls of Troy and thereby opened "la porta / onde uscì de' Romani il gentil seme" (*Inf.* 26.59–60).

on to tell of his relations with the Christians of his time, his words breathe the very atmosphere of Clementia:

> Vennermi poi parendo tanto santi,
>   che, quando Domizian li perseguette,
>   sanza mio lagrimar non fur lor pianti;
> e mentre che di là per me si stette,
>   io li sovvenni.
>
> (Purg. 22.82–86)

[They came then to seem to me so holy that when Domitian persecuted them, their wailing was not without my tears, and while I remained yonder I succored them.]

The righteous lives of Christians, he declares, made him despise all other sects (vv. 86–87). It is not difficult to hear in this a reminiscence of the poet's distancing of himself from traditional religion in the course of the *Thebaid* and his assignment of an increasing value to private virtue.

What might seem the most obvious linkage between Statius' poem and Dante's is in fact more difficult to assess. Statius received baptism, he tells us, "before I had led the Greeks to the rivers of Thebes in my verse" (22.88–89), an allusion which again seems to invite us to look for a latent allegory in the text of the *Thebaid*. Two passages suggest themselves: the Argives' arrival at the Theban rivers is clearly indicated (7.424–25), and as we have seen, the pseudo-Fulgentian commentary suggests an appropriate typological reading of the earlier encounter with Hypsipyle and the Nemean river Langia. But in both these episodes Statius is at pains to indicate the confusion of motive in the Argives' relation to the rivers rather than assign any definite significance to the encounter. In the Langia episode the thirst-maddened host begin by rejoicing together at the sight of the water but are soon fighting so desperately with one another to escape the river's strong current that they resemble conflicting armies (4.809–23). In the later scene the Argives are afraid to cross the river Asopus until, shamed and made less timid by the reckless plunge of Hippomedon, they follow him like cattle (7.425–40). If Dante is inviting us to associate either scene with Statius' baptism, it would seem that he perhaps does so in order to hint at Statius' uncertain motivation in embracing Christianity. The Theban scene in particular, with its emphasis on irresolution, suggests the "tepidezza" which had left Statius unable, "for fear," openly to declare his faith (*Purg.* 22.90–91).

There is, however, one striking moment in the first of these river scenes which, read in the perspective provided by Dante, suggests a significant, if indirect, linkage between the river and Statius' spiritual progress. Amid the frenzy of the Argives' assault on Langia, as they fight among themselves and continue to drink obsessively from the water they have fouled and muddied, an unnamed chieftain stands in midstream and offers his own prayer to the god of the river:

> "laetus eas, quacumque domo gelida ora resolvis
> inmortale tumens; neque enim tibi cana repostas
> Bruma nives raptasque alio de fonte refundit
> Arcus aquas gravidive indulgent nubila Cori,
> sed tuus et nulli ruis expugnabilis astro.
>   (*Theb.* 4.839–43)

> [May your course be happy, from whatever source you release
> your cool waters, issuing immortally; for the season of white
> frost does not fill you with its store of snow, nor the rainbow
> with waters stolen from another stream, nor does Corus,
> burdened with storm-clouds, favor you; your waters are your
> own, and your flow is unchecked by the influence of any star.]

Of all the moments of religious intuition in the *Thebaid* this is perhaps the most startlingly at odds with its context, and it points to a wealth of potential meaning which everything else about the scene seems calculated to obscure or deny. Before considering the implication of this moment at more length, we may note that the passage was clearly important to Dante: it is one of the sources of the lines in which Dante's Statius satisfies the thirst of the Pilgrim by explaining the climate of Purgatory:

> Per che non pioggia, non grando, non neve,
>   non rugiada, non brina più sù cade
>   che la scaletta di tre gradi breve;

nuvole spesse non paion né rade,
    né coruscar, né figlia di Taumante,
    che di là cangia sovente contrade.[23]
                        (*Purg.* 21.46–51)

[Wherefore neither rain, nor hail, nor snow, nor dew, nor hoar-
frost falls any higher than the short little stairway of three steps.
Clouds dense or thin do not appear, nor lightning-flash, nor
Thaumas' daughter who often changes her region yonder.]

The Langia episode clearly has a symbolic value in Dante's conception
of Statius. When Vergil, reporting to Statius the names of those of "your
own people" who languish with him in Limbo, mentions Hypsipyle, he
identifies her only as "she who showed Langia" (*Purg.* 22.109, 112). We
must see the Argive chieftain's prayer to the river, and his intuition that it
flows immortal from its unknown source, as exemplifying that quality in
the *Thebaid* which Dante must have valued at least as highly as the quasi-
Christian attitudes noted by Lewis: the deep sense it conveys of the separation of the lives of the spiritually starved humanity with whom it deals
from another level of reality, a world of purity and communal piety which
makes its existence known in sudden, powerful bursts of religious insight.
Such insight appears in a tentative and finally abortive form in Adrastus'
complex, almost tormented prayer to Apollo at the close of Book 1, in
which the dark associations of traditional mythology are unexpectedly
balanced in the final lines against a sense of the god's affinity with such
milder divinities as Osiris and Mithras (1.696–720). We can see it again as
a kind of poetic intuition in the speculations of Amphiaraus on the mysterious ability of birds to reveal to men the purposes of the gods.

Such bursts of insight are invariably brief, seemingly random, and
wholly unintegrated into the main action of the poem, but the Langia
episode, which represents the most extreme and most radically removed
of these visionary moments, set as it is within the larger isolation of the
Hypsipyle-Opheltes interlude, is unique also in that it has a certain causality

---

23. These lines also echo *Theb.* 2.32–57; see Padoan, "Il canto XXI del 'Purgatorio,'" 338.

of its own. The Argives do not come upon the river in a wholly random way, for Bacchus, to divert them from their campaign against his city, has ensured that Langia will continue flowing amid the general drought (4.716–17). They are, moreover, guided to the river by Hypsipyle, who thus assumes a potentially symbolic significance in the episode. In one aspect the Lemnian princess, whom the Argives encounter in a condition of utter exile, cut off, as she says, from her own heritage, and charged with the care of a child not her own (4.768–72), reflects in her own life the violently dislocating course of human history as the poem presents it. Her ministering to the needs of the thirsting army is conditioned by a Dido-like fellow feeling her misfortunes have taught her. At the same time her power to satisfy their thirst is a part of the design of the god, and her sudden apparition to the Argives, with the infant Opheltes at her breast, seems to them like a divine visitation (4.746–53); thus, though she herself disclaims divine power and is ignorant of Bacchus' role in the episode, she assumes the aura of a providential figure.

But neither the human dignity nor the quasi-divine office of Hypsipyle prepares us for the religious events to which the episode at the river gives rise, the unnamed chieftain's vision and the death and apotheosis of Opheltes. Hypsipyle's role in the first of these events is unwitting and accidental, and the death of Opheltes, miraculously significant to Amphiaraus and the Argives, is for her only a new reminder of the loss of her own children and the hopelessness of her subsequent life (5.608–35). Moreover, both the discovery of the river and the death of Opheltes generate reactions so violent that they threaten to turn into rioting if not all-out war. Hypsipyle is clearly powerless either to foresee or to control these effects, yet she is their unwitting cause, and in the second case brings her own life into jeopardy at the hands of Opheltes' father, Lycurgus.

In her dignity and her haplessness, her impulse to bring comfort and inspiration to others, and the futility and tragic isolation of her own life, Hypsipyle, even more than Amphiaraus, embodies the divided vision of human life in the *Thebaid*. Though blameless, and endowed with great humanity and moral courage, she is inescapably part of the violent course of human history, and is reduced, by suffering and the terrible consequences of her well-intended actions, to a point at which she wishes only to die (5.628–35). And it is only when she has reached this extreme of despair that providence intervenes in her life: her twin sons, guided, Statius tells us, by "wondrous fate" at the will of Bacchus (5.710–14), appear to rescue her, just as the Argives are about to go to war prematurely to defend her from the wrath of Lycurgus.

Hypsipyle's plight is in certain respects a counterpart to that of Statius himself, in that darkest mood in which he feels himself incapable of breaking away from his tale of a world in which history seems to come to nothing, the Statius who lets himself be drawn into the sufferings of his characters until his voice is indistinguishable from theirs, and who ends his narrative by lingering helplessly over the funeral pyre of Parthenopaeus. I would suggest that this is how Statius appeared to Dante as well, that Statius, as embodied in the *Thebaid,* is for Dante a kind of Hypsipyle. Dante hints at their identity by effectively identifying their roles: "she who showed Langia" did so at the behest of the poet who "brought the Greeks to the rivers of Thebes." Hindered by a profound irresolution from affirming for himself the implications of those moments of religious vision which punctuate the poem, Statius nonetheless makes them accessible to his readers, just as Hypsipyle, while viewing her own life as hopeless, plays a role in the providential economy and ministers to the "thirst" of others.[24] It is not only Vergil, Dante suggests, but his self-proclaimed disciple who "goes by night," yet provides light for those who come behind (22.67–69).

Hypsipyle is finally given a providential dispensation of her own, when she is discovered by her sons, who will (though Statius does not make this explicit) gain her freedom from Lycurgus' service and restore her to Lemnos, removing her once and for all from the tragic world of the poem.[25] No corresponding intervention redeems the conclusion of the *Thebaid,*[26] but here I would extend a tentative line of argument one final step, and argue that Dante himself plays the role of providence, and

---

24. On the relation of Hypsipyle to the recurring theme of thirst in the Statius cantos, see the suggestions of Caviglia, "Appunti," 269–72.

25. See Martinez, "Lament and Lamentations," 68.

26. I cannot accept the "redemptive" view of Theseus' role in the *Thebaid* imputed to Statius by Vessey, *Statius and the Thebaid,* 316. For persuasive opposing views, see Aricò, *Ricerche Staziane,* 109–31; Burgess, "Statius' Altar of Mercy," 339–49.

provides the affirmation which Statius had been powerless to make in his own person, by inventing for him a spiritual history which places both the poet and his poem in a new perspective. Like Hypsipyle's reunion with her sons, Statius' appearance in the *Purgatorio* is marked by ecstatic shouting and supernatural phenomena (*Theb.* 5.730–31; *Purg.* 20.127–37), and in both cases the event represents the reestablishment of a fundamental continuity: Hypsipyle's restoration to her heritage and her posterity corresponds to the establishment of Statius as an important link in the chain of influence which joins Dante to his own poetic heritage. Dante seems to confirm this association of poet, queen, and literary tradition later in the *Purgatorio,* when the two sons' discovery of Hypsipyle is evoked to set off Dante's encounter with Guido Guinizelli (26.94–96).

But Statius' role in the providential economy imposed on him by Dante is as unwitting as Hypsipyle's participation in the designs of Bacchus, and hence in the *Purgatorio,* too, it is important to recognize the limits of his knowledge. Its most striking feature is its wholly intuitive character. Statius is able to give an account of the unchanging phenomena of Purgatory, but he is frankly unable to explain what he nonetheless somehow knows—that there is change in Purgatory though there is no alteration in the nature of the place, that the mountain trembles for no natural reason whenever a soul is released from the process of its purgation. It is as though he had somehow received confirmation of that intuitive sense of an untroubled natural source world which he had put into the mouth of the Argive chieftain at the river Langia.

Statius on the Soul

Statius' word for the newly purified soul's discovery of its freedom to advance toward Paradise is "surprise" (22.61–63), and surprise, like intuition, is an essential element in the kind of experience with which he is identified in the *Purgatorio.*[27] We are surprised by his first, Christ-

---

27. Hawkins, "'Are You Here?'" does not mention the Statius cantos, but the surprises there are surely as thematically suggestive as, for example, the appearance of Ripheus or Trajan in Paradise.

like appearance to Dante and Vergil, and by his revelation of his identity; he himself seems surprised and baffled by his special knowledge of the miraculous nature of his experience and its setting. But all these surprising features of Statius' role are only preparatory for what is surely the greatest surprise of all, the fact that it is Statius who is given the responsibility of providing Dante with an explanation of the mysterious process of the creation of the human soul. This explanation, moreover, has been taken not only as Dante's most important statement on the soul but also as a significant step beyond scholastic orthodoxy, a uniquely personal, semimystical assertion of the soul's power to assimilate the divine.[28] Bold in itself, this discourse also constitutes Dante's boldest assertion of his freedom to read new meaning into ancient poetry: for the central feature of Statius' discourse, his description of how the powers of the natural organism are transformed and reoriented when it is informed by divine "vertù," transposes into medical-psychological terms the process whereby the goddess Virtus prepares the Theban hero Menoeceus for his immortalizing self-sacrifice in *Thebaid* 10. Statius' goddess leaps joyfully forth from heaven to inform Menoeceus' spirit with a new aspiration (*Theb.* 10.632–36), and though he experiences her informing presence as a form of possession, it differs from the traditional sacred rage in that Virtus becomes in effect his higher nature.[29] And as she rejoices at finding in Menoeceus a vessel worthy of receiving her (633–36), so in the narrative of Dante's Statius the response of the First Mover to the perfected natural creature is a joy which seems to serve as a catalyst for the inbreathing of a new "vertù" (*Purg.* 25.70–72).

But this remarkable use of allusion, in one sense the most flamboyant instance of the fictive religious typology on which Dante's exploitation of Statius depends, also defines the extremely selective terms on which Dante allows Statius' poetry to assume a significant role in his own scheme.

---

28. See Nardi, *Studi di filosofia medievale,* 54–68.

29. Though Menoeceus feels himself "possessed by a mighty power" ("multo possessus numine," 676) which drives him to seek his own death, Virtus is described as entering his breast gently and quietly to "leave herself in his heart" ("permulsit tacite seseque in corde reliquit," 673).

A remarkable feature of Dante's Statius' account of the animation of the mortal creature is the consistency with which it articulates and dramatizes the activity of the divine "alma" while stressing the passivity of the human vessel to the point of rendering it virtually inert. And this, too, corresponds to Statius' account of the experience of Menoeceus. It is Menoeceus' fierce bravery, attested by the heap of corpses that surrounds him (*Theb.* 10.650–55), which makes him fit to receive the summons of Virtus, but Statius' language hints that his martial self is being reduced to the status of a sacrificial animal ("neque te indecorem sacris," 650), and he is aware of the new spirit with which he is informed by Virtus only as a desire for death (677).[30] The simile of a tree blasted by lightning emphasizes again the sacrificial climax of his mortal existence, and his separation from the world is already under way when he lies to Creon, who, in a fit of uncharacteristic *pietas,* seeks to arrest him. The same sharp division between soul and body reappears in a more radical form in the discourse of Dante's Statius, who stresses only the soul's transcendent nature and destiny while saying as little as possible about its experience of its life in an earthly body.

An early sign of Statius' disregard for the merely human is his abstract treatment of procreation, and his apparent reluctance to acknowledge the female as such.[31] The process which leads to the mingling of "perfect" male blood with the blood of the "other" to form the human embryo in utero necessarily brings into play sexual passion and those parts of the body of which Statius says only that it is more seemly to be silent than to speak of them (*Purg.* 25.37–45), but Statius gives no hint of feeling or reciprocity, and his emphasis throughout is clinical and detached. The distinctively humanizing infusion of soul is described briefly,

---

30. Menoeceus' role as victim is further emphasized by his response to the summons of Virtus ("sequimur, divum quaecumque vocasti," 680), which echoes the response of the hapless Turnus to the exhortation of Iris in *Aen.* 9.21–22.

31. Freccero's otherwise insightful discussion of Statius' discourse disregards its repressive aspect; he sees the treatment of sexuality as a straightforward representation of natural creativity, analogous to the way in which "the poetic corpus is sired by the poet" (*Poetics,* 202).

and wholly in terms of the operation of the First Mover (70–74). Then, having acknowledged in a single line the existence of the new human creature, with its capacity for articulation and reflection, and illustrated the miracle of its creation with a memorable image of the making of wine (75–78), Statius immediately proceeds to undo the divine handiwork. As Menoeceus' ecstatic union with Virtus leads immediately to the death of his mortal self, so Dante's Statius, having traced the perfecting of the soul, moves forward abruptly to the *last* stage of its development, when it is separated from the flesh and enters the afterlife with its faculties intact (79–86). Henceforth Statius never looks back but instead goes on to dwell at length on the constitution of the "ombra," the shade state which is the modus vivendi of both Statius and Vergil in Purgatory. This shade is formed by very human feelings: "According as the desires and other affections prick us, the shade takes its form" (106–7). But we are given no earthly context for these feelings. For the purposes of Statius' discourse, the soul has no history.

In the curious disjunctions of Statius' pneumatology we may see Dante acknowledging the separation of worldly and spiritual concerns in Statius' own poetry and adapting it to his purposes. But Dante also shows himself aware of the vacillating character of Statius' religious intuitions in themselves, and their often uncertain relation to the enslaving repetitions of traditional cult. It is this uncertainty that accounts for the abrupt and fleeting character of the religious intuitions which punctuate the narrative of the *Thebaid,* and even with the larger perspective provided by his passage through Purgatory, Statius can convey a clear sense of the operation of the divine only by suppressing the earthly, human aspect of the soul's experience. There are hints of autonomy in the soul's activity: it is moved "per sé stessa" and "turns" on itself (75, 85). But all its significant experience comes to pass "mirabilmente," by the work of the First Mover. Only in death does it come to know "its own road," its destiny (87). Earthly life has no more inherent significance than those unnamed parts which effect physical generation in the "natural vessel" of the "other" (43–45).

Dante's own characters in the *Purgatorio* freely acknowledge the violence and discontinuity of their earthly lives, facts which, like the visible scar of Manfred in Canto 3, constitute the "brute details" of that human history which the *Commedia* redeems.[32] But Dante has wholly removed Statius from the historical world of his own poetry. Here again his position resembles that of Hypsipyle, the female character to whom the *Thebaid* grants the most prominent role, but whose pious existence is isolated from the action of the poem. Statius' instincts and Hypsipyle's together are reduced to the vessels of a higher inspiration which gives them a transcendent significance but does not relieve the human pain of their world.

Perhaps the most telling sign of Dante's restrictive treatment of Statius is the image with which his own Statius expresses the wonder of the inbreathing of the divine into the human organism:

> E perché meno ammiri la parola,
> > guarda il calor del sol che si fa vino,
> > giunto a l'omor che de la vite cola.
> > > (*Purg.* 25.76–78)

[And that you may marvel less at my words, look at the sun's heat, which is made wine when combined with the juice that flows from the vine.]

Vine and juice, here reduced to means whereby the sun's heat "si fa vino," "makes *itself* into wine," represent the merely human history which Statius' tentative sense of the divine fails to redeem.

Of course this comparison, which crowns Statius' account of the genesis of the soul, has broader implications. Like the spiritual capacities of the human organism, the power to collaborate in making wine is present only *in posse* in the grape, but the realization of this power has a radically transformative effect, which is here implicitly compared to the dynamic, ecstatic love of the pure soul for God. The *Thebaid* had compared the new dispensation represented by Clementia to the gifts of Ceres, agriculture and the Eleusinian mysteries. Dante in Canto 18 compares the zeal of the penitents who have conquered sloth to the energy of the Theban

---

32. See Freccero, *Poetics*, 198.

rites of Bacchus (18. 91–96). The lines just quoted evoke the cults of both these closely related deities and effect a union between them which becomes the image of a new, more profound mystery.[33]

Statius' discourse is the culmination of the concern with spiritual psychology that runs through the central cantos of the *Purgatorio*. This theme is introduced by Marco Lombardo's fanciful description of how the newly created soul responds, childlike, to the delightful variety of its earthly situation (*Purg.* 16.85–92). The passage strongly recalls Statius' description in the *Thebaid* of the infant Opheltes at play, and suggests that Dante read Statius' treatment of the infant god-to-be as a stage in the evolution of his treatment of spiritual psychology in the *Thebaid*. As Marco's "simple little soul," which knows nothing save its own impulse to be pleased, is beguiled by one trifling good after another, so Opheltes, lying unattended "in the lap of the vernal earth,"

> miratur nemorum strepitus aut obvia carpit
> aut patulo trahit ore diem nemorique malorum
> inscius et vitae multum securus inerrat.
>
> *(Theb.* 4.798–800)

> [wonders at rustlings in the woods, snatches at whatever
> he meets, takes in the day with open mouth, and strays
> through the grove, ignorant of danger and unconcerned
> for safety.]

---

33. Statius' image can hardly be referred to a specific source, but the imaginative typology it implies resonates with a passage from the commentary of Guillaume de Conches on Macrobius: "That Bacchus is said to be twice born, first of Semele, then of Jupiter's thigh at the time of his nativity, contains so much of truth that the vines (which we understand by Bacchus, for he is their god), impregnated by the sun's heat, become green— this is what Bacchus' first birth refers to—and later they grow until in summer they put forth grapes—and this is Bacchus' second birth"; cited from MS Vat. Pal. Lat. 953, f. 82va, by Dronke, *Fabula,* 29 (English), 71 (Latin). Elsewhere William imagines the priest of Bacchus making the god's winnowing fan (the "mystica uannus Iacchi" of Vergil, *Georg.* 1.166) the occasion for a sermon on the destiny of the "winnowed" (i.e., purified) soul; Dronke, *Fabula,* 22–23, 70.

These lines describe Opheltes' last waking moments. When we see him again he has fallen asleep, and he is stung as he sleeps by the tail of a huge serpent sacred to Jove. The serpent is wholly unaware of having wounded the child (5.538–39), no human being is present, and Opheltes passes from sleep to death in total isolation:

> fugit ilicet artus
> somnus, et in solam patuerunt lumina mortem.
> (*Theb.* 5.539–40)

[instantly sleep departed from his limbs, and his eyes opened upon death alone.]

Like Marco's "simple little soul," Opheltes knows nothing as he passes from life to death. The child does indeed seem to have lived only to die and become an object of worship, a symbol of the spiritual starvation of those who insist on his divine status. Statius' stark account of a transitional moment that reveals nothing but death points ironically to its meaninglessness as a spiritual event.

But the Argives' desperate need to discover something more in the event is significant in itself. Amid the bleakness of a discredited paganism they long to believe that a divine power recognizes and compassionates human suffering, and that through affirming the value of the innocence and purity embodied in Archimorus they can escape the curse that condemns their world to self-destructive violence. The same yearning emerges in Amphiaraus' imagining of the purer condition that enables birds to reveal hidden truths, or Thiodamas' intuition that beneath the chaotic surface of earthly life there exists a benevolent goddess Nature who has received Amphiaraus, clasping him lovingly to her bosom in acknowledgment of his goodness. The sequence of such moments of insight begins with the stark finality of the death of Opheltes and culminates in the triumphant affirmation of Menoeceus' ascent to heaven, while the attendant virtues who receive his abandoned body form a sort of *pietà* on the earth below (10.780–81). The knowledge Dante imputes to Statius in *Purgatorio* 25, his concise account of the soul's entry into the afterlife, is the culmination of this awareness. Only now, says Statius, does the soul come to know its destiny: "quivi conosce prima le sue strade" (v. 87). The line assumes an extra significance when placed in the mouth of Statius, and constitutes a victory for one whose own poetry has been marked so deeply by the desire for sure spiritual orientation.

And Statius' imaginative account of the genesis of the soul also has implications for Dante's conception of poetic creation. We should note how carefully and fully Statius details the handiwork, the "arte di Natura," that precedes the moment at which the divine "vertù" is actually breathed into the human embryo. The human creature is fully formed, endowed with its full complement of faculties and capacities, and the superadded virtue is essentially a knowledge, a sureness of orientation, which had not previously been present.[34] What the "motor primo" does in joyfully bestowing his "vertù" is explicitly a ratification of the artistry of Nature that has produced the integrity and beauty of the human creature; and Dante, in crediting Statius with this insight into the divine economy, is making a comparable claim for the integrity and validity of the art of poetry as embodied in Statius' epic, suggesting by his revisionary reading of Statius that the human poet has managed to create a vessel which needed only to be informed by divine "vertù" to become the vehicle of revelation. Dante brings Statius' art to its consummation when he breathes this revelatory power into the *Thebaid,* as Statius, discovering new meaning in the Vergilian lines he quotes, had conferred a tentatively similar status on the *Aeneid.*

Dante's creation of a fictive biography for Statius bears on his own career in other ways as well. It is a way of showing how something like the conversion of Statius could plausibly have happened, how a kind of providence could have disposed the interaction between the known events of the social, political, and religious past and the accidents of literary influence and artistic temperament in such a way as to bring about the creation of a canonical text in which both literary and spiritual history were fully expressed.[35] And what is presented conjecturally in the case of Statius assumes a more serious significance if we see it as a precedent for Dante's treatment of his own life as man, poet, and Christian. There is a marked similarity between Statius' final "surprise," his virtuoso

---

34. See, in addition to the discussion of Nardi cited in n. 25 above, Boyde, *Dante Philomythes,* 276–81.

35. See Martinez, "Dante and the Two Canons," 154–56.

account of the creative act of the First Mover as it breathes a "spirito novo" into the human embryo, and Dante's sudden and seemingly unpremeditated revelation of his own poetic power, the breathing of Love within him, in the previous canto (24.52–54).[36] The parallel reinforces the suggestion that in that remarkable moment, while the now-enlightened Bonagiunta stands by like Simeon beholding the infant Christ, Dante is claiming a transcendent status for his poetry. In effectively bypassing the tradition in which he had been schooled and deriving inspiration and authority directly from "Amor," he is collaborating in a process which resembles, as nearly as art or nature can, the creative activity of the "motor primo."[37]

But the centrality of Amor in Dante's account also points up the limitations of Statius' narrative of the soul as a model for Dante, limitations that will become clearer as Dante's own sense of his poetic gift is "refined" in the encounter with Guido and Arnaut that follows. Only the First Mover knows joy in Statius' discourse; it is radically distanced from the existential reality of human experience, and given the careful attention to procreation, the absence of any hint of the erotic is particularly striking. In this respect Statius' capacities and limitations define Dante's ongoing poetic task, the creation of a poetry which will express spiritual realities without disregarding the human desires that continue to inform his aspiration.

"I due poeti"

In addition to its bearing on Dante's poetics and poetic history, Statius' relationship with Vergil has a life of its own. It is important to remember that the Statius who appears in the *Purgatorio* is first and last a poet. In his own mind the catalyst of both his artistic and his spiritual vocation was his reading of Vergil, a reading marked by moments of discovery as intense and random as the visionary moments in his own poem, but which begins as a fundamentally nurturing experience:

---

36. See Mazzotta, *Dante, Poet*, 193–214; Freccero, *Poetics*, 202.
37. See Barolini, *Dante's Poets*, 89–91; Martinez, "The Pilgrim's Answer," 41–54.

Al mio ardor fuor seme le faville,
    che mi scaldar, de la divina fiamma
    onde sono allumati più di mille;
de l'Eneïda dico, la qual mamma
    fummi, e fummi nutrice, poetando:
    sanz' essa non fermai peso di dramma.
                    (*Purg.* 21.94–99)

[The sparks which warmed me from the divine flame whereby
more than a thousand have been kindled were the seeds of my
poetic fire: I mean the *Aeneid*. Which in poetry was both mother
and nurse to me—without it I had achieved little of worth.]

Throughout the cantos in which he first appears Statius hardly notices
Dante in his absorption with Vergil,[38] and Dante employs discreet humor
to dramatize this attachment. Even now, with centuries of purgatorial
hardship behind him, Statius can imagine deferring his entry into Paradise
for love of his mentor:

E per esser vivuto di là quando
    visse Virgilio, assentirei un sole
    più che non deggio al mio uscir di bando.
                    (*Purg.* 21.100–102)

[And to have lived yonder when Vergil lived I would consent to
one sun more than I owe to my coming forth from exile.]

The sentiment here expressed is of course utterly implausible: subject to
the spiritual psychology of Purgatory, Statius could hardly deny in himself the aspiration that he is now fully ready to pursue, let alone consign
himself to the darkness of pre-Christian paganism. But Statius' sin had
been prodigality, and there is something wonderfully prodigal about a
wish whose realization would effectively defer spiritual growth in favor
of the fullest possible experience of artistic discipleship. This reckless
desire to squander "one sun more than I owe" is all the more striking

---

38. See Whitfield, "Dante and Statius," 118.

in the mouth of the author of the *Thebaid*, where a year of exile counts for a good deal.

Vergil makes no response to Statius' warm praise, and silently imposes silence on Dante. That Dante proves unable to obey Vergil's command is crucial to the meaning of the episode. The silence by which Vergil is concealed suggests the restricted, and in a sense the negative, character of his authority, the fact that his poetry does not possess an inherent capacity to reveal truth. The long silence from which he had first emerged in the *Inferno* can only be broken by one who masters for himself Vergil's "bello stilo" and so can lay claim to the "forte a cantar" of a true poet. Hence Dante, rather than Vergil himself, must reveal Vergil's identity, and in doing so he both brings Vergil the poet into play and gains a necessary distance from his master. For Dante to have remained silent in obedience to Vergil's unuttered "taci" would have falsified the true nature of Vergil's influence; he would be subjecting his living will and imagination to the imagined authority of one who, as Statius will recognize, is essentially "vanitate" (21.135).

Dante's dilemma, in this situation governed entirely by the laws of "poetando," is worth examining closely:

> Or son io d'una parte e d'altra preso:
>   l'una mi fa tacer, l'altra scongiura
>   ch'io dica; ond' io sospiro . . .
> > (*Purg.* 21.115–17)

[Now am I caught on the one side and the other: the one makes me keep silence, the other conjures me to speak, so that I sigh . . .]

That Statius responds to Dante's smile, Vergil to his sigh, provides a gentle reminder of the aspects of their poetry that Dante wants to set in contrast. And when Statius is described as "conjuring" Dante into explaining the reason for his smile, we should recall that this verb appears only here and in Vergil's account of his subjection to the power of Erichtho (*Inf.* 9.23).[39]

---

39. I assume with the *E.D.* that *scongiura* is a variant form of *congiurare*, perhaps with a suggestion of urgent appeal rather than compulsion.

Here it is Dante who is conjured into drawing Vergil forth from the silent past. Without disturbing the genial atmosphere of the scene, Dante, with Statius as his surrogate, has managed to remind us of the dangers to which poetic influence can give rise, by touching, lightly but tellingly, on its necromantic aspect while at the same time opening the way for Statius' affirmation of the positive power that ancient poetry, fully assimilated, can exert.

It is remarkable that Vergil himself seems to recognize the potentially dangerous effect of his influence. Only when admonished by Vergil does Statius reawaken to the *vanitate* of their common condition, and by implication the vanity of his wish to have carried his experience of Vergil's influence to an impossible extreme. Dante had addressed Statius as "antico spirto" in preparing to reveal Vergil's identity (122), reminding us that the realization of Statius' wish would amount to abandoning himself to the world of the "antichi spiriti dolenti" (*Inf.* 1.116). Dante himself had experienced such a desire in a more radical form, under the spell of Vergilian language, on the shore of the river of *Inferno* 3, and Vergil's admonition had been necessary to recall him, traumatically, from a vicarious experience of Vergilian damnation.[40] Here that scene is restaged in an atmosphere of sheer innocuous "poetando," but we must take seriously the issues raised by the comic interplay between the two great poets.[41] Vergil, arresting Statius' attempt to embrace his feet, calls to mind the idolatry of the final lines of the *Thebaid,* where Statius, addressing his poem, warns it not to seek to rival the "divine *Aeneid*" but rather follow reverently in its footsteps (*Theb.* 12.816–17). We recognize once more that for Dante as for Statius, a too great attachment to Vergil—to poetry as such—can have an inhibiting effect on spiritual self-realization.

Again, when Vergil explains that his love for Statius was "kindled" by the "virtù" expressed in Statius' love for him (22.10–17), he tacitly corrects the prodigal Statius' claim that his poetic "ardor" had been kindled by the "divina fiamma" of the *Aeneid* (21.94–97). For the transmission of poetic "forte" must always be initiated by the disciple's loving appropriation of the master's power. That every word of Vergil's seems to Statius a token

---

40. See above, chap. 2, pp. 34–37.

41. On the function of comedy here, see Scrivano, "Stazio personaggio," 183–84.

of love (22.27) is due to his own loving nature, which his loving assimilation of the style of the *Aeneid* has enabled him to express. He later agrees to explain the origin and afterlife of the soul because, he says, he cannot deny Vergil (25.32–33), again indicating that Vergil had provided the articulating vehicle for his spiritual insight, a vehicle which, like the First Mover, he had appropriated and informed with love.

But Dante warns us against taking too seriously the role of Vergil in Statius' spiritual formation. However we understand Statius' notorious distortive reading of Vergil's "auri sacra fames" (*Aen.* 3.57; *Purg.* 22.37–42),[42] it clearly goes beyond the bounds of even the most radically exploitative medieval allegorizings of pagan poetry. By disregarding the authority, not just of Vergil's text, but of its syntax, Dante is acknowledging an arbitrariness which, as he was surely aware, implicates even his own much subtler appropriation of the *Thebaid*. Dante certainly believed that his poetry benefited in spiritually significant ways from his assimilation and reorientation of the insights of the Poeti, but he was also aware that his imaginative faculty was at the service of *ingenium* as well as religious vision,[43] that his dealings with ancient poetry were always to a greater or lesser extent a matter of "doing things with words."[44]

Statius and Vergil are placed in a similar perspective as the three poets resume their upward journey. Vergil takes charge, and Dante sustains the mood of the canto by emphasizing his role as disciple, following the two *poetae* and profiting from their discourse. But the tree that appears in the middle of their path, whose fruit Vergil and Statius may not eat (139–41), is a first clear sign of discrimination among them,[45] and the several mes-

---

42. The best case I have seen for taking Statius' reading seriously is that of Martinez, "La 'sacra fame dell'oro.'"

43. See Kleiner, *Mismapping the Underworld*, 71–84.

44. In keeping with this emphasis is the syntactic ambiguity of 125–26, where the "anima degna" whose "assent" makes them less unsure of the path might be Statius (as is usually assumed), or Vergil, whose willingness finally to reveal his identity has reaffirmed his disciples' sense of their vocation.

45. Dante has emphasized the linkage between Vergil and Statius, and their separateness from himself, in the later stages of the canto. They are twice referred to as "li poeti" (115, 139), they walk ahead talking (127–29), and they, but not Dante, approach the speaking tree (139).

sages emitted from within its foliage reveal the ethical significance of the prohibition. For Statius as well as Vergil the vision of paradisal bounty represented by the sweet fruit of the forbidden tree recalls a mythical golden age, a "primo tempo umano" which offered an abundance that required nothing of humanity, in which no standard existed to control indulgence, and which was inevitably lost through uncontainable human violence and greed. But rightly understood, the anonymous voice suggests, the original human condition was a kind of ascesis, an age of sufficiency: its simple resources were commensurate with the requirements of human sustenance, and consequently provided satisfaction rather than surfeit. This was the true Golden Age, which the Baptist sought to recover in his desert life, as a symbolic prefiguring of the renewal to be effected by the life and death of Christ. In comparison, the fantasy of abundance unfolded in Vergil's messianic Eclogue is as meaningless as the state of innocence in which Statius' Opheltes marvels at the variety of nature, or the condition of Marco's newborn "anima semplicetta."

Vergil and Statius contribute little to the next two cantos, but Canto 23 ends with Dante's explanation to Forese of Vergil's role in his journey:

> " . . . costui per la profonda
> notte menato m'ha d'i veri morti
> con questa vera carne che 'l seconda.
> Indi m'han tratto sù li suoi conforti,
> salendo e rigirando la montagna
> che drizza voi che 'l mondo fece torti.
> Tanto dice di farmi sua compagna
> che io sarò là dove fia Beatrice;
> quivi convien che sanza lui rimagna.
> Virgilio è questi che così mi dice."
>
> (*Purg.* 23.121–30)

[" . . . he it is that has led me through the profound night of the truly dead, in this true flesh which follows him. From there his counsels have drawn me up, ascending and circling this mountain, which makes you straight whom the world made crooked. So long he says that he will bear me company until

I shall be there where Beatrice will be: there must I remain
bereft of him. Vergil is he who tells me this."]

The length and placement of this passage are puzzling, since it intrudes
on Dante's engagement with friends and poets from the recent past, but
it has a pivotal function, defining once and for all the scope and limits of
Vergil's authority, and so setting off the series of encounters with living
poetry in the cantos that follow. Aside from a passing reference to the
"truly dead" and the naming of Beatrice, the passage contains no hint of
the spiritual significance of Dante's journey; even the Earthly Paradise is
identified simply as "là dove fia Beatrice," and as the place where Vergil
will leave him. And when Vergil is finally named, he is immediately contrasted with Statius, specified only as "quest' altro" (131), but then clearly
identified with the dynamic life of Purgatory, the shaking of the mountain and the spiritual release it signifies.

The point of the passage is underlined in the opening lines of Canto
24, where Dante unexpectedly picks up the thread, completing his account
of the still-unnamed Statius by noting that he ascends so slowly "out of
consideration for another" (24.8–9). Dante immediately changes the subject, but only after making plain the limited role that Vergil now plays.
At a stage when speech and ascent seem to complement each other, and
the travelers move forward "like a ship driven by a fair wind" (24.1–3),
Statius' deliberate matching of his pace to Vergil's shows that he is no
longer dependent on his poetic master.

Statius, too, will be reduced to a similar position. Vergil will defer to
Statius in the face of Dante's question about the posthumous existence
of the spirit (25.20–21), but Statius' great discourse will be his own final
contribution to Dante's development, and it seems clear that in providing
Statius with this authoritative role Dante is concerned chiefly to affirm
the validity of poetic insight in a way that pertains less to Statius' poem
than to his own. His attitude toward the two Poeti will continue to be one
of love and reverence, but already, and to a certain extent in spite of himself, he has ceased to require their guidance.

7

Lust, Poetry, and
the Earthly Paradise

Despite his seeming neglect of Vergil and Statius in Cantos 23 and 24, his striking declaration to Bonagiunta that he is guided by the inner voice of love, and the clear signs of his growing independence, Dante remains close to the ancient poets as they proceed, and identifies his experience with theirs. They are, he declares, "del mondo sì gran marescalchi" (*Purg.* 24.99), a phrase that seems to contrast the authority and power of their martial epics with the private, lyric inspiration Dante claims for himself, and suggests a lingering awe and dependence on his part. But as they proceed all three are clearly on the same level: They move in unison at the prohibitive command of another anonymous voice, they are addressed together as "voi sol tre" (133) by the fiery angel who directs them upward, and all three apparently ascend to the next terrace in total darkness.

But the final lines of Canto 24, which return us to the sphere of Dante's private imaginative experience, remind us of his unique situation:

> E quale, annunziatrice de li albori,
>   l'aura di maggio movesi e olezza,
>   tutta impregnata da l'erba e da' fiori;

tal mi senti' un vento dar per mezza
    la fronte, e ben senti' mover la piuma,
    che fé sentir d'ambrosïa l'orezza.
E senti' dir: "Beati cui alluma
    tanto di grazia, che l'amor del gusto
    nel petto lor troppo disir non fuma,
esurïendo sempre quanto è giusto!"

(*Purg.* 24.145–54)

[And as, heralding the dawn, the breeze of May stirs and smells
sweet, all impregnate with grass and with flowers, such a wind
I felt strike full on my brow, and right well I felt the pinions
move, which wafted ambrosial fragrance to my senses; and I
heard say, "Blessed are they who are so illumined by grace that
the love of taste kindles not too great desire in their breasts,
and who hunger always so far as is just."]

The heralding breeze, charged like Chaucer's April showers with the
"vertu" that will cause the earth to flourish, is an image of annunciation
and incarnation, foreshadowing the miraculous fertility of the Earthly Paradise and anticipating Dante's final readiness to enter it. The lush garden
world of the Golden Age has been disciplined as well, and relegated to an
appropriately symbolic role. In this moment of rich, synaesthetic awareness, the breeze on the Pilgrim's face is transformed insensibly to the touch
of the wing of the true herald, the angel who utters the quasi-beatitude
that completes the purgation of gluttony. A reciprocating transformation
is implicit in the ambiguity of the final line, where the literal disciplining of
physical appetite both completes the angel's homily and points beyond
itself to the "blessed hunger" for righteousness.[1] The message is close to
that of the scene which ends Canto 22, but here it is offered in wholly positive and implicitly sacramental terms, terms which carry Dante beyond the
imaginings of the *poetae* and show him, for a moment, effortlessly adapting the poetry of metamorphosis to a spiritual context.

---

1. With this suggestion the line recalls and in effect completes the recitation of the Beatitude (Matt. 5:6) begun by the angelic guide in 22.4–6.

Meeting Guido

The ascent to the seventh terrace which follows Statius' pneumatological discourse is in some respects the most difficult transition in the *Purgatorio*. The sin of lust is clearly one that Dante is reluctant to judge categorically, for it is the hardest of the sins to isolate and define. In dealing with it one can lose sight of what is essentially good in human desire, and restraint all too easily becomes prohibition. The examples cited by the penitents on this terrace illustrate the problem, for in every case chastity is affirmed by external authority rather than illustrated in experiential terms. Chastity is "imposed" ("imponne," 25.135) on husbands and wives by the institution of marriage; the harsh law of Diana forces Callisto, made pregnant through rape, into exile; even the virgin purity of Mary is appropriated, and any possibility of unchastity foreclosed, by God.

Certainly no useful definition of chastity emerges from the three cases, and none of them addressses the need for inner discipline as an antidote to lust. The uniquely perfect submissiveness of Mary sets an unattainable standard; the laws of marriage and social convention impose a kind of chastity, though one that admits of several definitions; but the militant chastity displayed in Diana's punishment of Callisto is a kind of inverted lust, a destructive force which, far from countering the ruthless desire of Jupiter or the jealousy of Juno, collaborates with them to ensure the total alienation of a common victim whose vowed chastity was taken by force.[2]

The recitation of each example is followed by the singing of the "Summae Deus clementiae," with its prayer for purity of heart and the purgation of sinful desire, which seems to point up the conspicuous failure of the chanted examples to address the psychology of lust. The tone

---

2. Jacoff, "The Rape / Rapture of Europa," 244–45, sees Dante's "misreading" of Ovid here as necessary to his pairing of Diana and Mary, though she also notes the very different treatment of Callisto / Helice in *Par.* 31.31–33.

If Dante's use of "Helice" for "Callisto" is deliberate, it may convey a further hint of the cruelty of her fate. Turned to a bear by Juno, she was later transformed by her assailant, Jupiter, into the "Great Bear," Ursa Major. "Helice" (spiral, twister), another name for this constellation, bears no reference to Callisto. Dante so names her again in *Par.* 31.32.

of Dante's concluding comment on the situation of the penitents is tinged
with something like sarcasm, and he can perhaps be heard questioning
the justice of their subjection:[3]

> E questo modo credo che lor basti
>   per tutto il tempo che 'l foco li abbruscia:
>   con tal cura conviene e con tai pasti
> che la piaga da sezzo si ricuscia.
>
> (*Purg.* 25.136–39)

> [And this fashion, I believe, suffices them for all the time
> the fire burns them: with such treatment and with such
> diet must the last wound of all be healed.]

The penitents, apparently ("credo," 136), are destined to move continually
back and forth between their chants, at one moment praying for inner
discipline, at the next confronting one or other of the three prohibitive
and perplexing examples, none of which exemplifies the self-control they
seek. No other passage in the *Purgatorio* presents moral instruction in so
arbitrary a fashion, or makes so clear the inadequacy of doctrine in the
absence of immediate experience. And nowhere is it more strongly suggested that the remedying of the sin in question requires a clearer understanding of what purgation must involve, and the intervention of something more than legalistic restraint.

It is thus appropriate and significant that Canto 26 represents the
purification of the lustful will, not as an exorcising of physical desire, but
as first and foremost a process of refinement, and one for which the art
of poetry can serve as a richly suggestive metaphor. As the canto begins,
the sun is low in the sky and Dante's body casts a shadow which makes the
fire appear more intense, enabling the penitents to recognize the extraordinary fact of his bodily presence. It is apparently in Dante's shadow that

---

3. Marti, "Il canto XXVI del 'Purgatorio,'" 610, remarks that Dante's tone
in these lines can seem both "complacently cruel" and tinged with "una sottile
amarezza d'ironia." He notes as well the hectic rhythm and obsessively repetitive
syntax of the description of the penance of the lustful (25.121–39).

the ensuing dialogue takes place, the shades careful to remain within the fire (26.14–15), Dante equally concerned to avoid it (25.116, 124–25). The wall of fire thus defines the terms on which Dante meets Guido Guinizelli, the poet who had inspired his early attempts to express in his own poetry a love which, while it takes its shape from natural desire, aspires to transcendence. Guido and his fellow sinners are being cleansed; their desire, it is suggested, will henceforth be free of every impulse but the pure love of God and humankind, while Dante is still opaque, uniquely privileged but at the same time trapped in his bodily self, his will contaminated by loves which confuse his impulse toward God. Guido is experiencing the purification prayed for in the "Summae Deus clementiae," while Dante must return to a world where the power of poetry to communicate spiritual intuition and the experience necessary to achieving purity of heart are inhibited by a blunt morality which suppresses or distorts desire instead of refining it. But the experience of a common desire is nonetheless a bond between them, and Guido, even amid his penitential suffering, acknowledges being so affected by Dante's address that an impression will remain even after he has completed his purgation and passed through Lethe (106–8). This "vestigio" is not simply gratitude for Dante's promise of "service," but a recognition of the affection that prompts it.[4]

In Guido's first address to Dante there is both tactful insight and the lyric urgency of a spirit "who burns in thirst and in fire."[5] Guido recognizes the reverence that makes Dante follow in the footsteps of the two Poeti, then quickly undoes the implication of courtly subjectivity in his reference to himself by indicating that not only he but all the penitents thirst for an explanation of Dante's presence. Guido has entered a state in which desire is free of ambiguity, and fire and thirst clearly have a

---

4. When Guido questions the truth of Dante's words, presumably a promise to ensure prayers on Guido's behalf, he distinguishes this promise from the affection attested by Dante's manner of speaking ("dire," 111, as opposed to the specific "parole" of the promise) and his facial expression ("guardar"). The use of "vestigio," markedly absent in Dante's later rendering of *Aen.* 4.23 (*Purg.* 30.48), suggests the stirring of a reciprocal affection in Guido.

5. Pertile, "*Purgatorio XXVI*," 382, notes the allusion to Guido's sonnet "Lo vostro bel saluto," lines 7–8.

sacramental purpose. His words anticipate the "novità" (26) of the two lines of souls whose conflicting desires are harmonized in the "accoglienza amica" of mutual charity (37), a bond which, as in the image of flocks of cranes impelled to fly in opposite directions (43–46), transcends nature.

That the astonishment of the penitent souls at the revelation of Dante's mortal state is compared to that of a "montanaro," newly arrived in the city, speaks both to their literal status as they ascend through Purgatory[6] and to the experience they have undergone. The image could imply crudeness and confusion, but the stylistic grace and intricacy of Guido's speeches, and later that of Arnaut, belies this. What they have attained is a state in which elegance and rusticity complement one another. Like the "montanaro," the penitents will become citified ("s'inurba," 69), or in Guido's image cloistered (127–29), in the heavenly Rome by virtue of having recovered the rusticity of innocence.

Dante's engagements with the ancient poets offer nothing comparable to his encounter with Guido. Poetic language, in the form of the "dolci detti" of the *stilnovo,* is inescapably the medium of their communication, but here it creates a bond far more intimate and intense than Dante's reverent assimilation of the style of Vergil.[7] The comparison of Dante's excitement as Guido names himself to that of the sons of Hypsipyle on discovering their mother makes this plain. The sons, roaming in search of Hypsipyle, overhear by chance fragments of an exchange between Tydeus and Lycurgus, and rush "through weapons and hosts" to save their mother from her threatened execution for having allowed the death of Archemorus. Their abrupt intrusion, marked by confused motives and issuing in an almost violent display of *pietas* (*Theb.* 5.720–22), suggests the conflicting forces at work in Statius' epic, and the impossibility, for a Christian poet, of assimilating its power in a fully coherent way. But as Dante silently contemplates one whose art is inseparably part of his own, while remaining fully aware of the fiery barrier that separates them, he and Guido are twinned by a common devotion to the "parlar

---

6. Koffler, "The Last Wound," 40–41.

7. Savarese, "Dante e il mestiere di poeta," 377, notes the internal motivation that distinguishes this moment from earlier encounters with poets, and rightly calls it "the most important chapter in Dante's literary autobiography."

materno," and the artistic superiority which Dante cannot help but declare defers to Guido's spiritual example.

So completely has literary tradition been subsumed by spiritual concerns that Guido is instantly dismissive of Dante's reverence, focused as it is on his poetic style. In referring Dante forward to Arnaut he is in no way diminishing his own authority, merely providing a further example of what purgation means for a poet, reminding Dante that style, as well as spirit, must be refined in a new way. And as Dante clearly implies, Arnaut's very status as "miglior fabbro" is implicitly a limitation, for what differentiates the Italians' poetry from that of Arnaut and his tradition is their appropriation of its masterly technique to represent new and more profound experience. Arnaut, like Ulysses, speaks from a virtual prison house of style, in a language which is unmistakably that of the courtly tradition he had helped to prepare for its transformation by Guido and his followers. Guido has learned to adapt his style to the demands of his place in Purgatory, and moves fishlike through the fiery element (134–35), but the static figure of Arnaut deploys an idiom still redolent of the "joi" and "dolor" which define the entrapment of courtly desire.[8] His only action is to conceal himself in the fire; the "fabbro" and his craft must be refined together.

Fathers and Sons

The pertinence of Arnaut's condition to Dante's is not immediately made clear. The opening lines of Canto 27 place the Pilgrim's situation in a larger perspective by an oddly detailed periphrasis, noting the position of the sun relative to Jerusalem, Spain, and India as a way of indicating that it is sunset in Purgatory. Jerusalem is identified as the place where God shed his blood (2), and the scope of this redemptive act is suggested by the world-encompassing panorama, but the imagery also conveys a strong sense of physical necessity. Spain has "fallen" into darkness, while the Ganges seems to burn under the noonday sun, and the evocation of an inexorable natural justice suggests that Purgatory, too, midway between

---

8. Bec, "La douleur," 546–52.

Indian noon and Spanish midnight, is subject to the same laws as the world of mortal beings.

The promise of the blood shed at Jerusalem ensures that the intense heats and deep darknesses of Purgatory are part of a providential design, but as the canto unfolds, Dante seems most involved with his physical situation. After the strong suggestion of self-canonization in Canto 26, he now reverts to a silent and almost passive state. His fear of the wall of flame becomes an immobilizing terror when the guiding angel commands him to enter the fire, and he remains "fermo e duro" (34), unpersuaded by Vergil's encouragements until drawn by the name of Beatrice. His response to the beloved name is ambiguously compared to the last gasp of Pyramus, who, hearing Thisbe's name, opens his eyes momentarily, only to close them again in death (37–39; *Met.* 4.142–46).

The ambiguity is significant. On the one hand Dante's evocation of the pathos of adolescent passion, like his earlier references to Ganymede and the boy Achilles, or his dream of the Siren, points to a lingering immaturity, all the more striking in that his experience of the lessons of Purgatory is nearly complete. The naming of Beatrice, like the reference to the Crucifixion in the canto's opening lines, conveys an assurance of providential control; but the shedding of Pyramus' blood, which Ovid with calculated bathos compares to a leak in a broken water pipe, and which, as Beatrice will recall (*Purg.* 33.69), affected only the color of the fruit of the mulberry, seems to parody the work of the blood shed at Jerusalem. Viewed in this way it is an appropriately demeaning image for the self Dante must now finally abandon once and for all, the connoisseur of pathos who had swooned on hearing the tale of Paolo and Francesca, and whose imaginative experience of love, even now, can be tainted by a self-deceiving *pietà*.[9]

But Dante's lines on the last moments of Pyramus are charged with religious suggestion, and the mulberry itself, with its blood-colored fruit,

---

9. Similarities between Dante's use of the Pyramus story and the story of Paolo and Francesca are noted by Picone, "*Purgatorio* XXVII," 396–97. Contini, "Alcuni appunti," 174, notes how readily the wall of fire that separates Dante and Beatrice (36) evokes the wall between the chambers of Pyramus and Thisbe (*Met.* 4.65–80).

is read in a well-attested exegetical tradition as standing for the Cross of Christ.[10] Fatal for Pyramus,[11] the love evoked by Vergil will be redemptive, for in the name of Beatrice is the promise of life, though Dante must evidently "die unto himself" to realize it, and this will require coming to terms with his sentimental and erotic nature in a more mature way.

In any case we should note that it is not passion itself, but the immature form it takes, that is here rebuked.[12] To a great extent the remaining cantos of the *Purgatorio,* and in many ways the *Paradiso* as well, are lessons regarding the nature of human desire, which, like Dante's impulse to give aesthetic form to his experience, must be refined, but can never be purged. Refinement leads to fuller realization, and the process will reach its climax, and with it the realization of all that Beatrice has been and meant for Dante, only in the great farewell of *Paradiso* 31, where man, poet, and pilgrim speak in unison.

In the meantime, though he seems unable to accept Vergil's assurances that the fire will not harm him,[13] Dante has also reverted to his earlier dependence on his "dolce padre" (52), who, after treating him as a willful child, to be rebuked and cajoled, will unexpectedly end the canto by declaring him sovereign over himself. The irony of Vergil's situation is nowhere more pronounced than here. Plainly excluded by angelic injunctions addressed to "holy souls," and those whom God has blessed (11, 58), he must nonetheless urge Dante forward with reminders of Beatrice, whose advent, as he must know, will mean his return to the lower world (23.127–30).

Dante ascends guarded fore and aft by the two Poeti (46–48), and when the setting of the sun obliges them to pause, he employs an elaborate and confusing simile to indicate his relation to them:

---

10. See Moevs, *Metaphysics,* 90–100.

11. In the *Integumenta Ovidii* of John of Garland, whose couplets commonly introduce individual tales in manuscripts of the *Metamorphoses,* the staining of the mulberry bush is "a sign that death is lurking in sweet love" (182).

12. This, too, can of course be read *in bono.* Moevs, *Metaphysics,* 100, sees in the childlike character of Dante's reaction to Vergil's naming of Beatrice the childlike trust that is essential to faith.

13. Dante's struggle here between "razionalità e trascendenza" is well analyzed by Barański, "Structural Retrospection," 18.

Quali si stanno ruminando manse
   le capre, state rapide e proterve
   sovra le cime avente che sien pranse,
tacite a l'ombra, mentre che 'l sol ferve,
   guardate dal pastor, che 'n su la verga
   poggiato s'è e lor di posa serve;
e quale il mandrïan che fori alberga,
   lungo il pecuglio suo queto pernotta,
   guardando perché fiera non lo sperga;
tali eravamo tutti e tre allotta,
   io come capra, ed ei come pastori,
   fasciati quinci e quindi d'alta grotta.
(Purg. 27.76–86)

[As goats, which have been swift and wayward on the peaks
before they are fed, become tranquil as they ruminate, silent
in the shade while the sun is hot, guarded by the shepherd
who leans upon his staff and tends their repose; and as the
herdsman, who lodges out of doors, passes the night beside
his quiet flock, watching lest a wild beast scatter it, such were
we then all three, I as a goat and they as shepherds, bounded
by the high rock on this side and that.]

This is Dante's last declaration of his dependence on the Poeti, and sounds
the first notes of an extended tribute to Vergil which will culminate in the
lament of Canto 30. The shift from the comparison of the more or less
emblematic "pastor" to that of the conscientious "mandrïan" seems to express a growing realization of the significance of the moment, and emphasizes the role of Vergil as guide and protector.[14] But as the long sentence
continues, Dante reverts to general terms; the reference to "tutti e tre"
renders the focus of the similes indeterminate, and when Dante distinguishes his position from that of the two *poetae* in the following line, Vergil has become once again a "pastor," his role merely emblematic and indistinguishable from that of Statius.

---

14. Hollander, "Le opere di Virgilio," 315, notes that the lines on the *man-*
drïan echo *Georg.* 4.433–35.

There is a strong elegiac strain in these lines, which recalls the one great declaration of personal feeling in Vergil's poetic corpus, the story of the ill-fated love of his fellow poet Gallus in the tenth and last of the *Eclogues,* and the acknowledgment of his own deep feeling for Gallus in that poem's final lines. Vergil's Gallus, having first written love elegies, had been consecrated as a poet of pastoral (*Ecl.* 6.64–73), but had been unable to free himself from his unrequited love, and reverted to his former role as a poet of fruitless passion: "Omnia uincit amor," Vergil's Gallus declares, "et nos cedamus amori" (*Ecl.* 10.69). Thus the poem proper ends.

In a coda to the *Eclogues,* which follows immediately, Vergil declares his love of Gallus, then in the final lines announces the end of his own career as a writer of pastoral:

surgamus: solet esse grauis cantantibus umbra,
iuniperi grauis umbra; nocent et frugibus umbrae.
ite domum saturae, uenit Hesperus, ite capellae.

(*Ecl.* 10.75–77)

[Let us rise: shade can be harmful to singers, harmful
the shade of the juniper; and shade harms the crops as
well. Go home well fed, for Hesperus is rising, go home,
my goats.]

Dante, who knew the *Eclogues* well,[15] clearly recalled these lines as he prepared to usher Vergil out of the *Commedia,* and the image of the departing poet, with the ambiguously menacing darkness gathering around him, must have had a deep meaning for him. Here that scene is reenacted. Having failed to bring his beloved Gallus to know the peace of the pastoral world, Vergil has apparently succeeded with Dante, once, like Gallus, a poet of love confused by passion, but now, like the goat of his simile, well fed and at peace, eager and ready to enter the true Arcadia which knows no harmful shadows. Vergil, meanwhile, the good shepherd who "lodges out of doors" (27.81), having seen Dante safely to the threshold of Paradise, has fulfilled his mission only to face exclusion and the

---

15. See Cioffi, "Il cantor," 100, and her review of criticism on the similes, 116–17n48.

inevitable return to Limbo, where fame alone can hold at bay the ever-encroaching darkness.

But Vergil's coda had included as well an acknowledgment of the power of his own love for Gallus, a love that is not tragic but profoundly natural, a feeling of growth which he compares to the burgeoning of a young tree in springtime. The expression of this love and the affirmation of its fundamental goodness are a confirmation of the integrity of his poetry and his confidence in his poetic powers, an essential preparation for the larger tasks Vergil would go on to perform. This understanding, too, is part of his legacy to Dante. He will end the canto by pronouncing Dante's will "libero, dritto e sano" (140), no longer liable to betrayal by his desires, and able to act "al suo senno" (141), so that the pursuit of pleasure ("piacere," 131) is now obligatory, a means to fulfillment rather than a danger.

This final bringing of "piacere," "arbitrio," and "senno" into harmony is foreshadowed by Dante's dream of Leah. "I'mi son Lia," she declares, "e vo movendo intorno / le belle mani a farmi una ghirlanda" (101–2). The first line clearly echoes Dante's account of how love inspires his poetry (24.52–54), and in fact Lia is the embodiment of this poetic, an image of pure feminine beauty that seems, like the verdure of Eden as described by Vergil (134–35), to become art of its own accord.[16] Nothing could be further from the dream of the Siren in Canto 19, or the imaginative process that caused her to appear beautiful; Dante as poet is now ready to experience imaginatively not only the consummation of earthly beauty in the Earthly Paradise[17] but also, through Beatrice, the more profound beauty mirrored by the figure of Rachel (104–6). In further confirmation of this move toward transcendence, Dante feels himself undergoing a metamorphosis of his own: at every step, "al volo mi sentia crescer le penne" (123).

Vergil's great final speech expresses with a fine concision the role of his wisdom and poetic artistry in Dante's regeneration, and then, Prospero-like, grants him his freedom:

---

16. See Picone, "*Purgatorio* XXVII," 399, for whom Lia represents "la felicità raggiungibile in questo mondo."

17. On Eden as "the most 'natural' place in the whole *Comedy*," see Kirkham, "*Purgatorio* XXVIII," 418–19.

Tratto t'ho qui con ingegno e con arte;
  lo tuo piacere omai prendi per duce;
  fuor se' de l'erte vie, fuor se' de l'arte.

(*Purg.* 27.130–32)

[I have brought you here with understanding and with art.
Take henceforth your own pleasure for your guide. Forth
you are from the steep ways, forth from the narrow.]

Despite its allusion to the "arcta via" of Matthew 7:14, the last line, with its almost fussy sound-play and punning, lends a certain irony to Vergil's declaration. His art and Dante's own poetic powers have been crucial to his progress thus far, but as "erte" jostles with "arte," art becomes *mere* art, a resource which has served its purpose, and Vergil appropriately goes on to confront Dante with the artless, authentic beauty of a place where he may sit in contemplation like Rachel, or with Lia adapt his own artistry to the richness of Nature. Vergil's praise of Paradise, which evokes the vivid imaginings of a pristine natural world that recur in all his own poetry,[18] is perhaps the one remotely Vergilian element in the speech, for Vergil has reached the very limit of his powers, and from now on will only gaze and wonder, like Dante himself.

Matelda

Dante, however, will continue to see Paradise with a poet's eyes, as he indicates, perhaps half-facetiously, by his elaborate but cliché description of the *schola cantorum* of the birds (28.16–18).[19] His artistic integrity is put

---

18. Ovid is commonly seen as the poet of the Golden Age most clearly implicated in Matelda's *corollario* (28.139–44; see Hawkins, *Dante's Testaments*, 181–82). But see Sabbatino, *L'Eden della nuova poesia*, 88–93, who notes that Ovid nowhere speaks of a *return* to the Golden Age, and that Vergil, on the basis of passages in the *Aeneid* as well as *Eclogue* 4, has an equally valid claim.

19. That the lines are conventional does not, of course, mean they are not meaningful. See Kirkham, "*Purgatorio XXVIII*," 425–27.

to a sterner test by the appearance, in a setting charged with erotic suggestion,[20] of a "donna soletta" who will later be identified as Matelda, but
who for the moment exists only as the fulfillment of a lyric dream, a living
Leah. Her beauty exists not only for her pleasure, but offers itself to the
viewer with an innocent assurance which makes all the more striking the
intense desire that she arouses in Dante. The Pilgrim's first response is to
appropriate her as a lyric image and "read" in her happy appearance a mirroring of the desire she arouses in him:

> Deh, bella donna, che a' raggi d'amore
>   ti scaldi, s'i' vo' credere a' sembianti
>   che soglion esser testimon del core . . .
> (Purg. 28.43–45)

[Pray, fair lady, who do warm yourself at love's beams,
if I may believe outward looks which are wont to be
testimony of the heart . . .]

The lines are hardly less conventional than the earlier treatment of bird-
song, a beautiful but generic response to the generic "donna," but the lines
that follow give them meaning:

> Tu mi fai rimembrar dove e qual era
>   Proserpina nel tempo che perdette
>   La madre lei, ed ella primavera.
> (Purg. 28.49–51)

[You make me recall where and what Proserpina was at the
time her mother lost her, and she the spring.]

The desire in these lines is real, and will become more intense as Matelda
draws closer and finally lifts her eyes, but it is disciplined by the poetic

---

20. Barolini, *Dante's Poets*, 148–53, demonstrates Dante's close dependence
on the *ballata* "In un boschetto trova' pasturella" of Guido Cavalcanti. See also
Hawkins, *Dante's Testaments*, 160–69.

forms in which it finds expression. In Dante's address to the "bella donna" *stilnovo* convention discovers its limits, as it seeks to contain a beauty in the creation of which it has played no part, and on which it can therefore make no legitimate claim. The comparison of Proserpina that follows points up the limitations of poetry itself. The imagining of Proserpine in the Vale of Enna represents, for Dante as for Milton, the closest ancient poetry could attain to intuiting a prelapsarian world, and the memory brings with it an acknowledgment that this world is lost. Like Milton Dante is acknowledging his own fallenness in evoking the myth, and affirming at the same time his solidarity with the tradition of the Poeti, whose aspirations have informed his own, and whose dreams will be vindicated by Matelda's generous suggestion in the canto's final lines.

The Last of Vergil

Vergil's complete silence after the great speech of Canto 27 and his *stupor* on beholding the sacred procession (29.56–57) make plain that he no longer has the power to act as guide, or even describe what he beholds.[21] Statius will scarcely be mentioned again. But even now Dante remains the disciple of the Poeti, reverting to the mode of the *Vita nuova,* but supplementing his lyric gestures by recalling classical archetypes.[22] Even before he has compared Matelda to Proserpina, his immediate reaction to her beauty recalls that of Ovid's Pluto, for whom seeing, loving, and ravishing are a single act (*Met.* 5.395).

But further allusions to Ovid suggest uncertainty. The light that shines forth from Matelda's eyes recalls the gaze of Venus, infected with

---

21. de Fazio, "*Purgatorio* XXIX," 440, notes the pertinence of the definition of *stupore* in *Conv.* 4.25.5, which cites the example of astonishment before a great work of art.

22. On the Ovidian references which follow, see Hawkins, *Dante's Testaments,* 187–93; as he notes, Ovid is here identified with "the postlapsarian imagination itself" (193). But while Hawkins sees the allusions as exposing Ovid's vision as "a distortion of Edenic reality," he does not acknowledge the effect of this distortion on Dante, whom he sees only as being "delivered" from Ovid's erroneous view.

love by Cupid (*Met.* 10.525–28), but the more significant allusion is to the death of the object of her love, Adonis. Dante's feelings as he gazes across the stream recall the futile "odio" of Leander (28.71–74), fearful of the stormy Hellespont, and pathetically aware of his youth and powerlessness.[23] These allusions strongly suggest on Dante's part a lack of confidence in his own powers, and the last lines of the canto confirm his lingering sense of dependency:

> Io mi rivolsi 'n dietro allora tutto
>   a' miei poeti, e vidi che con riso
>   udito avëan l'ultimo costrutto;
> poi a la bella donna torna' il viso.
>   (*Purg.* 28.145–48)

> [I turned then right round to my poets, and saw that with
> a smile they had heard these last words; then to the fair lady
> I turned my face.]

The "tutto" that completes the movement depicted in the first line makes plain the sense of urgency with which Dante turns,[24] and shows him wholly intent on determining the reaction of "his" poets to Matelda's confirmation of their vision of the Golden Age. Only when reassured by their smiles does he turn again toward Matelda, as he will turn again and again to seek guidance from the face of Beatrice.

For the moment Dante is clearly unready to follow Vergil's advice and let his own "piacere" be his guide. He is between two worlds: even as Matelda chants phrases from the Psalms, she appears to him like a nymph dancing through the shadows of the forest (29.1–6). Dante will repeat the two actions of turning to Vergil, then turning forward again, in the following canto, when what had appeared trees of gold are revealed as candlesticks (29.55–58). They will occur one last time, separated by a significant

---

23. With Singleton I assume that Dante's Leander is based on Ovid, *Heroides* 18 and 19, which make several references to his youth, the threat of discovery by his parents, and the possibility that he will fail to swim the Hellespont.

24. See Hawkins, *Dante's Testaments,* 127, on the similar effect of *volsimi* in 30.43.

interval, at the appearance of Beatrice (30.43–45, 62). But in the first case Vergil can only mirror Dante's "stupor" at what he sees, and when Dante turns again, Vergil will have left him "bereft of himself."

Dante's discovery of the disappearance of Vergil has been discussed so thoroughly, and so well,[25] that I have little to say about it, let alone much that is new. But the echoes of Vergil's own poetry which anticipate his vanishing are worth considering in the larger context of the later cantos of the *Purgatorio*. The death at 19 of Marcellus, who might well have succeeded Augustus as emperor of Rome, is recalled by the chanting of the beautiful but profoundly enigmatic "manibus, oh, date lilia plenis" (*Purg.* 30.21; *Aen.* 6.883), echoing Anchises' consecrating invocation of Marcellus in the final lines of his prophecy to Aeneas. The allusion is in one aspect a heralding of Beatrice, whose early death is essential to the sacred economy of Dante's poem,[26] but in its immediate context it is a more nearly tragic addition to the sequence of allusions to the youthful victims of uncontrolled desire, Pyramus, Adonis, and Leander, to whom Dante had earlier compared himself. In passing beyond these merely pathetic Ovidian figures to recall the profound loss incurred in Marcellus' early death, Dante acknowledges and honors Vergil's complex, uneasy vision of Augustan Rome.

The somber political implications of the reference to Marcellus are anticipated in yet another allusion to doomed youth, in Canto 29. The magnificence of the griffin's triumphal chariot, Dante declares, surpasses not only that of the chariots used to celebrate the triumph of a Scipio or Augustus, but even that of the chariot of the Sun,

> quel del Sol che, svïando, fu combusto
> per l'orazion de la Terra devota,
> quando fu Giove arcanamente giusto.
> (*Purg.* 29.118–20)

[that of the sun which, going astray, was consumed at devout Earth's prayer, when Jove in his secrecy was just.]

---

25. The two best discussions, in my view, are Hawkins, "Dido, Beatrice," and Jacoff, "Intertextualities in Arcadia," side by side in Jacoff and Schnapp, *Poetry of Allusion*, 113–44. For Hawkins, see also *Dante's Testaments*, 125–42.

26. See Mazzotta, *Dante*, 187.

The allusion is of course to Phaëthon's disastrous attempt to guide the chariot of his father, Apollo, and one purpose is doubtless to hint at Dante's presumption in offering his own largely uncanonical version of divine revelation.[27] But the preceding reference to Rome and its triumphs and the appended reminder that it was the appeal of Earth to Jove that led to the destruction of Phaëthon and his chariot set the passage in a Vergilian context, that of his great poem of the earth, the *Georgics*.

The first of the *Georgics* ends with a prayer for the end of the constant and widespread warfare that is one consequence of Augustus' imperial conquests. Fields lie barren, and farming tools have been turned to weapons. The final lines compare the wartorn world (and by implication Rome in particular) to a chariot out of control, no longer responsive to the guidance of the charioteer. This contrasting of warfare to agriculture and the sense that nature herself is violated by its effects are recurrent themes of Vergil's poetry. The same tension is present again in Anchises' lament for Marcellus, who will seem destined to carry forward the grim work of Augustus, but whose death in his youthful beauty and promise will make strong men weep and cover his tomb with flowers. Implied in Anchises' poignant memorial is the sadness that pervades the *Aeneid*, at the inevitable loss that is the price of conquest, and the repression of simple humanity required by the self-denying and ruthless *virtus* of the conqueror. The grief of Anchises anticipates the sorrow occasioned by the loss of Pallas and Camilla, who die with the promise of their virginal beauty and courage unfulfilled.

Vergil's keen responsiveness to the sacrifice of youth also anticipates the prominence of such deaths in Statius. The lines in which Dante laments his loss, with its threefold echoing of Vergil's name (30.49–51), will echo not only Vergil's own Orpheus mourning his lost Eurydice, but the final three lines of the narrative of the *Thebaid*, themselves a tribute to Vergil, in which Statius lingers over the pyre of the Arcadian boy-warrior Parthenopaeus, still beautiful in death, before going on to express his reverence for the "divine" *Aeneid* (*Theb.* 12.805–7, 816–17).[28]

---

27. See Hawkins, *Dante's Testaments*, 66–67.
28. See Jacoff, "Intertextualities in Arcadia," 138–44.

There remains to be considered the most famous Vergilian echo in the *Commedia,* Dante's version of the line in which Dido tells her sister Anna of the first stirrings of love for Aeneas: "conosco i segni de l'antica fiamma" (*Purg.* 30.48; *Aen.* 4.23). The line is not simply a translation; the substitution of "segni" (signs) for the Latin "vestigia" (traces) opens the way to a symbolic reading of Dante's "fiamma," and the suggestion of the "ancient flame" itself is controlled by the earlier reference to the "antico amor" that he had known while still a boy, and which the mysterious "virtù" of Beatrice's presence reawakens in him.[29] But by recalling the figure who, in the *Aeneid* as in the *Commedia,* can be said to be the personification of destructive passion, Dante is acknowledging with remarkable candor that he has yet to undergo the full effects of the fire that purges desire of its ambiguity, and so remains at a fundamental level imperfectly refined, too human to experience a wholly uncontaminated love. If we recall his encounter with Paolo and Francesca, paying the price of their illicit desire among the throng "ov'è Dido" (*Inf.* 5.85), we may perhaps see him here neutralizing the stigma of the medieval Dido's inescapable association with lust, acknowledging the humanity and generosity that are part of her love for Aeneas, and by implication vindicating those aspects of love which moral judgment too easily ignores.[30]

In parting from Dido, Aeneas had sacrificed something of his own humanity, and Dante, with the departure of Vergil, would seem similarly bound to forsake the world of all too human desire, and become the poet of transhuman reality. "Italiam non sponte sequor," Aeneas had declared when compelled by the gods to abandon Dido and Carthage (*Aen.* 4.361), and Dante, too, evoking the fatal passion of Dido to describe his own strong feelings, shows himself unable to surrender his earthly love and accept the new role for which his entire divinely ordained journey has been the preparation. Again, as when overcome by physical desire for Matelda, he retreats, passing through the memory of the confused desire of his boyhood to a state of poetic infancy in which he seeks to ground

---

29. See Hawkins, *Dante's Testaments,* 125–42; Freccero, *Poetics,* 208.

30. See Scrivano, "Il canto XXX del 'Purgatorio,'" 702, for whom the citation of Dido introduces a note "più densamente umano," and more "mature" as poetry than the tremblings of the previous line.

his turbulent emotion in the reassuring formulas of Vergil's deeply humane understanding of passion. The rhyming in the lines which describe his final turning to Vergil, "mamma," "dramma," "fiamma," echoes the passage in which Statius had expressed his great debt to the *Aeneid,* the nurse and mother of his own poetry (*Purg.* 21.94–99; above, chap. 6, p. 197).[31] Dante's language, in acknowledging the *Aeneid,* is also in an important sense addressed to Vergil himself, a Vergil whose profound humanity has survived Dante's every attempt to reduce him to a body of language and a model of style, as his Dido has resisted categorization in terms of moral allegory. Statius, in Dante's largely comic representation of poetic influence, had declared himself willing to have prolonged his stay in Purgatory if in return he had been able to know Vergil. But Dante, in terms which make clear his awareness of the religious implications of what he says, acknowledges a loss which, for a moment, outweighs the pleasure of having attained the Earthly Paradise.

Beatrice

From this point forward Dante is within the sphere of Beatrice, and classical allusion assumes a new significance. Shocked and shamed by Beatrice's first words, he lowers his eyes, sees himself reflected in the stream, and recoils in shame. The water, hitherto and henceforth a "rio," "fiumicello," or "fiume," becomes for this one moment a "chiaro fonte" (76), inviting us to associate Dante's glance with that of Narcissus, but perhaps more immediately with that of the Lover of the *Roman de la Rose,* whose first experience of love takes place at Narcissus' fountain. Dante, like Narcissus, has been deceived by false beauty, and the attending angels seem, like Ovid's Naiads, to sympathize with his plight, but he has come, like Guillaume's Amant, to the source of a transformative experience which, unlike that of l'Amant, will reveal to him wonders which Guillaume's imagery merely suggests.

It is an experience for which Dante is hardly prepared. The obstacle is an inability to trust the promptings of the desire he feels, so that the clear fountain, with its archetypal suggestion of the rich possibilities of love,

---

31. See Jacoff, "Intertextualities in Arcadia," 143–44.

presents a threat rather than an invitation. Beatrice's words repeatedly point to his immaturity, and reduce him in his own eyes to a "fanciullo," silenced by shame (31.64–67), but a more telling comment is implicit in his comparison of his reluctance to gaze at Beatrice with the resistance of a tree which is finally uprooted by wind:

> Con men di resistenza si dibarba
> > robusto cerro, o vero al nostral vento
> > o vero a quel de la terra di Iarba,
> ch'io non levai al suo comando il mento.
> > > > (*Purg.* 31.70–73)

[With less resistance is the sturdy oak uprooted, whether by wind of ours or by that which blows from Iarbas' land, than at her command I raised my chin.]

The image sets Dante's submission to Beatrice in contrast to the simile that describes Aeneas' agonized but firm resistance to the entreaties of Dido (*Aen.* 4.441–49). The odd substitution of "our" wind for Vergil's Alpine blasts suggests the intimacy and pathos of the moment, but the added allusion to "la terra di Iarba" places it in a larger context.

In *Aeneid* 4, the powerful African King Iarbas, first protector and then rejected suitor of Dido, is named by Dido's sister Anna in the course of her attempt to persuade the queen to give in to her love of Aeneas. Dido had rejected Iarbas out of declared fidelity to the memory of her dead husband, Sychaeus, but Anna scorns this devotion to "ashes and buried shades" (*Aen.* 4.34), and points to the proximity of Iarbas' kingdom as a threat from which Aeneas, borne to Carthage by destiny, will protect her. Iarbas himself appears later in Book 4, offering angry prayers to Jupiter and expressing his contempt for the Phrygian origins of Aeneas and the Trojans, "this Paris with his eunuch companions" (198–218). It is in response to Iarbas' prayer that Jupiter sends Mercury to command that Aeneas leave Carthage and pursue his destiny.

That Beatrice should here play Iarbas to Dante's Dido, reinforcing his feminization by her humiliating reference to his beard (74–75), is a measure of Dante's demoralization at this point, hardly less telling than his earlier reference to the "antica fiamma" of Dido's passion. Here the reminder is of Dido's inescapable guilt and its punishment, and there is no extenuating hint of her vulnerability and humanity. Abandoned by Aeneas as a result of Iarbas' prayers, she will descend to the underworld, there to renew her devotion to her true husband, Sychaeus. Dante, too, subjected to Beatrice's Iarbas-like scorn at his having betrayed her memory and embraced a new and finally deceiving love, is brought to reacknowl-edge his love for her, only to be seemingly rejected. The ultimately beloved Beatrice is at once the agent of his punishment and the measure of his guilt, and Dante, menaced by her complex power over him, succumbs to a profound confusion:

> di tutte altre cose qual mi torse
>   più nel suo amor, più mi si fé nemica.
>   Tanta riconoscenza il cor mi morse,
> ch'io caddi vinto . . .
>
> (Purg. 31.86–89)

[of all other things, that which had most turned me to love of it became most hateful to me. Such contrition stung my heart that I fell overcome . . .]

It is perhaps taking absurd advantage of a certain syntactic ambiguity, but I would suggest that "of all other things, that which had most turned me to love of it," and which is now all the more hateful, can bear more than one meaning. Normally and sensibly glossed as the misguided love which had lured him away from Beatrice, it can also be taken as referring to Beatrice herself. On this reading the cause of Dante's swoon would be the unendurable pain of recognizing the terrible, impossible contradiction involved in momentarily hating the agent of his own salvation, who is, moreover, the object of his deepest human feelings.[32] Like his earlier faint-ing, on the shores of Acheron and in the presence of Francesca, this mo-

---

32. As Durling and Martinez observe in their edition of the *Purgatorio,* the complex significance of "riconoscenza" (88), makes this passage "particularly untranslatable." Cp. "riconoscendo" in line 66.

mentary rejection of Beatrice, if such it be, involves an imagining of spiritual death caused by the insidious working of desire, and again he recovers only after having wholly abandoned himself to an experience of which he understands only that Beatrice was its cause (89–90).

A second, more clearly significant loss of consciousness takes place in the following canto. A curious simile which links the circling of the holy procession to the maneuver of a retreating army by playing on the meaning of "salvation" ("salvarsi," 32.19) seems intended to show the inappropriateness in this context of any hint of the poetry of war. As Dante follows the procession, he reminds us of the presence of his companions, Matelda, the "bella donna" who had "drawn him to the ford" (28),[33] and Statius, invisible in the three preceding cantos. The associations of these figures with Dante's merely poetic experience are distanced as the three together walk to the rhythm of an angelic song (33), and the sense of a new departure is given further point by the reminder that the "alta selva" of Paradise is "empty through fault of her who believed the serpent" (31–32), an allusion which effectively renders null and void the classical terms in which Dante had previously described it.

Dante compares, or rather declines to compare, the sleep that now siezes him to that imposed on Argus by Mercury in Ovid's tale of Io (64–66; *Met.* 1.682–721). He claims to be unable to describe Argus' slumber, and leaves it to "one that can depict slumber well" (69). This may be a confession of inadequacy: only a perfect representation of Argus' charmed sleep could provide an adequate comparison for his own. But it is perhaps better taken as a dismissal of this task of representation (already well accomplished by Ovid) as being irrelevant to his new situation. To have done no more than mention the name of Argus and the circumstances of his fatal slumber is sufficient to make his point, and provide the necessary foil to the significant transition Dante's own sleep effects.[34]

---

33. Pace Singleton, who sees in this line only a reference to *Purg.* 31.91–104, the use of "bella donna" and the suggestiveness of "trasse" also recall Dante's first encounter with Matelda.

34. On this contrast, and the relation of the naming of Argus here to that in *Purg.* 29.95, see Barolini, "Arachne, Argus, and St. John," 216–20.

As Dante reminds us, Argus had fallen asleep "hearing of Syrinx" (65). Mercury, intending to tell the tale of Pan and Syrinx, had told only of the divine beauty of the desirable but resolutely chaste nymph. Left untold is Pan's vain pursuit of Syrinx, who escaped ravishment through her transformation to a cluster of sighing reeds, which Pan then fashioned into an instrument of music to which he gave the name of Syrinx. This classic Ovidian account of the creation of art belongs to a world which Dante has left behind. Unlike Argus, who, possessed of the imagined beauty of Syrinx, passes from consciousness to sleep and instant death, Dante awakens from his slumber, aroused by a "splendor" to behold the living Matelda, who is again recalled, significantly, in terms of their first meeting at the stream (84; cp. 31.92). Like the world of Ovidian change, that encounter, redolent of the atmosphere of Dante's love poetry, is set in a distancing perspective, but Dante's recurrent memory of it makes plain that natural desire is still alive in him.[35] It is only after Matelda has guided his eyes to Beatrice that he hears foretold the final, total transformation of his imaginative world, and is invited to review his own evolving condition. From the lyric poet whose squandered passion she will later compare to the blood of Pyramus which stained the mulberry (33.69), he has been and will again be transformed into a denizen of the Earthly Paradise, a "silvano" like the inhabitants of Vergil's primitive Italy,[36] before becoming once and for all a citizen of the City of God, the true Rome, the city not of Caesar or Cato but of Christ.

---

35. Beatrice will point to this with her reference to Pyramus and the mulberry (33.69), a final reminder of how the pathos of love continues to resist Dante's spiritual aspiration. See Moevs, *Metaphysics,* 105–6.

36. "Silvanus" was the god worshiped by the first inhabitants of Latium (*Aen.* 8.600–602). Dante's appropriation of the term is perhaps intended to contrast his present status in the Earthly Paradise, a poetic fiction, and his future, authentic "citizenship" in Paradise.

8

Paradiso

In the *Paradiso* the world of classical poetry remains significantly present. In this realm where all is "transhuman," and much is beyond Dante's power to comprehend or represent, the discourse of the saints and soldiers of the heavenly city is nonetheless focused to a remarkable degree on the human world. In its larger trajectory, of course, the *Paradiso* describes a mystical journey, an *itinerarium mentis in Deum,* and the emphasis on earthly reform, after reaching a climax in Cacciaguida's great charge to Dante in Canto 17, diminishes thereafter. But as Ugo Dotti argues, the order and harmony and above all the justice that constitute the happiness of the beatific state are perhaps most significant insofar as they exemplify the happiness to which the earthly city might aspire. For saints and statesmen alike, dedication to attaining this happiness for mankind is the highest earthly calling.[1]

The voices of the Poeti are a continual undertone in the early cantos, but a new influence is exerted by two dialogues centered on Roman philosopher-statesmen, the *Consolatio* of Boethius and the *Somnium Scipionis,* the visionary conclusion of Cicero's now-fragmented treatise *De re*

---

1. *Divina Commedia,* 104–21.

publica. Both of these works are structured largely by a dialectical interplay between celestial vision and political and ethical wisdom, and from
Beatrice's first rebuking of Dante's "falso imaginar" (1.88–90) to the moment when Bernard "terminates his desire" with a final vision of Beatrice
in glory (31.65–66), the dialogues of the *Paradiso* show clear traces of their
influence.

Boethius' prisoner, bitterly disillusioned by the failure of his political
career and what seems the insuperable power of Fortune, is restored to his
proper self by Philosophy's celebration of the order of the Platonic universe. "Hausi caelum et mentem recepi," he tells us on first recognizing
Philosophy (*Cons*. 1, *pr*. 3.1), and the focus of her consolation is largely an
elaboration on this causal relationship between Platonic cosmology and
self-knowledge, aimed at bringing him back to that state in which his mind
"ran along heavenly paths" and Philosophy "formed his character and
the whole purpose of his life on the model of the celestial order" (1, *metr*.
2.6–7; 1, *pr*. 4.4).

Cicero's Scipio Africanus is made to recognize that a justly ordered
city is of all earthly things the most pleasing to God, and that he will attain
heaven only by cultivating justice and piety in his public role (*Somn*. 3.5).
But he is repeatedly warned also not to let his thoughts dwell on the
world. It is contemplation of the ordered beauty of the universe that will
instill in him an awareness of the heavenly origin and destiny of his spirit,
thus ensuring that he will conduct his life with dignity and purpose, and
remain free of earthly attachments.

Dante, too, must learn both that the peace and harmony of heaven
are an infinitely desirable state, ineffably superior to anything human art
or genius could emulate, and that it is nonetheless in the human world
that his duty lies. Like Scipio he will return emboldened, in the face of
ominous prophecies regarding his worldly life, by the knowledge that his
is a high and praiseworthy calling, that his poem will be a force for good.
Before being made explicit in the meeting with Cacciaguida, his mission,
too, is adumbrated in terms of celestial order:

> Quando la rota che tu sempiterni
>   desiderato, a sé mi fece atteso
>   con l'armonia che temperi e discerni, . . .
>
> (Par. 1.76–78)

[When the revolution which Thou, by being desired, makest
eternal turned my attention to itself by the harmony which
Thou dost temper and distinguish . . .]

The phrase "sempiterni / desiderato" expresses with wonderful concision
the centripetal power of the love with which not just the Primum mobile,
but the whole of creation responds to God, a love which Dante is now experiencing with a new immediacy. But in the final line, whose language
is drawn directly from the *Somnium Scipionis,*[2] the divine harmonizing of
the spheres is simultaneously offered as a model for the aesthetic creation
which will be Dante's contribution to the reform of the earthly city, his
equivalent to the ordering power of political wisdom.

That the desire for God is thus inseparably linked with the creation of
order in the earthly city illustrates a pattern fundamental to the *Paradiso.*
The currents of energy that flow between the Paradise Dante imagines
and the world he has ostensibly left behind are perhaps the most important feature of this cantica, and the harsh and worldly tone in which
the blessed spirits refer to one another and to the sins of humankind can
be disconcerting. We do not expect the career of St. Dominic to be described in terms whose grimness recalls Justinian's account of the history
of Roman conquest, or hear a gratuitously harsh condemnation of lust
mar an otherwise benign confession of youthful folly. Folquet de Mar-
seille, the author of this condemnation, can go on to revel in the bliss of
his condition and its promise for the world below:

> Qui si rimira ne l'arte ch'addorna
>   cotanto affetto, e discernesi 'l bene
>   per che 'l mondo di sù quel di giù torna.
>   (*Par.* 9.106–8)

[Here we contemplate the art which so much love adorns,
and we discern the good by reason of which the world below
again becomes the world above.]

But despite the ineffable joy which surrounds them, Dante's blessed souls
often seem, like Vergil's Venus, Juno, and Jupiter, to be preoccupied with

---

2. *Somn.* 5.1, quoted by Singleton in his note on line 78.

the "mondo di giù," and the consuming love they feel is often perceptibly marked by the "vestigio" of an earthly attachment.

Inspiration and Apollo: The Poetics of the Paradiso

That classical poetry, and Ovid in particular, will have a significant role in the *Paradiso* is boldly announced by the invocation of Apollo, with its references to Parnassus and, in a second appeal for inspiration, the satyr Marsyas.[3] Much of what Dante will see in Paradise is beyond his power to express (*Par.* 1.5–9), but it is clear nonetheless that he regards the task ahead as an exciting challenge to his powers as a poet, and that achieving it will be a triumph. He asks to be made a "vessel" of Apollo's power, a poetic counterpart to St. Paul, the "vas d'elezïone" (*Inf.* 2.28), but as the Epistle to Can Grande points out, he asks to be rewarded as well as inspired: Apollo's "valor," he hopes, will render him worthy to receive from the god the laurel crown.[4]

The pain of separation from bodily existence in the world will be compensated by a new birth; both are expressed in the reimagining of the flaying of Marsyas as "drawing him from himself" (*Met.* 6.385) in a positive way, effecting his release from his mortal body.[5] In Ovid's brief narrative Marsyas had remained obdurately untransformed, a mass of tormented flesh, and the only metamorphosis had been the creation of a clear river from the tears of the rustic deities and countryfolk who mourned his loss. Here any hint of pastoral nostalgia has been cut away, but Marsyas' body has become itself an almost maternal "vaso," a "vagina" from which he emerges to symbolize Dante's passage from the Earthly Paradise, where he had been, like Marsyas, a "silvano" (*Purg.* 33.100), to a new imaginative and visionary state.

---

3. Brownlee, "Pauline Vision," 204, shows persuasively how the *Metamorphoses* function here as a "privileged model text."

4. The Epistle divides lines 13–27 into two parts, the first invoking the god, the second persuasively restating Dante's petition and "remunerationem quandam prenuntians."

5. On the allusion, see Hollander, *Allegory,* 215–16.

But Ovid's Marsyas, even in his torment, had remained devoted to the Olympian gods (*Met.* 6.393), and Dante, too, remains persistently attached to the conventions of ancient poetry. Milton will invoke the Holy Spirit rather than the traditional Muse. Dante seeks rather to augment the inspiration of the Muses, to whom one peak of Parnassus is dedicated, with the mountain's second peak, sacred to Apollo. The god is asked to enter Dante's breast, a prayer which, followed as it is by the naming of Marsyas, evokes the tormented inspiration of the priestess or Sibyl. But Apollo is also bidden to make Dante his instrument,[6] and he alone can inspire and reward the poetry to which Dante aspires.

The two peaks of Parnassus are standard poetic lore (*Met.* 1.316; 2.221; *Theb.* 7.346), but the only detailed account of the mountain's form and history, and the most likely basis for Dante's reference, occurs in Book 5 of Lucan's *Pharsalia*. In a scene that parallels Sextus Pompey's visit to Erichtho, Appius Claudius, anxious about the impending battle, seeks from the Delphic oracle a prophecy of his fate. Before the priestess responds to his request, Lucan provides an account of how the great flood had once submerged one of Parnassus' peaks, and of the founding of the oracle by Apollo, who had discovered that here the earth "breathed forth divine truth" (*Phars.* 5.83). He then offers elaborate speculations about the unknown god of great wisdom who has chosen to dwell beneath the ground in this place, and whose inspiration seems to emanate from both earth and heaven (93–96).

In certain respects the shrine resembles Statius' altar of Clementia, though in a predictably fatalistic Lucanian version:

> Hoc tamen expositum cunctis nullique negatum
> numen ab humani solum se labe furoris
> uindicat. Haut illic tacito mala uota susurro
> concipiunt; nam fixa canens mutandaque nulli
> mortales optare uetat.
>
> (*Phars.* 5.102–6)

---

6. The use of "tue" for *tu* in line 19 suggests the breathy note of the flute, as if Apollo were being asked to literally "play" Dante. Ovid nowhere indicates, as the mythographers do, that Apollo played the lyre in his contest with Marsyas. *Met.* 6.384 could easily be taken as implying that he had played the flute.

[Open to all, denied to none, only this holy place can claim to be free of the taint of human madness. None here whisper the wicked prayers they harbor; for since the oracle tells only of fixed events that none may alter, it forbids mortals to hope.]

In the context of the *Pharsalia* this oracle is another of Lucan's religious dead ends, a benign alternative to Erichtho's magic, but no less futile.[7] The world has grown so wicked that kings now fear to consult the oracle, and Appius' intrusion is the first in many years. The oracle possesses boundless knowledge: when the priestess is possessed by the god, "all time converges, all history oppresses her suffering breast" (177–78). But the priestess strongly resists being possessed, first lying to Appius and then feigning possession before finally submitting to the god. Even then, after yielding an ambiguous assurance of Appius' own survival, her voice is suppressed by Apollo, the oracle falls silent, and Lucan suggests that the prophecies unuttered were too awful to be revealed (193–208). The Lucan who will go on to offer an expert review of the extremes of blasphemy in the Erichtho episode is here rendered silent by imaginings he dare not reveal.[8]

In considering what this episode might have suggested to Dante, I would note first the peculiar status of Apollo. The mountain, Lucan tells us, is sacred also to Bacchus, and the Thebans have traditionally held festivals there in which the two gods were worshiped as one ("numine mixto," 72). Even at Delphi Lucan's Apollo is and is not the presiding deity. It is he who inspires the priestess to prophesy, but in so doing he is apparently only the agent of a higher god—a god whose power, as Lucan suggests in a uniquely affirmative moment, may even transcend that of fate:

Quis latet hic superum? quod numen ab aethere pressum
dignatur caecas inclusum habitare cauernas?
quis terram caeli patitur deus omnia cursus
aeterni secreta tenens mundoque futuri
conscius ac populis sese proferre paratus

---

7. See Ahl, *Lucan*, 125–28; Narducci, *La provvidenza crudele*, 64–66.

8. See Masters, *Poetry and Civil War,* 147–48, who suggests that Erichtho and the Delphic priestess define "the split in Lucan's poetic persona."

contactumque ferens hominis magnusque potensque,
siue canit fatum, seu quod iubet ille canendo
fit fatum? Forsan terris inserta regendis
aere libratum uacuo quae sustinet orbem,
totius pars magna Iouis Cirrhaea per antra
exit et aetherio trahitur conexa Tonanti.

(*Phars.* 5.86–96)

[Which of the gods is concealed here? What power borne
down from heaven deigns to dwell shut up in this dark cavern?
What heavenly god endures earthly existence, possessed of
all the secrets of the divine order of events, imparting to the
world knowledge of the future, willing to manifest himself to
mortal people, not shunning human contact? He is great and
powerful, whether he predicts fated events, or fated events
occur because his prophecy commands. Perhaps a great portion of the power of all-powerful Jove, which holds the world
stable in empty space, abides here to rule the earth, and what
issues from the Cirrhean cavern and is received there is linked
to the will of the heavenly thunderer.]

This is straightforward Stoic theology, unambiguous in itself, but its value
for Lucan is equivocal. We are given no sign of the power of this evidently
benign deity, and it is easy to accept, despite its context of falsehood, the
suggestion of the priestess that Apollo finds no one in the modern world
worthy of receiving the wisdom he controls (139–40). Here as so often
in the *Pharsalia*, Lucan gives the impression of writing under a curse, capable of imagining a world ordered and guided by a benevolent god, but
persuaded that his own world is cut off from any such guidance. Again,
one of the priestess' "lies" suggests itself:

Muto Parnasos hiatu
conticuit pressitque deum, seu spiritus istas
destituit fauces mundique in deuia uersum
duxit iter . . .

(*Phars.* 5.131–34)

[Parnassus, its cavern mute, has ceased to speak and buried its god; perhaps the spirit has forsaken this cavemouth and changed its course to some new part of the world . . .]

For Lucan and his poem this is in fact the case. When the priestess declares that though heaven has silenced the oracle the verses of the Sibyl are sufficient for Rome (136–38), she is in effect advising the reader to seek in the *Aeneid* the sense of destiny that the *Pharsalia* is doomed to withold.

Dante, by invoking the second peak of Parnassus, is "reawakening the oracle," restoring Apollo to his vatic function,[9] and putting him at the service of a higher god who possesses truly all the attributes Lucan had imagined. The comparison of Marsyas is a measure of the boldness of Dante's venture, and the awe he feels in contemplating it.[10] He is entering an "arena" (18) where he will be tested like a gladiator or martyr.[11] The crowning laurel, to which he refers a second time, will be the token of his victory (25–27), a victory which, he suggests, will revive the glory of the triumphs of the *poetae,* and those of the "Caesars" on whom their poems have bestowed the reward of fame. Thus will be fully accomplished a poetic task which involves both a radical new departure and the renewal of the classical tradition, a process which had begun with the emergence of Vergil from "long silence" in *Inferno* 1.

Poetry and Truth

As Kevin Brownlee has made clear, Dante's allusions to the myth of Marsyas and to that of Glaucus, which follows, are complementary: Marsyas stands for Dante the poet in his new artistic role, while Glaucus' beautiful

---

9. Cp. Boccaccio's declaration, *Lettere edite e inedite,* 184, that Petrarch, by his recuperation of the classical past, had "restored Apollo to his throne," and "ascended to the very peaks of Parnassus" (a phrase which perhaps recalls *Par.* 1.16–18). The passage is cited by Mazzotta, *Worlds of Petrarch,* 18.

10. See Mazzotta, *Dante's Vision,* 193–95.

11. See Schnapp, *Transfiguration,* 216, in the course of a discussion of Dante's "poetics of martyrdom" (170–238).

account of his transformation into a sea god marks the limits of poetry's power to represent the experience Dante the pilgrim now undergoes as he gazes at Beatrice (65–69).[12] But taken as a whole Ovid's story of Glaucus, which seems to lend itself so readily to Dante's purposes, bears a broader and more complex relation to his situation, and provides a distorted mirror version of Dante's progress to this crucial moment, when he will pass beyond human experience.

Midway in Ovid's summary of the journeying of Aeneas, at the point when the Trojans are approaching the Sicilian coast and the cliff of Scylla, he suspends the Vergilian narrative and inserts an account of the earlier life of Scylla as a human being (*Met.* 13.730–14.74). Once a beautiful and resolutely chaste maiden, she rejected the love of the sea god Glaucus, even after having heard his enchanting account of his transformation. Glaucus then sought to win her by enlisting the magical powers of Circe, who became herself enamored of him, and when he rejected Circe's offer of love because of an unswerving devotion to Scylla, Circe sought a perverse revenge by transforming Scylla into a monster.

Glaucus' experience as Ovid traces it belies the profound effect of his metamorphosis. Once turned into a sea god, he undergoes an elaborate purification at the hands of the higher sea gods, then experiences a further transformation of which he has no memory, but which, he declares, has left him changed in both body and mind (*Met.* 13.949–59). He nevertheless succumbs to a very human passion for Scylla, and it is in anger at his rejection that he seeks the aid of Circe. At her cruel punishment of Scylla he can only weep.

Dante experiences a more decisive metamorphosis. Sternly rebuked for having wavered in his devotion to Beatrice, he now rediscovers his earthly beloved transformed, and is endowed by her with a new degree of imaginative power (46–54). Only then, realizing himself in a new element, a daylight illumined as if by another sun, does he gaze on Beatrice and undergo his own transformation. The transformation of Scylla at the hands of the daughter of the sun had left Glaucus, despite his deification, helpless, bound by an unquenchable passion which seems to undo the

---

12. See Brownlee, "Pauline Vision," 213; also Hollander, *Allegory,* 216–20.

work of the purifying rituals he had undergone. But in Dante, though he will never completely transcend his earthly love of Beatrice, or purge it of its erotic elements, passion itself is transformed, and becomes a redemptive force, sustained by the love of the transformed Beatrice, whose true value he now becomes imaginatively capable of apprehending. Through her his desire becomes part of that universal desire to which God responds with a perpetually sustaining love ("tu sempiterni / desiderato," 76–77).

Dante's appropriation of Ovidian myth in this opening canto defines in absolute terms the limits of his ability, of poetry's ability, to represent his experience. But as in the *Purgatorio,* Dante has remained true to the essential character of the tales he deploys. He has seen in the fate of Marsyas, not just another instance of divine cruelty, but a meditation on inspiration as "tragic ordeal."[13] He recognizes in the transformation of Ovid's Glaucus an experience which, if not as perfectly homologous with his own as is sometimes suggested, stands in an archetypal relation to it. Marsyas remains utterly untransformed, and Glaucus transformed remains subject to mortal passion, but Picone is not wrong in asserting that we can see in Dante's use of both stories the "confirmation and completion" of a meaning which Ovid had suggested.[14]

Always close to the surface of Dante's mind in this opening canto is the language that describes the "ecstasy" of Paul and the spiritual psychology of the New Testament, and establishing a complementary relation between biblical and classical allusion is essential to Dante's purpose.[15] The exordium to Canto 2, on the other hand, comes close to being sheer "poetry." The single sustained metaphor of voyaging governs the first fifteen lines, assimilating mythological detail as it proceeds, and leading smoothly into a detailed allusion to the Argonauts—like Dante voyagers on a sea hitherto untraveled[16]—and the heroism of Jason. Dante's vessel, which sings as it sails ("cantando varca," 3) recalls not only Dante's

---

13. Wind, *Pagan Mysteries,* 143.

14. See Picone, "Dante e i miti," 30–32.

15. See Brownlee, "Pauline Vision," 202–8; Rigo, *Memoria classica,* 60–67.

16. As Hollander notes, *Allegory,* 222, line 7 echoes Ovid, *Met.* 6.721: "per mare non notum prima petiere carina."

earlier account of the emergence of his poetry (*Purg.* 24.52–54), but also the *Thebaid,* and Hypsipyle's beautiful account of the arrival of the Argonauts at Lemnos, announced by the song of Orpheus which makes the oarsmen forget their labor and calms the very waves (*Theb.* 5.340–45). Poetic inspiration is now defined in an orderly way. Apollo, as at Lucan's Delphi, is subordinated to a higher power: here it is Minerva who inspires ("spira," 8; cp. 1.19), filling the sails of Dante's vessel, while Apollo mans the helm, and "new Muses" chart its course.[17] Three lines intrude the non-nautical image of the biblical bread of angels and those wise enough to hunger for it, but these are then, as it were, drawn into Dante's wake, subsumed to the larger metaphoric pattern as the allegory of voyage is brought to its graceful completion.

Much of the meaning of this passage is indicated by what follows immediately, as Dante describes his translation to the sphere of the Moon. Unlike the journey of the Argonauts, the ascent is swift, effortless, and almost imperceptible. The guidance of mythical powers becomes the inborn desire for God, and the uncharted sea and far-off Colchis are replaced by the mysterious immateriality of the cloudlike Moon, in which Dante, penetrating its surface like a beam of light, leaves no trace (34–36). But we know that even the evocative description of this "eternal pearl" (34) falls short of the reality Dante has experienced, as the sea journey of the canto's opening lines cannot adequately suggest the ascent that follows. Even the learned few who most hunger for wisdom are as voyagers on an unknown sea, and despite the preparation implied by "navigio" (14),[18] they can make way only by following closely in the "furrow" of Dante's wake. For the sea they seek to cross, like the surface of the lunar sphere, will preserve no trace of his voyage, and the sustaining love of Beatrice, like the arts of Medea which enabled Jason to perform the feats that so astonished the Argonauts, exerts its power only for him.

---

17. I choose to read "nove" as "new" rather than "nine," because I can see no reason for Dante's calling on *all* the Muses here, and good reason for his invoking new Muses, uniquely able to define the course of this radically new voyage.

18. The term, used only here, indicates a larger seagoing vessel, as opposed to the *barca* of *Par.* 1.1, or the *navicella* of Dante's still-unrevivified *ingegno* in *Purg.* 1.2.

But despite the radical difference between the projects of Jason and Dante, the palpable imagery of plowing draws them together. The yoking of the bulls of Mars, with their feet of bronze and iron-tipped horns, clearly corresponds to the task of adapting classical poetry to a radically new purpose, a purpose which poetry alone can accomplish, and one which effects a unique linkage between story and poetic vehicle. For as Freccero has declared, Paradise and the poetry which represents it are coextensive; Paradise can exist, for us as for Dante, only through metaphor.[19]

The supernatural guidance of the two ladies is essential in both cases. The immunity secretly provided to Jason by Medea, which enables him to appear superhumanly heroic, taints his success with an element of falsehood, pointing to the ambiguity of his motives in pursuing the golden fleece and anticipating his later betrayal of Medea. Dante would seem to be beyond suspicion in this regard, but his motives, too, like the substances that compose the lunar sphere, are of varying quality:

> Quel sol che pria d'amor mi scaldò 'l petto,
>   di bella verità m'avea scoverto,
>   provando e riprovando, il dolce aspetto; . . .
>   (*Par.* 3.1–3)

> [That sun which first had heated my breast with love,
>   proving and refuting had uncovered to me the sweet
>   aspect of fair truth, . . .]

The prosaic "provando e riprovando" stands out incongruously amid the lyric diction of these lines, and points to the equivocal status of Beatrice's arguments in the previous canto. As Beatrice moves between physics and metaphysics, practical experiment and superintellectual "luce vivace," so Dante's response to her discourse expresses the different levels at which he feels love for her. The "sun" that once warmed his breast was Beatrice; the "sweet aspect of fair truth" which he now beholds is Beatrice; what draws Dante toward understanding is not proof and refutation but the fact that it is Beatrice who provides them.

---

19. *Poetics*, 212.

In a sense Dante has already here committed the error he will describe a few lines further on, an error "contrary to that which kindled love between the man and the fountain" (17–18). Narcissus had imagined he saw in the fountain's reflection another person; Dante will mistake for reflections what are actually spiritual beings. But in the canto's opening lines his perception is both true and false. He describes in Beatrice (but is then distracted from addressing) a figure who is, like the image loved by Narcissus, the inevitable projection of his own desire, yet is at the same time a living spirit. Like Narcissus, Dante will discover his error as regards the faces of Piccarda and her companions, but the contradiction in his perception of Beatrice is undetectable, for his subjective imagining and the desire which provokes it are indistinguishable from the attractive power of his true perception of her as his "dolce guida," the "sweet aspect" of truth itself.

In the opening invocation of the *Paradiso* Dante had addressed Apollo as at once the beginning and the end of his project, which is inspired by the god and thus made worthy of the god's reward, "l'amato alloro" (15), the tree for which, in its original human form, Apollo had felt passionate desire, but which is now a sacred symbol. The ultimate paradigm for this twofold relationship to the god is that described in the opening lines of Canto 10, where creation itself is seen as a work of art (10–11), the expression of the love which God feels for the Son, a love which we emulate when we see the universe as his handiwork. At this level poetic tradition is left behind. No amount of "genius, art, or practice" could represent a reality which takes Dante unawares, like a man "before his first thought" (10.43–44, 35–36).[20]

Beatrice, like Apollo, is finally only a means to this vision, the focal point of the process through which imaginative desire is transformed into spiritual aspiration. Like Paradise itself, Beatrice can now exist for Dante only in terms of poetry, "those words that praise my lady" (*Vita nuova* 18.6); she will always be at once real and imaginary, truth and "falso imaginar." In this respect Dante's perception of her corresponds to how she

---

20. As Moevs remarks, *Metaphysics*, 87, "for the Dante of the *Comedy*, what alone can change us is . . . beauty-truth itself: Beatrice, . . . the *riso de l'universo*, . . . a cosmic power of attraction or love so intense that it steals the mind and heart from themselves."

herself apparently regards the cosmic mythology of Plato and his world, false as doctrine but perhaps true as poetry (4.49–63).[21] But Beatrice is something more, not only the inspiration and in a sense the end, but also the medium of his vision. Apollo must finally accept the transformation of Daphne into "l'amato alloro" as a barrier to the fulfillment of his desire, but Beatrice enables Dante to pass beyond such barriers, and recognize how radically reality is transformed in heaven. The ambiguity of his anti-Narcissistic situation in Canto 3 is provisionally resolved when, having failed to discover behind him the originals of what he takes to be reflected faces, he turns back to be instantly enveloped in the light of Beatrice's smile and her "occhi santi" (18–24), and discover through her the reality of his situation. But later, in the heaven of the sun, where the truth implicit in the cosmos so dazzles him that even Beatrice is momentarily "eclipsed," her smile miraculously enables him to contemplate many objects, simultaneously and without dividing the focus of his vision, his "mente unita" (59–63).

Ancient Examples

In the course of Canto 4 the relation of representation to truth is addressed in various ways. The simplest is wordplay: Beatrice's discourse includes several lines which play with crucial terms—"ingiusta / giustizia" (67), "pietà / spietato" (105)—which recall Pier della Vigna, and his account of how his fear of scorn "ingiusto fece me contra me giusto" (*Inf.* 13.72). In Pier's case the antithesis had expressed his irredeemably divided condition. As deployed by Beatrice, the combination of what Pertile calls "forceful compression and artificial preciosity" expresses the inevitable inadequacy of language to the intricacy of theological truth, where such contradictions are reconciled.[22]

---

21. Singleton aptly cites the commentary of Thomas on Aristotle's *De caelo et mundo* (Lib. 2, lect. 22.8) that while some argue for a figurative, some for a literal interpretation of Plato's imagery, the important question is where the truth lies. Beatrice, like Thomas, leaves open the question of how to read Plato.

22. See Pertile, "*Paradiso IV*," 58–60.

At a more complex level, Beatrice uses pagan and Christian exempla to make a similar point. Discussing the failure of Piccarda and Costanza to return immediately to the cloister when free to do so, Beatrice contrasts their failure of will with the resolution of St. Lawrence, mocking his tormentors as he is burned to death, and Mucius Scaevola, who punished his failure to murder Porsenna by burning his right hand (82–86). Though Mucius' sacrifice was recognized by Dante as historical (*Conv.* 4.5.13; *Mon.* 2.5.14), the comparison of his act with Lawrence's points up limitations that resemble those of the motifs of classical poetry as compared to truth. Like the suicide of Cato, the self-torture of Mucius is the expression of a circumscribed, political virtue that can only prove itself by self-display, whereas Lawrence, forced to endure torture, is sustained by his faith in a power beyond himself. The examples which follow further illustrate the contradictions to which pagan virtue is subject. The story of Alcmaeon, who killed his mother at the command of his father, thus performing an impious act out of *pietà*, is another example of the inevitably "mixed" character of this virtue (100–105), and in Canto 5 Agamemnon's sacrifice of Iphigenia to honor a vow is dismissed as "stolto" (6.68).

Ancient example and divine purpose come together in a more complex way in the discourse of Justinian in Canto 6, an argument for the providential course of Roman history and the sacredness of Rome's mission to rule justly a world at peace. Justinian's personal history is a virtual allegory of the conception of justice he embodies. Having first accepted the Monophysite heresy, and so denied the human nature of Christ, he was led to orthodoxy by Pope Agapetus, and thereafter moved in step with the Church ("con la Chiesa mossi i piedi," 22), thus affirming the distinct but balanced and harmonious relation between secular and ecclesiastical authority. Only then was he empowered to codify Roman law, for only then could he recognize the proper role of secular power—recognize, for example, that Christ had acknowledged the authority of Rome in assenting to be born "sub edicto romane auctoritatis," a decree perhaps issued "by divine inspiration through Caesar" (*Mon.* 2.10.6; 11.5–7; Luke 2.1).[23] Thus enlightened he was divinely prompted to give himself wholly

---

23. See Woodhouse, *Dante and Governance,* 9.

to the task of editing the laws, leaving it to his general Belisarius, guided by the hand of God, to expand and secure the imperial territories (23–27). Now, after the "milizia" of earthly life, he sits enthroned, like all the blessed, in "eternal triumph" (5.115–16).

In his blessed state Justinian claims to understand the dual nature of Christ as clearly as an earthly mind like Dante's understands the contradictory relation of truth and falsehood (19–21). It is significant of his crucial role that his recognition of the importance of codifying the essential elements of the law should have come as a consequence of his accepting this great exception to the principle of noncontradiction.[24] Just as the opposition of human and divine is neutralized in Christ, so Christ's birth and death not only vividly affirm the authority of Rome and its laws, but at the same time reveal the order of history in a new way, such that Rome's ascendancy can be seen to have played only an ancillary, albeit essential, role in the providential scheme. In this broader perspective, the Code of Justinian, a task to which he was prompted by God, becomes the basis for maintaining justice and political stability in a Christian empire, the bequest to the post-Roman world of a Rome which has accomplished its secular but divinely ordained purpose.

Justinian has little to say about the new order in its political aspect. It first emerges in the powerful opening tercet, in which Constantine's relocation of the seat of empire to the east is defined as "counter to the course of the heavens," and so counter to the evolution that had begun with Aeneas' journey to the west (2–3).[25] Justinian offers no comment on this move, but we know that it was accompanied by Constantine's conferral of temporal power on the Roman Church, an act whose legitimacy Dante elsewhere strenuously denied, as granting the Church a false political authority (*Mon.* 3.10). Justinian's review clearly aims to counter this error by reaffirming the autonomy of the secular power within its own

---

24. See Mazzotta, *Dante's Vision,* 104, though he also asserts there that "Agapetus' faith, in which Justinian came to believe, coincided with logic's analytical distinctions," a claim which seems to deny this crucial exception.

25. As many commentators have noted, the opening lines of the canto imitate the opening of *Aen.* 3, where Aeneas prepares to journey westward in response to divine omens.

sphere. While acknowledging the spiritual authority of the Church, he insists repeatedly that his own authority as emperor, legislator, and commander in chief stemmed directly from God.

The second book of the *Monarchia* had been devoted to demonstrating that the ascendancy of pre-Christian Rome, too, was overseen by God. The view of Roman history that Justinian presents is similar but more ambiguous, reducing this history to a string of military victories, punctuated by reference to legends of other kinds. The "virtù" that made Rome deserving of reverence (34–35), a theme on which the *Monarchia* had dwelled at length (2.3), is traced back by Justinian to "the hour when Pallas died" (35–36). The virtue in question may thus be that of Pallas himself, whose loss drove Aeneas to seek revenge by killing Turnus, thereby completing the Trojan conquest of Latium; or it may be the *virtus* that is a constant in the character of Aeneas, but which in this last decisive action gave way to "furious wrath" (*Aen.* 12.946; *Mon.* 2.9.14).

In either case this virtue bears only an oblique relation to the larger historical pattern Justinian will trace.[26] Facing death, Pallas prays to Hercules, who weeps at his inability to save him from his fate, but is admonished by Jupiter, who reminds him that while Pallas' death is inevitable, "to extend one's fame by deeds is the work of virtue" ("hoc uirtutis opus," *Aen.* 10.468–69). Aeneas, before his final encounter with Turnus, tells his son Ascanius, "learn bravery ["uirtutem"] from me, and the true task, but good fortune from others" (12.435–36). For both heroes life is fatally circumscribed by the obligation, heroic or political, to accomplish the true task of *virtus*, and even the reward of fame is precarious: Aeneas ends his address to Ascanius by urging him, when he shall realize the "great rewards" for which he is destined, to remember the "exempla tuorum" which are all that will survive of his father and his uncle Hector (436–40).

Justinian's Roman panorama thus begins on a profoundly Vergilian note, but in what follows, though the tone remains elevated and the phrasing at several points recalls Vergil and Lucan, the only clear evocation of

---

26. Mariotti, *Scritti medievali*, 94–95, argues that *virtù* as used by Justinian must be understood, not as civil or military *virtus*, but as an "efficacy" conferred by grace and unattainable by human means. But heroic *virtus*, too, is clearly in play here.

ancient poetry will be a brief, haunting allusion to Hector (68). It is Justinian's constant reference to the "sacrosanto segno" (32) of the eagle—the emblem, at once political and religious, of Rome's unfolding purpose—that provides continuity. The purpose of the next sixty lines, like that of the second book of the *Monarchia*, is to trace how Rome was led by Providence to the attainment of dominion over a peaceful world. But we see this narrative as it appears "on the stage of the world,"[27] and as it proceeds the providential pattern is hard to discern. There is no more reference to "virtù": a string of famous names is linked without comment to decisive events, glorious or ignominious, all attributed syntactically to the Roman eagle, "l'uccel di Dio." The era of the seven kings is bracketed by the "wrong" of the Sabine women and the rape of Lucretia (40–41); Caesar's conquests in transalpine Europe are interspersed with references to Pharsalia and other internecine conflicts, and Justinian, speaking after the fact, cannot, like Anchises, urge restraint on the powers he names (cp. *Aen.* 6.832–35). Even the final events which ensured Octavian's ascent to imperial rank are presented in an atmosphere of infernal gloom. Brutus and Cassius "howl in hell," not at their terrible punishment for the murder of Caesar, but at the deeds of Octavian; and Cleopatra, condemned to the circle of the lustful, still weeps for the death of Antony (73–78).

After the achievement of the Pax Augusta, Rome remains the agent of violence, "avenging" the wrath of God by decreeing the death of Christ, and then, under Titus, takes revenge on the perpetrators of this act of vengeance by destroying Jerusalem. The survey ends by noting the renewal of the imperial mission in Charlemagne's defense of the Church against the invading Lombards, but its net effect is to emphasize the randomness and violence of the events that led to the decisive triumph of the Roman eagle. It is as though Justinian, who purged the law of its superfluous elements, were deliberately ignoring the *Monarchia*'s elaborate philosophico-legal justifications of the exercise of Roman power, which emphasize the "common good" (*Mon.* 2.5.26) and "the goal of the human race" (2.6.5). Instead he reduces the history of Rome to a tale of sheer force, governed, in ways beyond human understanding, by Providence.

---

27. Mazzotta, *Dante, Poet*, 181.

The chivalrous notion of "trial by combat" (2.9) can hardly be made to bear on the conflicts of Caesar and Pompey, or Octavian and Antony. No duel, indeed, could meet Dante's strict definition (2.9.2), and those which most nearly do so are the stuff of heroic legend, proper only to the stories of Pallas, the Horatii, or Hector, whose ancestral *virtus* alone, it would seem, confers such nobility as Rome can claim.[28] Significantly the following canto will consider several modes of virtue, and nobility will be seen as grounded in the disciplined exercise of the *virtù* of will (7.25, 78).

But as Justinian himself acknowledges, his account of Roman history, disjointed and chaotic from an earthly standpoint, is significant only insofar as it prepares the world for events in relation to which the imperial mission will be reduced to a subordinate but collaborative role. The vast sweep of his discourse, which has paired the fall of Troy with the founding of Constantinople, and moved from the Troad to Spain and back again to the shores of the Red Sea, now recedes:

> Ma ciò che 'l segno che parlar mi face
> > fatto avea prima e poi era fatturo
> > per lo regno mortal ch'a lui soggiace,
> diventa in apparenza poco e scuro,
> > se in mano al terzo Cesare si mira
> > con occhio chiaro e con affetto puro.
> > > (*Par.* 6.82–87)

[But what the standard that makes me speak had done before, and after was to do throughout the mortal realm subject unto it, becomes in appearance little and obscure if it be looked on in the hand of the third Caesar with clear eye and pure affection.]

The reminder that Justinian himself is inspired by the eagle of God, itself the agent of Providence, recalls us to the spiritual purpose of his discourse.

---

28. See *Mon.* 2.3.3–4, where the nobility that justifies the ascendancy of Rome is said to be grounded in "virtue," and Dante adds that the ennobling virtue may be one's own or that of one's forebears.

In the following lines time itself is divided by the participles *fatto* and *fatturo,* removing the empire for a time from its dominant role, and reducing it abruptly to a "mortal realm." We are in the Christian era, and what now unfolds must be viewed with fresh eyes and in a new spirit. History hitherto had been a means to an end, but now for a time human and sacred history can be viewed as one. Rome has achieved its place in the world by force, but now the purpose of empire in enacting and enforcing its laws and decrees is to bring its instruments of justice into harmony with the "living justice" of God.

In this perspective Justinian's Roman history is as much as anything else a lesson in the inscrutability of the divine plan. From the death of Pallas to the (unmentioned) death of Caesar and the final triumph of Augustus, a causality is operative in which not just epic heroism, but rape, murder, and civil war become means to the ultimate goal of world peace. Justinian in his blessed state can see with "occhio chiaro" a justice inaccessible to those who still dwell in that "regno mortal" where true and false, good and bad, are forever irreconcilable. As Beatrice had explained in Canto 4, doubt concerning the justice of God is a consequence of faith, a necessary stage in acknowledging his power (4.67–69), and in Canto 7 the paradoxical relation of divine to human justice is addressed in theological terms.

Venus and Dido

In Canto 8 we have imperceptibly entered the heaven of Venus. The limits of earthly vision are again in question, and the opening lines condemn as a dangerous superstition Venus' power to inflict "mad love." This "ancient error" of "the ancient people" is illustrated by reference to Vergil, and throughout this canto and the next ancient poetry is set in a complex perspective.[29] But Dante goes on to acknowledge, candidly and suggestively, the fundamental role of Venus, declaring that it is she "from whom

---

29. Barolini, *Dante's Poets,* 61, rightly enough, sees an "implied corrective" of classical poetry in these cantos, but as I will try to show, the correction works both ways.

I take my start,"[30] and describing her relation to the sun in erotic terms.[31] If ancient myth has misrepresented her, the power she exercises is nonetheless real, and to confirm that Dante has entered her sphere, poetry and theology conspire in rendering Beatrice still more beautiful (14–15).

In this context, where the power of Venus is both affirmed and qualified, the reference to Dido deserves special attention. As related by Vergil, her story is the classic illustration of the power of Venus, and the moment to which Dante alludes, when she is drawn to take Cupid, disguised as the child Ascanius, on her lap (*Par.* 8.9; *Aen.* 1.718), marks a crucial stage in her victimization. Dante, it would seem, has chosen to deny Dido's story its tragic power by redeeming Venus, denying her mythic role as the source of erotic madness. Dido may then be seen reduced, as so often, to a fictive illustration of uncontrolled desire, justly relegated to the circle of the lustful in hell, and she will soon be recalled again, as in the *Inferno,* as having betrayed her marriage vows (9.97–98).

In fact the heaven of Venus is more tolerant of fleshly desire than Dante's introductory lines may suggest. In the following canto both Cunizza and Folco will speak frankly of having been overcome by the influence of the goddess (9.33); for them the "antico errore" that affirms her erotic power had expressed a reality. Folco, indeed, will explicitly compare her effect on himself to the burning desire of Dido (9.97; *Aen.* 4.54, 68), acknowledging a youthful folly ("che si convenne al pelo," 99) for which he no longer feels contrition.

But while Folco's candid acknowledgment of the sins of his youth seems of a piece with Dante's frank declaration that it is from Venus that he "takes his start" (8.10), his reference to Dido as having wronged both her dead husband, Sychaeus, and Aeneas' lost Creusa (97) is surprisingly

---

30. The phrase "onde io principio piglio" closely echoes *Purg.* 18.64–65, where reason is defined as "il principio onde si piglia / ragion di meritare," as it discriminates among good and evil desires that originate in the "prima voglia" (59); here *ragion,* like the "proof and refutation" performed by Beatrice (*Par.* 3.3), is superseded by the power of Venus.

31. The syntax of "la stella / che 'l sol vagheggia" (11–12) may indicate either the response of the sun to the beauty of Venus or an attractive power exercised by Venus herself.

and, Dante suggests, excessively harsh. Folco goes on to cite other classical examples of extreme passion (100–102), but Dido alone is singled out for censure. Phyllis, abandoned by Demophoön, blamed only him for her betrayal (*Her.* 2), and Folco, too, sees her only as "deceived." Hercules, unlike Dido, betrayed his still-living wife in his fatal infatuation with Iole (*Met.* 9.137–46; *Her.* 9), but is recalled tenderly by Folco as having "enclosed [Iole] in his heart." Yet Dido, who had clearly acknowledged her infidelity to the ashes of Sychaeus (*Aen.* 4.550–52), and blamed herself bitterly for succumbing to a desire which she believed at the same time to be fated, and thus irresistible, remains the archexample of "mad love" as guilt, and undergoes a damnation she herself had foreseen (*Aen.* 4.24–29) but had been unable to avoid.[32]

That Folco refers to Dido as having betrayed not only Sychaeus but Creusa seems simply cruel, ignoring as it does the fact that Aeneas, too, had betrayed a dead spouse, and that he, unlike Dido, had no thought of marriage in reciprocating her desire. Folco's harsh judgment recalls *Inferno* 5, where Dido is paired with Semiramis, and recalled as

> colei che s'ancise amorosa,
> e ruppe fede al cener di Sicheo.
> (*Inf.* 5.61–62)

[she who slew herself for love, and broke faith to the ashes of Sychaeus.]

By reversing the sequence of events, these lines obscure the extent to which shame at having betrayed Sychaeus was one of the many causes of Dido's suicide. They ignore as well the quasi-absolution that Vergil would grant to Dido's shade, whom we last see in the underworld, fleeing Aeneas to rejoin a Sychaeus who now "responds to her pain, and matches her love with his" (*Aen.* 6.474).

Dante, at last in the presence of Beatrice, could describe his feelings only by recourse to the words in which Dido had described the first

---

32. A redeeming view of Dido is offered by Dotti, *Divina Commedia*, 33–41; see also Bono, *Literary Transvaluation*, 11–38.

stirrings of her desire for Aeneas. They are also of course Vergil's words, and Vergil, like Dido, is damned, while Dante, like Aeneas, pursues his higher destiny. It can be argued that by twice editing Dido's story *in malo* and allowing Folco to judge her so severely, Dante is again challenging us with the inscrutability of divine judgment, which redeems the harlot Rahab but condemns women so virtuous as Lucretia and Hypsipyle to Limbo. And perhaps Dante's very affinity with Dido, which emerges so clearly in his encounter with Beatrice, is now to be seen as a weakness, an impulse which must be exorcised if he is to understand and emulate the radical separation from worldly desire of the souls he encounters here.

But the anti-Vergilian harshness of the condemnation of Dido calls attention to itself in another way as well. Like the dubious exemplary value of the allusion to Diana and Callisto at the end of *Purgatorio* 25, it suggests an ambivalence in Dante regarding the condemnation being voiced. Again we are made to recognize the inevitably arbitrary character of any human attempt to pass final judgment on human desire. Constrained by the doctrinal system of his poem, Dante could hardly accord so powerful a figure as Dido the privilege he will extend to Trajan or Ripheus. But by the extraordinary device of assigning her final condemnation to a spirit who ostensibly sees with the "clear eye and pure affection" of the blessed, yet whose judgment can be seen as arbitrary and unfair, he goads us to recall the generosity and nobility of Vergil's heroine, a victim of the cruel power of "durus amor" (*Aen.* 6.442), and makes us recognize how much is lost when tragic passion is simply condemned.

As in his treatment of Ugolino, Dante here seems to acknowledge an aspect of human experience for which his Christian universe has no place, but which refuses to be ignored. Here, however, he has gone a step further and exposed the inadequacy of the moral judgments imposed on Dido's actions. Ugolino is no doubt as sinned against as sinning; but Dido, in her greatness of spirit, rises above her accuser. Recurring again and again to Dante's mind, and resisting his every attempt to categorize her, she has finally become the example through whom Dante, in profound sympathy with Vergil, affirms the essential integrity of human desire.

Juno and Dominic

Canto 12 begins with a careful description of how, as Thomas Aquinas ends his praise of St. Francis and rejoins the cluster of spirits who surround him, a second singing circle encloses the first,

> e moto a moto e canto a canto colse;
> canto che tanto vince nostre muse,
> nostre serene in quelle dolci tube,
> quanto primo splendor quel ch'e' refuse.
> <div align="right">(<i>Par.</i> 12.6–9)</div>

[and matches motion with motion and song with song; song which, in those sweet pipes, as much surpasses our Muses, our Sirens, as a first splendor that which it throws back.]

The simple repetition of "moto" and "canto" in the first line is linked to what follows by the "canto . . . tanto" of the second, which is then linked anaphorically to the third by "nostre muse," / "nostre sirene," followed in the fourth by the description of what might be called a visual echo. There is a sequence to this wordplay: it begins in a divine simultaneity and harmony which are then compared to inspired emulation (the Muses), then specious imitation (the Sirens), and finally the passive reflection generated by a brilliant light.

This diminuendo is echoed in an elaborately convoluted simile, charged with allusions that seem oddly out of keeping with what will follow:

> Come si volgon per tenera nube
>   due archi paralelli e concolori,
>   quando Iunone a sua ancella iube,
> nascendo di quel d'entro quel di fori,
>   a guisa del parlar di quella vaga
>   ch'amor consunse come sol vapori,
> e fanno qui la gente esser presaga,
>   per lo patto che Dio con Noè puose,
>   del mondo che già mai non più s'allaga.
> <div align="right">(<i>Par.</i> 12.10–18)</div>

[As two bows, parallel and like in color, bend across a thin cloud
when Juno gives the order to her handmaid—the one without
born of the one within, like the voice of that wandering nymph
whom love consumed as the sun does vapors—and make the
people here presage, by reason of the covenant that God made
with Noah, that the world shall never again be flooded . . .]

Like the preceding lines, in which the celestial music is said to excel that
of both the Muses and the Sirens,[33] this passage seems unnecessarily detailed, and commentators have understandably found it cumbersome
and hard to interpret.[34] The augmentation of the original simile by the
reference to Echo is especially puzzling. The comparison of her wasting
away to that of vapors, presumably those that produce the rainbow and
are then consumed by the sun, brings the simile to a rather disconcerting
climax, by effecting the disappearance of its central image. This abruptly
reappears as Noah's rainbow in the final tercet, but the unambiguous significance of this final image, "set in the clouds" by God, only emphasizes
by contrast the puzzling movement of the simile as a whole and its allusions to Juno, Iris, and Echo.

The complicating of our ability to read by these seemingly intrusive
references is perhaps deliberate. In the canto the simile introduces, the
career of St. Dominic and an important aspect of the glorious mission of
the Church will be invested with much of the ambiguity of the history of
Rome as presented by Vergil, Ovid, and Dante's Justinian, so that Bonaventure's narrative must be read in a way very different from Thomas's
presentation of Francis, which it claims to complement. The difficulty
of the simile may be intended as a foreshadowing of this interpretive
challenge, and so I will examine it more closely, with an eye especially to
Dante's evocation of the complex role of Juno in Vergil and Ovid.

There are several occasions in both poets when Juno manifests her
will by sending Iris and her rainbow down to the mortal world. They
typically show the goddess aspiring to a role she cannot fulfill, emulating the power of fate but doomed to failure by her passsionate nature

---

33. I can see no basis for Singleton's claim that "serena" here denotes simply
"one who sings," as opposed to its clearly pejorative significance in *Purg.* 19.

34. Bosco and Reggio find the details of the simile "un po' ingombranti."

and irrational motivation. Dido is the central figure in the most memorable of these episodes, the conclusion of *Aeneid* 4. Juno, who has been complicit in engineering Dido's fatal love, finally feels pity for the dying queen, whom, as a suicide, Persephone has declined to release from her torment. She sends Iris to cut the vital thread, and Dido's spirit, like the rainbow on which Iris descends, vanishes into the air (*Aen.* 4.693–705).

The episode constitutes, by classical standards, an authentic theophany. Iris' divine authority is confirmed by her decisive actions and the formulaic utterance, ending in the quasi-liturgical "teque isto corpore soluo" (703), which affirms that Dido's suicide is untainted by sin.[35] Whatever her motivation, Juno, through Iris, is clearly doing the decent thing.

In *Aeneid* 5, driven by her abiding hostility to Aeneas and the Trojans, Juno sends Iris to their encampment in Sicily, where she assumes the form of the matron Beroe, and seeks to incite the other Trojan women to burn the ships and so put an end to their endless voyaging. Her eloquence speaks to the women's deepest longings, but creates only confusion. Recognized as a goddess in disguise, Iris takes wing in her proper form, while the women become a frenzied mob and attack the fleet, only to be thwarted when Jupiter answers Aeneas' prayer with a heavy shower of rain (5.606–99).

In *Aeneid* 9 Iris, sent again by Juno, appears briefly to Turnus, urging him in Aeneas' absence to attack the Trojans' camp and destroy their ships (9.1–24), but this attempt, too, is forestalled by Jupiter at the urging of Cybele, who had granted Aeneas trees from her sacred forest to build the Trojan fleet. The ships are transformed into sea creatures and swim to deep water (9.77–122). Having goaded Turnus to madness by her false assurance of an easy victory, Iris is soon compelled to go forth again, this time dispatched by Jove, at whose command she delivers to Juno a harsh order to cease her machinations.

Iris descends again in *Metamorphoses* 11, where Alcyone, unaware that her husband, Ceyx, has drowned at sea, wearies Juno with ceaseless prayers for his safe return. Iris is sent to order the god of Sleep to send a

---

35. See Pease, *Aeneidos Liber Quartus*, 529–37. That Dido is freed from the taint of suicide is confirmed by her reappearance, not among the suicides, but with the victims of the cruelty of love (*Aen.* 6.440–75).

dream-spirit in the form of Ceyx to inform Alcyone of his death (*Met.* 11.583–632). Neither Juno nor Iris takes part in the Ovidian episode explicitly recalled by Dante, the pining away of Echo, but we should remember that it was Juno who began Echo's misfortunes by curbing her powers of speech, as revenge for the nymph's having repeatedly warned Jove of her attempts to expose his infidelities (*Met.* 3.362–69).

All these episodes display Juno's violent passions, her chronic sense of wrong, and her ceaseless and futile desire to alter the destined order of events. As she contemplates Dido's death throes, she is called "Juno omnipotens" (693), but in fact her larger designs on Dido and Aeneas have utterly failed; Jove has intervened to ensure that Aeneas will resume his destined voyage, and Dido's great love now ends in tragic disaster. That Juno twice attempts to destroy the Trojan fleet suggests her obsession with fates she cannot withstand, and even her relatively minor Ovidian interventions prove futile. Her cruel disillusioning of Alcyone, which drives the widowed queen to attempt suicide, is countered by "the pitying gods," who turn Alcyone and Ceyx into seabirds. (*Met.* 11.641–48). And her punishing of Echo is a halfway measure of gratuitous cruelty, provoked by her inability to curb the lust of Jove, and finally cast into shadow by the beauty and pathos of Echo's final transformation.

But though Juno is unable to alter fate, chastise Jove, or control her own strong passions, she is nonetheless powerful. She is arguably the central figure in the plot of the *Aeneid*,[36] and Vergil cannot even begin his narrative until he has spent thirty lines explaining the complex of motives, great and small, for her hatred of Troy. Her power manifests itself, moreover, not only within the narrative, but at the level of epic decorum. Throughout the poem her mad scheming and the madness it provokes undermine the dignity of the heroic enterprise, reducing the epic world to a tangle of plots and counterplots. Her interventions in history divert Aeneas from his divinely sanctioned mission, visit disaster on Juno's own city, Carthage, and create the conditions under which, despite her prayers, Italy is not only conquered, but laid waste. Juno stands for nothing, and the rainbow of Iris, her emissary, is an emblem of false promise. As the deceptively

---

36. See Johnson, *Darkness Visible*, 7–11.

majestic descent of Iris at the end of *Aeneid* 4 obscures the tragic majesty of Dido, so the larger effect of Juno on the poem as a whole is to demean piety and heroism, and cast Rome and its destiny in an equivocal light.

Juno's role is thus defined largely by her disruptive challenges to the power of destiny, challenges which inevitably prove futile. The ascendancy of Rome which she has failed to prevent can be seen as foreshadowing the foundational achievements of Francis and Dominic. Their lives are made to define a new heroic order, heralded by the lucid and compact vision of sacred history with which Thomas introduces the life of Francis (11.28–34). Both Thomas and Bonaventure stress the continuity of purpose in the work of these two princes of the Church, such that to praise one is to define the praiseworthiness of the other (11.40–42; 12.34–36).

But the simile and its allusions to the work of Juno are an ominous preface to Bonaventure's encomium of Dominic. The initial image of the double rainbow seems intended as an illustration of perfect consonance, an appropriate preface to the harmonizing of Dominic's work with that of Francis. But the added allusions to Juno's reckless and deceptive deployment of Iris and her jealous curtailment of the speech of Echo are signs that celebrating Dominic will be a more difficult task than Thomas' praising of Francis.

Thomas' charismatic Francis appears first as a mythic presence, a sun who stimulates the earth by his great virtue, then joins with his Lady, Poverty, in a love allegory which becomes for a moment a courtly idyll; their marvelous joy inspires others to emulation, and the Franciscan order arises spontaneously:

> La lor concordia e i lor lieti sembianti,
>   amore e maraviglia e dolce sguardo
>   faceino esser cagion di pensier santi.
>   (*Par.* 11.76–78)

> [Their harmony and joyous semblance made love and wonder
>   and tender looks the cause of holy thoughts.]

Ennobled by love, Francis appeals "royally" to Innocent III to sanction the Franciscan rule (91–92), and from this point the narrative is largely a history of the work of the order.

Francis' life is manifestly Christlike: its defining moment, his marriage
to Poverty, is described in terms which recall Thomas' prefatory reference
to the union of Christ with the Church, a passage marked by a strong
erotic undertone:

> però che andasse ver' lo suo diletto
> la sposa di colui ch'ad alte grida
> disposò lei col sangue benedetto.
>
> (*Par.* 11.31–33)

[that the Bride of Him who, with loud cries, espoused her
with the blessed blood, might go to her Delight.]

At the literal level the description of Francis' marriage appears very
different:

> ché per tal donna, giovinetto, in guerra
> del padre corse, a cui, come a la morte,
> la porta del piacer nessun diserra.
>
> (*Par.* 11.58–60)

[for, while still a youth, he rushed into strife against his
father for such a lady, to whom, as to death, none willingly
unbars the door.]

But the syntax of these lines, like Vergil's words as interpreted by Statius,
is malleable. The "guerra del padre" is on one level Francis' defiance of his
father's anger at his renouncing of his patrimony. The proverb recalled in
the following lines clearly requires that "del piacer" be adverbial. But "the
war of the father" can also be read, not as a campaign against an earthly
parent, but as undertaken, like the earthly mission of Christ, at the bidding of the heavenly Father, to rebuke a Church too worldly to recognize
holy poverty as worthy to pass through "la porta del piacer" and attain
the promised "diletto."

So understood, Francis' embrace of extreme poverty, a radical and
daunting vocation which alienated his father and made Pope Innocent
hesitate to sanction the early Franciscans, becomes the aspect in which

he most resembles Christ; for like Christ, he will be "miraculously de-spised," and will triumph through self-abasement (90, 111). From the win-ning of his first disciples to his final reception of the stigmata, his every act is an imitation of Christ and, as Thomas indicates in calling him "seraphic" (37), an expression of love for God.

What is metaphorical in the presentation of Francis takes concrete form in Bonaventure's encomium of Dominic. He, too, is both lover and "champion," but the latter role predominates. The saga of his life is stud-ded with military imagery, and though he is identified first as "gardener," messenger, and teacher, he is increasingly depicted as a warrior in the cause of orthodoxy. The terms of his marriage to Faith and the dowries of "mutual salvation" they exchange (12.61–63) have a legalistic ring, and suggest a relationship like that of state and Church.

And in fact Dominic's role recalls in several ways the secular mis-sion of Rome. As Rome's great task, in Anchises' famous formula, was "to spare the humble and cast down the proud" (*Aen.* 6.853), so Dominic is first described as "benigno a' suoi e a' nemici crudo" (57). But we hear little of his benignity; his power asserts itself most strongly where it most encounters obstinacy (101–2), and though he is the founder of a great fraternal order, there is no talk, as with Francis, of followers drawn by love to follow in his footsteps. Granted license to make war against heresy, and armed "with doctrine and with will" (97), he goes forth "like a tor-rent" (99), recalling the river imagery with which Lucan marks the prog-ress of Caesar's march on Rome, and like Caesar's, his campaign is de-scribed as civil war ("civil briga," 108). Thomas' Francis had been the living embodiment of humility and ecstatic piety, the perfect exemplar of Chris-tian devotion, but Bonaventure's Dominic and the doctrine he wields are tools, at times virtually weapons, of God and His Church. The torrential force of his assault on the "mondo errante" (94) is derived from the higher power ("alta vena," 99) which is its source, but the forceful language of Bonaventure's description of the campaigns licensed by this higher power hints at an unwieldy, even violent impulse.[37]

---

37. Though Dominic's campaigns are described as "civil briga" (108), the phrase "mondo errante," which recalls Dante's claim that in addressing his canzone "Le dolci rime d'amor" as "Contra-li-erranti mia" he is alluding to the

There can be no questioning the respect with which Dominic is presented, but it is clear that in Dante's eyes his life and work did not lend themselves to the reverently idealizing treatment accorded Francis. Bonaventure, himself the biographer of Francis, is plainly unable to echo Thomas by providing the clear correspondences seemingly promised in the previous canto (11.40–42). In Paradise all differences are reconciled, and the two saints can doubtless be seen to have "warred" to the same end (11.35), but Bonaventure offers no such clarifying perspective to his mortal audience. That Dominic's militant championing of orthodoxy could take harsh forms is strongly suggested,[38] and Bonaventure's account includes no such iconic moments as those which punctuate Francis' career. Though Dominic is always and everywhere the servant of the Church, he can be said to exercise the Church's equivalent to the power of the secular arm, seeking always to maintain and extend its supremacy over a doctrinally unified Christendom. And like doctrine itself, which strengthens faith but gives rise to disputes that can lead to schism, his wide-ranging mission plays a potentially paradoxical role, for there is a strong suggestion that his zeal to "defend" the Church (107) and ensure the unity and hegemony of Christian belief aggravated the embattled position of the Church in the world.

It is such problems as these, I think, that explain Dante's having introduced his portrayal of this "paladino" with the complex simile discussed above. In pursuing heresy too forcefully, the Church risks usurping to itself the proper function of the state (as indeed was the case during the early stages of the Dominicans' work on behalf of the Inquisition). When religious zeal and martial *virtù* enter into an unholy alliance, a sort of "Juno principle" can begin to operate. We are surely invited to see in Juno's disputatious character and her perpetual hatred of

---

Summa contra gentiles of Thomas (*Conv.* 4.30.3), is perhaps a reminder that the Dominicans' warfare extended beyond the curbing of Christian heresy. Dante may be recalling the intensity of Dominican disputations with Jewish masters, and the often biased rigor of the "trials" to which these opponents were sometimes subjected.

38. Noteworthy in this regard is the use of "crudo" to characterize Dominic in his assault on heresy (57), the only instance outside the *Inferno* in which this term is applied to an individual.

the Trojans a warning of the dangers to which a single-minded militancy, even in the cause of Truth, might lead, its liability to foment dissent in seeking to eliminate it, and to make the trappings of divine sanction, like the rainbow of Iris, a disguise for unwarranted aggression. Even Ovid's Juno, an almost pathetic parody of Vergil's, who squanders her power in vindictive assaults on human women ravished by Jove, serves to suggest the unwieldiness of the blunt instrument of persecution. Her reduction of Echo's speech to a repetition of the words of others is an all too apt reminder of the specious character of any orthodoxy imposed by force.

The world defined by allusion to Lucan, Vergil, and Ovid has become the strife-torn secular world of Dante's day, with which the Church must coexist, but which it emulates at its peril. Francis is a recurring presence in the later cantos, and Dante's own experience will exhibit a markedly Franciscan character, but Dominic's work is acknowledged only here, and in terms which even Bonaventure, himself made beautiful by love (31), cannot make spiritually appealing.

Cacciaguida

Language assumes a new significance as Dante ascends. Awed by the splendor of the circle of Mars he cries out "Eliòs!" (14.96) with a spontaneity like that of the followers who first responded to the seraphic radiance of Francis. This word, which Dante the scholar understood as a synthesis of Greek and Hebrew, is to be understood here as wholly unpremeditated, an outward expression of that instinctive, prayerful speech "which is one in all men" (14.89). The Pilgrim has entered a realm beyond thought, where "art and genius" are meaningless as applied to poetic language, referable at best to such practical tasks as building (116–17), and as distant from the ravishing song that envelops Dante as are the spirits in the sphere of Mars from the motes of dust to which he compares them (112–14). Like the radiance of the eyes of Beatrice, the music he hears elicits only an uncomprehending love (124–29).

After such assurances Dante's encounter with Cacciaguida must be understood as an extraordinary indulgence in poetic license, complementing the indulgence of family pride and the score-settling references to contemporary Florence with which the episode abounds. From the initial comparison of Cacciaguida to Anchises, overjoyed at the sight of Aeneas, we are in Elysium as well as Paradise,[39] and after he has greeted the Pilgrim in richly allusive Latin we can hardly take seriously Dante's claim that the speech which follows was too profound to be intelligible to a mortal (15.37–42); by Canto 17 it has become "preciso / latin" (17.34–35). Cacciaguida, unique in this respect among the blessed spirits, has yearned Anchises-like for his promised meeting with one who still belongs to the world, and Dante confesses that their communion caused him, even in heaven, to glory in his ancestry (16.1–6). Suspended, with Cacciaguida and Beatrice "quinci e quindi," like the Church flanked by Dominic and Francis (15.33; cp. 11.36), he feels uplifted, made "more than himself" by a "baldezza" that is surely grounded in family pride (16.17–18), while at the same time reduced to an awed respect which recalls his meeting with Farinata. Beatrice indulges these all-too-human responses with a very human smile (16.13–15).

Aeneas is given by Anchises a broad vision of the future of the city whose destiny he bears, a city "blest in its progeny" (*Aen.* 6.781), the race of heroes, kings, and Caesars who will make it great. Cacciaguida looks back in time, and describes for Dante the simple beauty of life in a modest and homogeneous Florence, conscious of its Roman heritage, a life both "glorious and just" (16.151–52). He gives vent to their common detestation of the greed and depravity of Dante's city, but then places the city's decline in perspective:

> le cittadi termine hanno.
> Le vostre cose tutte hanno lor morte,
> sì come voi; ma celasi in alcuna
> che dura molto, e le vite son corte.
> E come 'l volger del ciel de la luna
> cuopre e discuopre i liti sanza posa,
> cosi fa di Fiorenza la Fortuna.
>
> (*Par.* 16.78–84)

---

39. This sense is reinforced by clear allusions to the *Somnium Scipionis*. See Schnapp, *Transfiguration*, 59–62. But see also below, p. 260, n. 41.

[. . . cities have their term. Your affairs all have their death,
even as have you; but it is concealed in some things that
last long, whereas life is short. And as the revolution of
the heaven of the moon covers and uncovers the shores
without pause, so Fortune does with Florence.]

Aeneas had learned from Anchises, to his horror, that life is endless; that
we pass from the world to an afterlife where we undergo punishment
and purification, only to enter the world again, impelled by a "cruel desire
for light" in which Aeneas sees epitomized the wretched human condition (*Aen.* 6.713–21, 735–51).[40] Dante's final transcendence of earthly life
is assured, but the lesson he must learn about the finitude of human
achievement is hardly less grim. Aeneas had also been shown a city-to-
be, a vision of promise. Cacciaguida's evocation of the Florence of his
time only makes clearer the extent, and the inevitability, of the city's fall.[41]
Dante himself will be a victim of the perfidy of the corrupted city that
he both loathes and loves, and he must learn to accept his disenfranchised
condition. His imperial dream will remain unfulfilled, and his only political reward will be the conscious integrity of a party of one (17.68–69).
Not surprisingly the wisdom of Boethius is a clear undertone in Cacciaguida's prophecy, and the consciousness that he will be following in
Boethius' footsteps is perhaps Dante's only consolation.[42]

The allusion to Phaëthon that opens Canto 17, and expresses Dante's
need to learn what the future holds, together with Cacciaguida's comparison of his coming exile to that of Hippolytus (46–48) point up the complexity of Dante's position. Read *in bono* they serve to set off by contrast the
triumph he will achieve.[43] Dante, unlike Phaëthon, will complete the heav-

---

40. See Putnam, "Virgil's Inferno," 98; Schnapp, *Transfiguration*, 30–31.

41. See Schnapp, *Transfiguration*, 49–51.

42. On the Boethian elements in this scene, see Schnapp, *Transfiguration*,
11–12, 228n–229n; Ferrante, *Political Vision*, 279–80. A clear echo occurs in
17.130–32, based on *Cons.* 3, *pr.* 1.13–14. Cacciaguida's description of his own passage "from martyrdom to this peace" (15.148) echoes Thomas' lines on Boethius
(10.128–29).

43. See Schnapp, "Dante's Ovidian Self-Correction," 217–23; Picone, "Dante,
Ovidio, e la poesia dell'esilio," 20–21.

enly journey which he, like Phaëthon, had called on Apollo to make possible; and the Hippolytus whose exile anticipates his own is not Euripides' zealot, but the Hippolytus who, according to a legend perhaps invented by Vergil, and appropriated by Ovid (*Aen.* 7.765–77; *Met.* 15.506–46), is restored to life by the arts of Aesculapius and returns to the world as the Italian deity Virbius, whose name is glossed by Servius as "bis-vir," "twice-man."[44] But whereas Vergil's Virbius is a minor figure, living out his divine life "ignobly," deep in the Italian woods (*Aen.* 7.776–77), Dante, restored to poetic life and inspired by Vergil, will accomplish great things.

But if such a reading justifies Cacciaguida's comparison of what he foresees to an organ's sweet harmony (43–45), there is a darker undertone in these allusions. Like all Dante's appropriations of the Poeti, they bear not only on his poetic journey but also on his situation in the world. His presumption in assuming the role of reformer and prophet is hardly less than that of Phaëthon, and his fearless virtue, like the purity of Hippolytus, will make him enemies. As the strongly hortatory tone of Cacciaguida's final words makes clear, persevering in his mission will require patience, and above all courage.

Cacciaguida's first instruction to Dante had been bracing:

> la voce tua sicura, balda e lieta
>   suoni la volontà, suoni 'l disio!
>   (*Par.* 15.67–68)

> [Let your voice, confident and bold and glad, sound forth the will, sound forth the desire.]

His own speech meets this high standard. His revelations concerning Dante's future life are "chiose," clarifying glosses on what had been hinted ambiguously earlier in the poem, and his words are delivered "con preciso latin" (17.34–35). This may be Latin itself, or an older and presumably purer and more dignified form of the Florentine vernacular, but it is above all clear (34), and the same criteria are operative in his final advice to

---

44. Servius, *In Aeneidem* 7.761 (Thilo-Hagen, vol. 2, 193). See also Chiarenza, "Hippolytus' Exile," and "Time and Eternity," 138–46.

Dante. He must make plain what he has seen, loudly proclaim the truth
without fear of giving offense in high places. Thus he will gain honor,
and it is to prepare him for this duty that throughout his journey he has
been shown only the souls of great men (17.128–38).

This last assertion can hardly be reconciled with Dante's experience or
our own, but it sheds light on Cacciaguida's own code of values. He speaks
as a soldier, and conceives Dante's poetic power as a defiant shout, a
peremptory challenge to the high and mighty, so that the poem-to-be becomes in his view virtually a crusade.[45] The Aeneas-like position in which
he places Dante, the markedly classical character of his exhortation,[46] and
the promise of honor as reward, all attest to the heroic nature of the task he
defines. His insistence that Dante cast aside falsehood distances the *Commedia* from classical epic *fabula,* but Dante's mission finally bears as directly
on the earthly city, past and to come, as that with which Anchises charges
Aeneas.[47] The signs of Cacciaguida's transcendent perspective are inex-
tricably combined with reminders of the human concerns that he shares
with Dante, and the secular experience that shapes his view of Dante's
mission.

Dante has chosen this moment, when he is on the point of ascending
to the new poetic height marked by his invocation of the "diva Pegasëa"
(18.82–87), to declare himself once and for all a reformer, a poet of the
earthly city. The memory of *Aeneid* 6 and the *Somnium Scipionis* is nowhere

---

45. See della Coletta, *"Paradiso* XV," 213: By emulating Cacciaguida's eloquence, Dante will become "the second Alighieri crusader, the authoritative mediator of the languages of sacred love and martial ardor."

46. Cacciaguida's comparison of Dante's "grido" to the wind, "which smites
most upon the loftiest summits" (133–34), recalls Horace, *Odes* 2.10.9–12, a warning to Licinius of the danger of being overbold, and Ovid, *Remedia amoris* 369,
on the envy encountered by Homer and Vergil. (Both passages are quoted by
Abelard, *Historia calamitatum,* ed. Monfrin, lines 121, 803–4.) Dante has made
the wind a metaphor for the courage and the quasi-prophetic power his own undertaking will require, but its association with envy is perhaps to be recalled also,
as a reminder that these cantos include what Momigliano called "i discorsi più
gelosi della *Commedia*" (*Dante, Manzoni, Verga,* 33).

47. Schnapp, *Transfiguration,* 141–49, provides a full and careful discussion
of the contrasting roles of Cacciaguida and Anchises.

more clearly present than here,[48] and Dante is aware that the missions entrusted to Aeneas and Scipio, though denied the guidance of Truth, required spiritual as well as political dedication,[49] that in his own undertaking he is following in their footsteps, carrying forward the tradition of Cicero and Vergil.

Justice

Canto 18 begins with a long, delicious interval of self-abandonment to the spell of Beatrice's beauty, prompted by the "amoroso suono" of her voice (7), and ending only with her reminder that her eyes are just one manifestation of Paradise (21). But after a final joyful glance as Dante ascends to the sphere of Jupiter, Beatrice is not mentioned again until the beginning of Canto 21. Her withdrawal gives a unique quality to the intervening cantos, which can be said to reinaugurate Dante's earthly mission as a poet of social reform, first tracing justice to its source in the unfathomable mind of God, then acknowledging the difficulty for existential man of believing that this justice is operative in his earthly experience.

The imagery that attends Dante's ascent suggests that one consequence of this new departure will be a diminished emphasis on subjective feeling. Though Beatrice appears still more beautiful, the "dilettanza" Dante now feels in beholding her contains no apparent trace of the erotic, but only confirms that he has risen to a higher sphere, and suggests to him the satisfaction one feels in "doing well" (58–60). This new, chastened response to Beatrice is complemented by the image which introduces the sphere of Jupiter:

48. On the presence of the *Somnium Scipionis*, see Dotti, *Divina Commedia*, 104–8. As Dotti observes, 7–8, Dante's poem here appears as a "grido di battaglia" for reform: "il suo obiettivo ultimo non fu la Città di Dio eternamente fiorente in beatitudine, ma il rinnovamento della Città dell'uomo. . . . L'imprescindibile modello celeste, si direbbe, è posto al servizio della redenzione del quaggiù."

49. Schnapp, *Transfiguration*, 14, seems to ignore this aspect in asserting that while Dante's mission is meaningful in itself, those offered to Aeneas and Scipio are only means to "a simple escape from the prison of history."

E qual è 'l trasmutare in picciol varco
   di tempo in bianca donna, quando 'l volto
   suo si discarchi di vergogna il carco,
tal fu ne li occhi miei, quando fui vòlto,
   per lo candor de la temprata stella
   sesta.

                     (*Par.* 18.64–68)

[And such change as comes in a moment over the face of a
pale lady, when her countenance frees itself from a burden
of modest shame, was presented to my eyes when I turned,
because of the whiteness of the temperate sixth star.]

The lady's release from "modest shame" corresponds to Dante's more
chaste and temperate response to the newly enhanced beauty of Beatrice,
in a sphere where the "sfavillar de l'amor" (71) of the blessed souls expresses itself in the disciplined form of a written message.

    With a final glance at Beatrice, Dante enters the sphere of Jupiter,
and reveals a new sense of the mission of his poetry, invoking an un-
specified Muse, a "Pegasean goddess,"

                 che li 'ngegni
fai glorïosi e rendili longevi,
ed essi teco le cittadi e ' regni.

              (*Par.* 18.82–84)

[you who give glory unto men of genius and render them
long-lived, as they, through you, the cities and kingdoms.]

The process whereby this divine Muse, through the mediating "ingegno"
of the poet, gives enduring form to the principles of just government
(18.82–87) parallels the work of the Divine Mind which, through the
"temperata complessione" of Jupiter (*Conv.* 2.13.25), manifests justice to
the world (18.115–17). For earthly justice in its larger meaning is an art, the
work of the supreme artist whose concern for social order extends to teaching birds how to form their nests (109–11).

Deprived for the moment of Beatrice's mediating presence, Dante in Canto 19 is put firmly in his place for his nagging but unuttered concern regarding the fate of virtuous persons who live and die without knowledge of Christ. Before dealing with this question, the Eagle formed by the constellation of just souls, speaking in their unanimous voice as Justice itself, describes the depth of the divine judgment in vivid and forceful terms. By so doing it has in effect already answered Dante, and its address to the question which Dante has raised "so incessantly" (69) seems almost angry. It rebukes Dante's presumption in the language of the Book of Job, cites biblical authority as sufficient to suppress open doubt, then flaps its wings and concludes its "answer" in terms which seem to foreclose further discussion:

> "Quali
> son le mie note a te, che non le 'ntendi,
> tal è il giudicio etterno a voi mortali."
> (*Par.* 19.97–99)

["As are my notes to you who understand them not, such is the Eternal Judgment to you mortals."]

But of course the Eagle's answer does not end here. He goes on to assert the absolute necessity of belief in Christ, but then hints at the possibility of belief in Christ before the Crucifixion, and declares that ignorance of Christ will be judged far less harshly than pretended faith (103–8). Followed as it is by the claim that the final Judgment which condemns the false Christian will make an Ethiopian "eternally rich" (109–11), this seems to promise a way of meeting Dante's concern. But the Eagle's words are cryptic. As Barański notes, the canto is charged with the terminology of signification, and clearly invites the exegesis appropriate to a deeply symbolic religious text.[50]

The Eagle reopens the question of salvation in more accessible terms in Canto 20, identifying the diverse representatives of justice who form

---

50. Barański, "*Paradiso* XIX," 285–86. But see also Foster, *Two Dantes*, 137–55, for a coherent reading largely in terms of Thomist theology.

its eye and brow. In each case the just man is identified and his salvation vindicated in terms of his own intentions, regardless of the results of his actions and apart from any intervention of grace, though it is through the grace now conferred on him that he realizes the implications of his life. The net result of the Eagle's revelations is to confirm its earlier insistence that God's judgments are unfathomable, but they also serve as a rich and broadly affirmative commentary on Dante's own artistic project.

Also significant for Dante's undertaking are the souls who form the eye of the Eagle. Dante's sense of affinity with David is clear from his portrayal of him in *Purgatorio* 10, and the same biblical episode is recalled here.[51] That David is identified by his role as psalmist affirms the value of poetry as a vehicle of justice, and his placement as the pupil of the Eagle's eye makes him an emblem of the poetic task Dante is in the process of defining for himself. Trajan, first damned, then saved, can be seen as a "type" of the Dante who has known both hell and Paradise, and he, too, is an emblematic figure, an embodiment of the often contradictory but ultimately positive role of the Empire in Dante's vision of providential history. The meaning of Hezekiah for Dante is again both personal and political: as ruler in Jerusalem he took on himself the guilt he saw manifested in the city's oppression by the Assyrians, and his repentance and concern for Israel were rewarded by divine protection. Later, "sick unto death," and feeling himself on the brink of the pit of Sheol, he prayed again and was granted a prolongation of life, as Dante, close to spiritual death, received not only a renewal of life, but the promise of salvation.[52]

A great deal of Dante's vision of history is compressed in the Eagle's reference to Constantine:

> sotto buona intenzion che fé mal frutto
> per cedere al pastor si fece greco:
> ora conosce come il mal dedutto
> dal suo bene operar non li è nocivo,
> avvegna che sia 'l mondo indi distrutto.
> (*Par.* 20.56–60)

---

51. See above, chap. 5, pp. 135–36; and 2 Kings 6:2–17.
52. See Charity, *Events and Their Afterlife*, 230; 2 Kings 18–20.

[with a good intention which bore bad fruit, he made himself
Greek, together with the laws and me, in order to give place to
the Pastor. Now he knows how the evil derived from his good
action does not harm him, even though the world should be
destroyed thereby.]

Dante could hardly go further in condemning the Donation of Constantine, a historical disaster whose implications for Dante's world have yet to
be fully realized. What is more remarkable is that the destruction of the
world is mentioned, not to emphasize the evil results of the Donation,
but to declare their irrelevance to the spiritual status of Constantine himself. Even though the world, in the absence of a single, all-governing emperor, is chronically riven by violence, so that justice and happiness are
unattainable, men who dedicate themselves to attaining peace and justice
can triumph, making a conquest of the divine will through the love and
hope expressed in their lives (94–99); for God wills to suffer the violence
of love.[53]

It is in the light of these lines that we can best understand the presence of Ripheus, Vergil's "iustissimus unus" (Aen. 2.426), whose devotion
to the right, as Aeneas notes bitterly, could not save him from the doom
decreed by the gods, but whose fate has now been undone by divine grace
(70–71). The salvation of this figure, for whose very existence Vergil is
the sole authority, underlines the irony of the damnation of Vergil himself. For some critics it is at the same time a declaration that Vergil's damnation is deliberate, that Dante found him unworthy of salvation.[54] But it
can also be seen as a vindication of Vergil's sense of justice: if the pagan
gods ignored Vergil's insistence on Ripheus' virtue, the true God agrees
with him.[55] And Vergil's invention of the Ripheus whom Dante now can-
onizes places him squarely in the tradition of poets whom the "diva Pe-
gasea" empowers. Ripheus' devotion to justice becomes a foreshadowing of the mission to be carried out by Rome, and makes him a type of

53. See Took, "Justice and the Just Ruler," 150–51. As Took notes, lines 94–95
restate in positive terms the grim reflection of Matt. 11:12: "regnum caelorum vim
patitur et violenti rapiunt illud."

54. See Hollander, Virgilio dantesco, 99; Barolini, Dante's Poets, 254–56.

55. See Chiarenza, "Paradiso XX," 303–4.

the emperor of Dante's imperial dream, reminding us of all that Dante's political ideology owes to the *Aeneid.*[56]

To make Ripheus' salvation an occasion for speculation about Vergil's is to risk missing the point of the canto, to presume to see to the bottom of the sea of divine justice. It is probably idle to point out that Paul was thought to have wept over the grave of Vergil, and longed to have seen him a Christian, as Gregory had prayed for the soul of Trajan,[57] or that Constantine's reversal of the westward course of empire disrupted a providential design to which Vergil had been the first to bear witness. It could be answered that the fatalistic "dis aliter visum" (*Aen.* 2.428) appended to Vergil's celebration of Ripheus is sufficient evidence of an inability to wholeheartedly affirm this providential vision, a spiritual defect deserving of damnation. What is certain is that Vergil's invention is here clearly fundamental to Dante's project as represented emblematically in this canto, a final demonstration of Dante's willingness to extend and validate the vision tentatively expressed in the *Aeneid,* liberating Ripheus from the confusion of history, and transforming the stark inevitability of his Vergilian fate into the ultimate demonstration of the mysterious workings of divine justice.

Poetry in Perspective

The abrupt reversion to Beatrice which opens Canto 21 reminds us that she has been virtually absent during Dante's interview with the Eagle. In retrospect this episode can be seen as a special dispensation to Dante as poet, a validation of the synthesis of traditions and the unprecedented exercises in poetic license that have enabled him to express imaginatively his complex sense of the operation of justice in history. Ascending to the sphere of Saturn after this intense focus on the world, he is abruptly recalled to the theological reality of his situation by Beatrice, who— merciful where Ovid's Juno had been cruelly vindictive—withholds her smile lest it turn him to ashes, as Semele, tricked by Juno, was destroyed by the visitation of Jove in his cosmic majesty (21.4–6; *Met.* 3.259–309). The absent smile, like the absence of song in this sphere, suggests that the in-

---

56. See Davis, *Dante and Rome,* 103–5.
57. See Comparetti, *Vergil in the Middle Ages,* 98.

dulgences of "poetando" are inappropriate here, and this is confirmed by the spirit of Peter Damian, who explains both phenomena as illustrating the economy of love in the higher heavens, where the joy of beholding God, no longer mediated by the imagery of natural things, is precisely proportionate to the intensity with which each soul is illumined (88–90).[58]

Ascending to the sphere of the fixed stars in Canto 22, Dante enters Gemini, the sign which marked his birth, and immediately feels himself at the source of his inspiration as a poet. His prayer to the constellation "from which I derive all my genius" (113–14) attests the perspective he has attained, his ability at last to see his poetry as integrated with the order of things, and the world as "a totality of internal relations rooted in and recapitulated by poetic metaphor."[59] Here he is bidden for the first time to look down. What he sees, Beatrice tells him, will prepare him to participate fully in the vision to come (130–32), by exposing the "vil sembiante" of the world as a thing to be rejected once and for all. But like Scipio he cannot make this final gesture, as the final lines of his prayer to the Gemini had made clear:

> A voi divotamente ora sospira
>   l'anima mia, per acquistar virtute
>   al passo forte che a sé la tira.
>   (*Par.* 22.121–23)

> [To you my soul now devoutly sighs, that it may acquire virtue
>   for the hard pass which draws it to itself.]

The "passo forte" is in one sense clearly the challenge that lies immediately ahead, that of making his eyes sufficiently "clear and keen" to assimilate the vision of the highest heaven to which he is being drawn. But it also denotes the task of representation, of integrating this vision into his poem, and this task, as we have seen, will draw him back to earth, to the "passo" of exile and the thankless labor of the reformer.

It is in the light of this awareness that Dante, looking down, identifies the planets, not by their conventional mythic names, but by those

---

58. See Wilson, *"Paradiso XXII,"* 322–23.

59. Mazzotta, *Dante's Vision,* 169.

of the older, parent gods, Latona, Hyperion, Maia, Dione, who were displaced by their children, the Olympians. The effect is to remind us of the inevitability of change. Saturn himself belongs to this earlier generation, and we have already been reminded that he presided over the world of the Golden Age, when evil was unknown (21.26–27). That world inevitably gave way to the increasing wickedness of the human world, as the life of cloistered simplicity, adorned with fruit and flowers in the discourses of Peter Damian and Benedict, has given way to the present decadence of the monastic orders.

The *Aeneid* had given tentative expression to Vergil's dream of a new Golden Age, a re-creation of the primordial, Saturnian Italy in a world prepared by the Pax Augusta, a dream all too easily broken by the "horrida bella" which dominate the poem. Dante, angered and demoralized by the corruption of his world, reveals only by way of cryptic signs his vision of world empire. But in the sense he conveys of stages of world history succeeding one another, old orders giving way to new, clearly present in this brief cosmic vision, lies his challenge and his hope, the hope which, as Beatrice will declare, sustains him in the unceasing war waged by the Church Militant (25.52–57).

Looking upward again, Dante sees the splendor of the higher heaven continually increasing. The joy in Beatrice's face is beyond description (23.24), and his chastened poetic self, deliberately retreating from the impossibility of describing the unendurable radiance of the sun that manifests Christ, attempts only to suggest its clarity by the comparison of the moon's pure light in a clear sky (25–33). Beatrice, too, is now indescribable, as Dante's noninvocation of Polyhymnia and her sisters makes clear (55–60).

This humbled view of his creative powers had been anticipated in the opening lines of Canto 25, where the poet, clearly speaking from the exile foretold by Cacciaguida, imagines returning to Florence "as a poet" to receive his long overdue reward. Only here, and only in anticipation, does he confer on himself the title of "poeta," a vernacular poet, and by so doing he declares himself the first and sole true poet of the postclassical world.[60]

---

60. For Tavoni, "Il nome di poeta," 571, Dante's use of this term suggests "il sogno di un inaudito alloro poetico volgare." See also Barolini, *Dante's Poets,* 269–77; Brownlee, "Why the Angels Speak Italian," 605–10.

But the claiming of this title is accompanied by a concession: Dante explicitly acknowledges that he is not the sole author of this "sacred" poem, "to which both heaven and earth have set hand" (2). He is truly a poet insofar as he is not only a true disciple of the Poeti and a master "fabbro" in his own right but also God's "scribe" (*Par.* 10.27),[61] authorized like John to "write in a book" what has been revealed to him. The ceremony he anticipates will be less a laureation than a quasi-sacrament, a new baptism that will reconfirm the faith that has already gained him his more significant coronation by Peter (8–12).

The passage, moreover, is not an expression of regret for Dante's banishment, but rather a confirmation of the necessity of exile to his discovery of his true mission. It is in exile, as Cacciaguida had implied, that Dante will learn to speak "con altra voce," the "grido" of the "vox clamantis in deserto." Beatrice expresses the same idea in her curious interruption of St. James, declaring that it has been granted Dante to come "from Egypt to Jerusalem" (25.55–56), and though he must return to the world to complete his mission as a soldier, he will return clad in "altro vello," gray-haired and reconsecrated,[62] to visit wrath on his own Egypt, but also to deliver a message of hope (25.59–60).

The status of the poem itself, a product of human art and so destined to pass from memory, is addressed in Canto 26. Dante's amazement on learning that he is in the presence of Adam is carefully described:

> Come la fronda che flette la cima
>   nel transito del vento, e poi si leva
>   per la propria virtù che la soblima,
> fec' io in tanto in quant' ella diceva.
>   (*Par.* 26.85–88)

---

61. In using this term, which appears only here, Dante is perhaps claiming to have surpassed Alan of Lille who, at the midpoint of his *Anticlaudianus* (5.273), prepares to describe the higher heavens with a prayer in which he declares himself "the pen of the poem, not the scribe or author." See Dronke, *Dante and Medieval Latin,* 8–14.

62. On *vello* as symbolic of Dante's prophetic role (and as having nothing to do with Dante's hair), see Sarolli, "Dante's Katabasis," 92–104.

[As the bough which bends its top at passing of the wind,
and then uplifts itself by its own virtue which raises it,
so did I while she was speaking.]

At the heart of this simile is an allusion to the second *metrum* of Book 3 of Boethius' *Consolatio,* which shows "natura potens" providentially sustaining the life of the universe by imposing the unbreakable bonds of her law. The opening lines of the *metrum* present a straightforward picture of Nature's rule:

Quantas rerum flectat habenas
natura potens, quibus immensum
legibus orbem prouida seruet
stringatque ligans inresoluto
singula nexu . . .
    (*Cons.* 3, *metr.* 2.1–5)

[How powerful Nature plies the reins of creation, by what
laws she sees to the preservation of the universe and draws all
things together, binding them with an unbroken bond . . .]

The power of natural law is then illustrated by the images of captive lions, a caged bird, and a sapling trained to bend downward. In each example the discipline of "natura potens" is illustrated by an artificial constraint, imposed by men and seemingly at odds with the creature's natural impulse toward self-fulfillment. The tree image is the clearest illustration of this:

Validis quondam uiribus acta
pronum flectit uirga cacumen;
hanc si curuans dextra remisit,
recto spectat uertice caelum.
    (*Cons.* 3, *metr.* 2.27–30)

[Compelled by great strength a sapling bends its top
downward; but if the bending hand releases it, it looks
to the sky with head erect.]

The tree which reasserts its inherent impulse to stand erect and "look to the sky" is for both poets an image for self-realization. Dante, uplifted by "la propria virtù," is instinctively responding to the idea of human perfection associated with Adam, and Adam, drawn to recall his "animal" existence in the world,[63] expresses a reciprocal "affetto" (98), the reawakened human impulse perceptible through the light which "covers" him.

Justinian had claimed to see the dual nature of Christ better than Dante could see the contradictory relation of true and false (6.19–21), and Adam's discourse begins with a similar comparison of his own power to read Dante's thoughts to the limited certitude Dante is capable of attaining. Having himself possessed and then lost perfect certitude,[64] Adam understands the limitation of Dante's powers, and he understands as well the Pilgrim's eagerness for knowledge. It is significant that his answer to Dante's several questions begins with a compact definition of the sinful excess to which this eagerness can lead, "il trapassar del segno" (117), which led to his banishment from Eden, a way of denoting the sin of pride which has important implications for Dante himself.

The "segno" can be broadly defined as marking the limits of human possibility. Adam's transgressing of the limit imposed by God to eat of the forbidden fruit had been provoked by a prideful desire to achieve an "excellence," a degree of perfection, beyond the power of flesh and blood to attain.[65] The thirst for knowledge had led Ulysses, here as everywhere a type of Dante, to pass beyond the pillars with which Hercules had

---

63. On the perfection associated with Adam in medieval thought, see Cremona, "*Paradiso* XXVI," 184; Thomas, *Summa theol.* 1.q.94; *Quaest. de veritate* 18.6. "Animal" and "perfection" have already been brought together in Thomas' assertion of God's power to create a being endowed with "tutta l'animal perfezïone" (13.83).

64. Both Augustine, *De libero arbitrio* 3.18, and Thomas, *Summa theol.* 1.94.a.4, consider that unfallen Adam, unlike Dante, could not be deceived as to the truth.

65. See Thomas, *Summa theol.* 2.2.q.163, a.1; also *Eth. nicom.* 1, lec. 18, on relative and absolute "excellence," the former being worthy of "praise," the latter of "honor," a term Dante tends to reserve for artistic excellence, as in *Inf.* 4.72–93. The standard of poetic excellence is of course Vergil, who had noted in *Inf.* 4 that the poets of Limbo "did well" in showing him honor.

signified ("segnò," *Inf.* 26.108) the proper limits of exploration. Dante's completion of Ulysses' voyage has been accomplished through grace, but despite his privileged status he repeatedly indicates his awareness of having sought to push beyond the limits of language in an attempt to record the impact of heavenly glory on his overtaxed sensory powers,[66] to make human "segni" mean more than they can, to achieve a work of greater excellence than that of any previous poet.

The ultimate excellence would be the recovery of the language of Eden, where Adam's every word had an archetypal significance expressive of his perfect knowledge. All the more significant, then, is the meditation on language which Adam now offers. Language, like any human resource, is finite, transitory, changeable *ad placitum,* and to attempt to exceed its limits is to undertake an "ovra inconsummabile" like that of Nimrod (125–26):

> ché 'l uso d'i mortali é come fronda
> in ramo, che sen va e altra vene.
> > *(Par.* 26.137–38)

> [for the usage of mortals is as a leaf on a branch,
> which goes away and another comes.]

The linkage of "fronda" and "ramo" in these lines deserves notice. Earlier in the canto, recalling Boethius, Dante had compared himself, not to a tree, but to a "fronda," a leafy branch. Early in the *Inferno,* on the shores of the Styx, he had tacitly identified himself with a "ramo" in his reworking of Vergil's simile describing the clustered spirits of the damned (*Inf.* 3.112–14).[67] There the bough had lost its leaves; here bough and foliage come together again, only to be separated again by time and the work of nature.

---

66. Moevs, *Metaphysics,* 101–2, emphasizes the sensory aspect of the "trapassar del segno": "To overstep the *segno* is . . . to seek more from the ego and the senses, from finite being, than what they can provide. . . . [T]he illusion that the final fulfillment of desire and understanding can be wrung from the world."

67. See above, chap. 2, pp. 35–36.

The three passages are closely related. The impulse to Adamic "rectitude" illustrated by the Boethian simile is the fair-haired sister of the vicarious submission to Vergilian damnation on the shores of the Styx. Each in its way implies a kind of poetic overreaching, and in the lines just quoted the two together are gently chastised by the Horatian reminder that language, too, decays, the new continually replacing the old (*Ars poetica* 60–62). Horace notes also that the old can be reborn, but we have learned that this can happen only insofar as it is appropriated to new purposes, released from "long silence" by a new voice. There could hardly be a better confirmation of this than Dante's own triumphant use of the *volgare,* and while Horace's Latin voice, speaking to the ages, is clearly audible under the vernacular surface of Dante's lines, reminding us that the voice of Dante, too, will one day be silenced, it is Vergil who is plainly implicated. "Virgilio," named for the last time in the *Commedia* by Adam, is rhymed with "essilio," as by Vergil himself on meeting Statius (*Purg.* 21.14–18),[68] and his Limbo, like all of hell, is finally a place of mourning ("ambascia," 133). "We are owed to death, we and all that is ours," Horace says (*Ars* 63); even the fame of the heroes and authors enshrined in Limbo will fade as new "magnanimi" displace the old in cultural memory.

After these strongly elegiac reflections, the few brief classical references in Canto 27 add a further note of finality. The bizarre simile which indicates how anger has reddened the face of Peter (13–15) is more confusing than illuminating, and it seems almost a redundant afterthought. To imagine Jove and Mars, first as birds, then as exchanging plumage (27.13–15), is to rob the classical pantheon, and perhaps the universe itself, of inherent meaning, to reduce them to images almost arbitrarily chosen from a conventional repertory. It is as if ancient poetry were being deliberately mocked. In Canto 29 we will see a more coherent but similarly reductive reference to the planetary gods, as "the two children of Latona," and a complex, precise description of the vernal equinox

---

68. See Brownlee, "Language and Desire," 53–54, who notes that Vergil as *autore* and his almost sacred "volume" (*Inf.* 1.84–85) have been displaced by the "verace autore" (26.40) and the "volume" that contains the universe (33.86).

become a figure for Beatrice's momentary glance at the point of light which manifests God.[69]

Later in the present canto, prompted by Beatrice, Dante gazes downward into the world,

> sì ch'io vedea di là da Gade il varco
> folle d'Ulisse, e di qua presso il lito
> nel qual si fece Europa dolce carco.
> (*Par.* 27.82–84)

[so that, on the one hand, beyond Cadiz, I saw the mad track of Ulysses, and on the other nearly to the shore where Europa made herself a sweet burden.]

A great deal of mythic history is distilled in these emblematic figures: the finally futile enterprise of the Homeric hero; the divine rape which caused the westward journey of Cadmus, the founding of Thebes, and in effect the first involvement of Europe in world history. Dante's vantage point, as he reminds us, is the sign of the Gemini, "the nest of Leda" (98). From Leda's ravishment by Jove were born not only Castor and Pollux but also Helen and Clytemnestra—or in Yeats' terse summary, "Troy's broken wall, and Agamemnon dead."

All of this is finally framed by the lines that register Dante's inability to retain his final vision:

> Un punto solo m'è maggior letargo
> che venticinque secoli a la 'mpresa
> che fé Nettuno ammirar l'ombra d'Argo.
> (*Par.* 33.94–96)

---

69. The sun and moon, positioned for an instant precisely on opposite sides of the earth, are the essential elements of the simile, and Dante's naming of Latona, rather than Apollo and Diana, is perhaps intended to screen out literary associations and restrict them to their cosmic function, in a simile which aims to show the instantaneity of Beatrice's glance. See Payton, "*Paradiso* XXIX," 438–39; and for the larger, transitional significance of the simile, Moevs, *Metaphysics,* 151–60.

[A single moment makes for me greater oblivion than five and twenty centuries have wrought upon the enterprise that made Neptune wonder at the shadow of the Argo.]

With the naming of the Argo, Dante's final historical vision is complete. The voyage of the Argo and the final voyage of Ulysses represent the beginning and end of pre-Roman, mythic history as transmitted by the Poeti. In spanning the ages and linking himself to the Argonauts, Dante is declaring his own poem a radically new departure, one that could have been imagined only in a dim and shadowy form by ancient poetry, here emblematized by the wondering gaze of Neptune.[70] But Neptune's perspective is also Dante's, insofar as he remains the mortal man and poet who must redescend into the world, preserving only a remote and dreamlike version of his visionary experience.[71] To the end, poetry, the universe of the Poeti, remains, like being itself, a "gran mar," mirroring the unfathomable depth of God, and it remains the element in which Dante's poet-self will always have his being.

70. On Jason's voyage as a prefiguring of Dante's, see Hollander, *Allegory*, 220–32. Brownlee, "Jason's Voyage," 172, notes that these lines recall *Roman de la Rose* 9501–516. But Dante has replaced the rage of Jean de Meun's Neptune with wonder.

71. As Hollander observes, *Allegory*, 227, Dante's journey is over. "In the midst of his description of the Godhead he has become the Poet, has finished being the Pilgrim." See also Freccero, *Poetics*, 219.

Bibliography

A Note on Texts

All quotations from the *Commedia* are from the edition of Charles Singleton (6 vols.; Princeton: Princeton University Press, 1970–75). My text for Vergil is the edition of R. A. B. Mynors (Oxford: Oxford University Press, 1972); for Ovid's *Metamorphoses*, that of W. S. Anderson (Leipzig: Teubner, 1977); for Lucan, that of Abel Bourgery, revised by Paul Jal (2 vols.; Paris: "Les Belles Lettres," 1997); for the *Thebaid* of Statius, that of Alfred Klotz, revised by Thomas C. Klinnert (Leipzig: Teubner, 1973). The translations of passages from the *Commedia* are Singleton's. Those from the Latin poets and other texts are my own.

Other Works Cited

I. Works of Dante

Commedia secondo l'antica vulgata. Edited by Giorgio Petrocchi. 2 vols. Milan: Società dantesca italiana, 1966–67.
Divina Commedia. Edited by Umberto Bosco and Giovanni Reggio. 3 vols. Florence: F. Le Monnier, 1982–83.
Divina Commedia. Edited by Carlo Grabher. Milan-Messina: Giuseppe Principato, 1966.
Divine Comedy. Edited and translated by Robert Durling and Ronald Martinez. Vol. 1, *Inferno*; vol. 2, *Purgatorio*. New York: Oxford University Press, 1996, 2003.
Divine Comedy. Edited and translated by Mark Musa. 6 vols. Bloomington: Indiana University Press, 1995–2004.
Divine Comedy. Edited and translated by John D. Sinclair. 3 vols. Oxford: Oxford University Press, 1939.

Inferno. Edited by Robert Hollander, translated by Robert Hollander and Jean Hollander. New York: Doubleday, 2000.

Purgatorio. Edited by Robert Hollander, translated by Robert Hollander and Jean Hollander. New York: Doubleday, 2003.

Convivio. Edited by Cesare Vasoli. In Dante Alighieri, *Opere minori*, vol. 1.2. Milan-Naples: Ricciardi, 1988.

De vulgari eloquentia. Edited by Pier Vincenzo Mengaldo. In Dante Alighieri, *Opere minori*, vol. 2, 3–237. Milan-Naples: Ricciardi, 1979.

Epistole. Edited by Arsenio Frugoni and Giorgio Brugnoli. In Dante Alighieri, *Opere minori*, vol. 2, 507–643. Milan-Naples: Ricciardi, 1979.

Monarchia. Edited by Bruno Nardi. In Dante Alighieri, *Opere minori*, vol. 2, 241–503. Milan-Naples: Ricciardi, 1979.

Vita nuova. Edited by Domenico de Robertis. In Dante Alighieri, *Opere minori*, vol. 1.1, 3–247. Milan-Naples: Ricciardi, 1984.

II. Primary Sources

Abelard, Peter. *Historia calamitatum.* Edited by Jacques Monfrin. Paris: J. Vrin, 1959.

Alain de Lille. *Anticlaudianus.* Edited by Robert Bossuat. Paris: J. Vrin, 1955.

Boccaccio, Giovanni. *Esposizioni sopra il Dante.* Edited by Giorgio Padoan. Tutte le opere di Giovanni Boccaccio, vol. 6. Padua: Mondadori, 1959.

———. *Lettere edite ed inedite.* Edited by Francesco Corazzini. Florence: Sansoni, 1877.

Boethius. *Consolatio Philosophiae.* Edited by Ludwig Bieler. Corpus Christianorum 94. Turnhout: Brepols, 1957.

Cicero. *Somnium Scipionis.* Edited by James Willis. Macrobius, *Opera*, vol. 2, 155–63. Leipzig: Teubner, 1963.

Eneas. Edited by J.-J. Salverda de Grave. 2 vols. Paris: Honoré Champion, 1964–68.

Fulgentius. *Mitologiae.* Edited by Rudolph Halm. In Fulgentius, *Opera*, 3–80. Leipzig: Teubner, 1898.

John of Garland. *Integumenta Ovidii.* Edited by Fausto Ghisalberti. Messina: Giuseppe Principato, 1933.

Scriptores rerum mythicarum. Edited by G. H. Bode. 2 vols. Hildesheim: George Olms, 1968.

Servius. *Commentary on Vergil.* Edited by Georg Thilo and Hermann Hagen. 3 vols. in 4. Leipzig: Teubner, 1881–1902.

Super Thebaidem. Edited by Rudolph Halm. In Fulgentius, *Opera*, 180–86. Leipzig: Teubner, 1898.

Villani, Giovanni. *Nuova cronica.* Edited by Giuseppe Porta. Parma: U. Guanda, 1990.

III. *Secondary Sources*

Note: Where an essay has been printed more than once, I have normally cited only the most recent, or what I take to be the most readily available printing. When a book has appeared in more than one edition I cite only the most recent edition.

Ahl, Frederick M. *Lucan: An Introduction.* Ithaca: Cornell University Press, 1976.

Aricò, Giuseppe. *Ricerche Staziane.* Palermo: Grafiche Cappugi, 1972.

Armour, Peter. "Brunetto, the Stoic Pessimist." *Dante Studies* 112 (1994): 1–18.

Arnold, Matthew. "The Study of Poetry." In Arnold, *Essays in Criticism: Second Series*, 1–55. London: MacMillan, 1888.

Auerbach, Erich. *Dante, Poet of the Secular World.* Translated by Ralph Mannheim. Chicago: University of Chicago Press, 1961.

———. "'Figura.'" In Auerbach, *Scenes from the Drama of European Literature*, 1–76. Minneapolis: University of Minnesota Press, 1984.

Balducci, M. A. *Classicismo dantesco: Miti e simboli della morte e della vita nella Divina Commedia.* Florence: Le Lettere, 2004.

Ball, Robert. "Theological Semantics: Virgil's *Pietas* and Dante's *Pieta*." In *The Poetry of Allusion: Virgil and Ovid in Dante's "Commedia,"* edited by Rachel Jacoff and Jeffrey Schnapp, 19–36, 249–58. Stanford: Stanford University Press, 1991.

Barchiesi, Marino. "Catarsi classica e 'medicina dantesca' (dal canto XX dell'Inferno)." *Letture Classensi* 4 (1973): 11–124.

Barański, Zygmunt G. "Structural Retrospection in Dante's *Comedy*." *Italian Studies* 41 (1986): 1–23.

———. "*Paradiso* XIX." In *Lectura Dantis Virginiana* I. Dante's *Inferno*: Introductory Readings, 277–99. *Lectura Dantis* 6: Supplement, 1992.

———, ed. *Seminario Dantesco Internazionale—International Dante Seminar 1.* Società Dantesca Italiana, Quaderno 7. Florence: Società Dantesca Italiana, 1997.

Barkan, Leonard. *The Gods Made Flesh: Metamorphosis and the Pursuit of Paganism.* New Haven: Yale University Press, 1986.

Barolini, Teodolinda. *Dante's Poets: Textuality and Truth in the "Comedy."* Princeton: Princeton University Press, 1984.

———. "Arachne, Argus, and St. John: Transgressive Art in Dante and Ovid." *Medievalia* 13 (1989): 207–26.

———. *The undivine Comedy: Detheologizing Dante.* Princeton: Princeton University Press, 1992.

Bec, Pierre. "La douleur et son univers poétique chez Bernard de Ventadour." *Cahiers de civilization médiévale* 11 (1968): 545–71; 12 (1969): 25–33.

Biow, Douglas. "From Ignorance to Knowledge: The Marvellous in *Inferno* 13." In *The Poetry of Allusion: Virgil and Ovid in Dante's "Commedia."* Edited by

Rachel Jacoff and Jeffrey Schnapp, 45–61, 261–64. Stanford: Stanford University Press, 1991.

Boitani, Piero. *L'ombra di Ulisse: Figure di un mito.* Bologna: Il Mulino, 1992.

Bon, Cristina. "Lucano all'*Inferno.*" In *La Divina foresta: Studi danteschi,* edited by Francesco Spera, 71–104. Naples: M. d'Auria, 2006.

Bono, Barbara J. *Literary Transvaluation from Vergilian Epic to Shakespearean Tragicomedy.* Berkeley: University of California Press, 1984.

Borges, Jorge Luis. "El falso problema de Ugolino." In *Nueve ensayos dantescos,* 29–34. Madrid: Alianza Editorial, 1982. Translated by Nicoletta Alegi in *Critical Essays on Dante,* 185–88, edited by Giuseppe Mazzotta. Boston: Twayne, 1991.

Boswell, John E. "Dante and the Sodomites." *Dante Studies* 112 (1994): 63–76.

Botterill, Stephen. "*Inferno* XII." In *Lectura Dantis Virginiana* I. Dante's *Inferno:* Introductory Readings, 149–62. *Lectura Dantis* 6: Supplement, 1992.

Boyde, Patrick. "*Inferno* XIII." In *Cambridge Readings in Dante's "Comedy,"* edited by Kenelm Foster and Patrick Boyde, 1–22. Cambridge: Cambridge University Press, 1981.

———. *Dante Philomythes and Philosopher: Man in the Cosmos.* Cambridge: Cambridge University Press, 1981.

Brooks, R. A. "*Discolor Aura*: Reflections on the Golden Bough." *American Journal of Philology* 74 (1953): 260–80.

Brownlee, Kevin. "Why the Angels Speak Italian: Dante as Vernacular *Poeta* in *Paradiso* XXV." *Poetics Today* 5 (1984): 597–610.

———. "Language and Desire in *Paradiso* XXVI." *Lectura Dantis* 6 (1990): 47–59.

———. "Pauline Vision and Ovidian Speech in *Paradiso* 1." In *The Poetry of Allusion: Virgil and Ovid in Dante's "Commedia,"* edited by Rachel Jacoff and Jeffrey Schnapp, 202–13, 286–89. Stanford: Stanford University Press, 1991.

———. "Jason's Voyage and the Poetics of Rewriting: The *Fiore* and the *Roman de la Rose.*" In *The Fiore in Context: Dante, France, Tuscany,* edited by Zygmunt G. Barański and Patrick Boyde, 167–84. Notre Dame: University of Notre Dame Press, 1997.

Burgess, John F. "Statius' Altar of Mercy." *Classical Quarterly,* n.s. 22 (1972): 339–49.

Caviglia, Francesco. "Appunti sulla presenza di Stazio nella *Commedia.*" *Rivista di cultura classica e medievale* 16 (1974): 267–79.

Cestaro, Gary P. *Dante and the Grammar of the Nursing Body.* Notre Dame: University of Notre Dame Press, 2003.

Charity, A. C. *Events and Their Afterlife: The Dialectics of Christian Typology in the Bible and in Dante.* Cambridge: Cambridge University Press, 1966.

Chiarenza, Marguerite. "Hippolytus' Exile: *Paradiso* XVII, vv. 46–48." *Dante Studies* 84 (1966): 65–68.

———. "Time and Eternity in the Myths of *Paradiso* XVII." In *Dante, Petrarch, Boccaccio: Studies in the Italian Trecento in Honor of Charles S. Singleton*, edited by Aldo S. Bernardo and Anthony L. Pellegrini, 133–50. Binghamton, NY: Center for Medieval and Early Renaissance Studies, State University of New York at Binghamton, 1983.

———. "*Paradiso* XX." In *Lectura Dantis Virginiana* III. Dante's *Paradiso*: Introductory Readings, 300–307. *Lectura Dantis* 16–17, 1995.

Cioffi, Caron. "'Il cantor de' bucolici carmi': The Influence of Virgilian Pastoral on Dante's Depiction of the Earthly Paradise." In *Lectura Dantis Newberryana* 1, edited by Paolo Cherchi and Antonio Mastrobuono, 93–22. Evanston, IL: Northwestern University Press, 1988.

———. "The Anxieties of Ovidian Influence: Theft in *Inferno* XXIV and XXV." *Dante Studies* 112 (1994): 77–100.

Clay, Diskin. "The Metamorphosis of Ovid in Dante's *Commedia*." In *Dante: Mito e Poesia. Atti del secondo Seminario dantesco internazionale (Ascona, 1997)*, edited by Michelangelo Picone and Tatiana Crivelli, 69–85. Florence: F. Cesati, 1999.

Comparetti, Domenico. *Vergil in the Middle Ages*. Translated by F. M. Benecke. Princeton: Princeton University Press, 1997.

Consoli, Domenico. *Significato del Virgilio Dantesco*. Florence: Le Monnier, 1967.

Conte, Gian Biagio. *The Rhetoric of Imitation: Genre and Poetic Memory in Virgil and Other Latin Poets*. Ithaca: Cornell University Press, 1986.

Contini, Gianfranco. "Alcuni appunti su *Purgatorio* 27." In Contini, *Un'idea di Dante: Saggi Danteschi*, 171–90. Turin: G. Einaudi, 1976.

Cremona, Joseph. "*Paradiso* XXVI." In *Cambridge Readings in Dante's "Comedy,"* edited by Kenelm Foster and Patrick Boyde, 174–90. Cambridge: Cambridge University Press, 1981.

Danese, Roberto M. "L'anticosmo di Eritto e il capovolgimento dell'Inferno virgiliano (Lucano, *Phars.* 6, 333 sgg.)." *Atti della Accademia Nazionale dei Lincei: Memorie,* ser. 9, vol. 3 (1992): 197–265.

Davis, Charles T. *Dante and the Idea of Rome*. Oxford: Oxford University Press, 1957.

de Angelis, Violetta. ". . . e l'ultimo Lucano." In *Dante e la "bella scola" della poesia: Autorità e sfida poetica*, edited by Amilcare A. Iannucci, 145–203. Ravenna: Longo, 1993.

———. "Il testo di Lucano, Dante e Petrarca." In *Seminario Dantesco Internazionale—International Dante Seminar* 1, edited by Zygmunt G. Barański, 67–109. Società Dantesca Italiana, Quaderno 7. Florence: Società Dantesca Italiana, 1997.

de Fazio, Marina. "*Purgatorio* XXIX." In *Lectura Dantis Virginiana* II. Dante's *Purgatorio*: Introductory Readings, 433–47. *Lectura Dantis* 12: Supplement, 1993.

della Coletta, Cristina. "*Paradiso* XV." In *Lectura Dantis Virginiana* II. Dante's *Purgatorio*: Introductory Readings, 213–28. *Lectura Dantis* 12: Supplement, 1993.

Dewar, Michael. "*Siquid habent ueri uatum praesagia:* Ovid in the 1st–5th Centuries A.D." In *Brill's Companion to Ovid,* edited by Barbara W. Boyd, 383–412. Leiden: Brill, 2002.

Dotti, Ugo. *La Divina Commedia e la città dell'uomo: Introduzione alla lettura di Dante.* Rome: Donzelli, 1996.

Dragonetti, Roger. *Dante, pèlerin de la Sainte Face.* Ghent: Romanica Gandensia, 1968.

Dronke, Peter. *Fabula: Explorations into the Uses of Myth in Medieval Platonism.* Leiden: Brill, 1974.

———. *Dante and Medieval Latin Traditions.* Cambridge: Cambridge University Press, 1986.

Durling, Robert, and Ronald Martinez. *Time and the Crystal: Studies in Dante's "Rime Petrose."* Berkeley: University of California Press, 1990.

Eliot, T. S. "Tradition and the Individual Talent." In Eliot, *Selected Essays,* 1–32. London: Faber, 1951.

Enciclopedia dantesca. 5 vols. Rome: Istituto della Enciclopedia italiana, 1970–78.

Enterline, Lynn. *The Rhetoric of the Body from Ovid to Shakespeare.* Cambridge: Cambridge University Press, 2000.

Farrell, Joseph. *Vergil's Georgics and the Traditions of Ancient Epic.* New York: Oxford University Press, 1991.

Feeney, D. C. "History and Revelation in Virgil's Underworld." *Proceedings of the Cambridge Philological Society* 32 (1986): 1–24.

Ferrante, Joan. *The Political Vision of the "Divine Comedy."* Princeton: Princeton University Press, 1984.

Ford, Andrew. *Homer: The Poetry of the Past.* Ithaca: Cornell University Press, 1992.

Foster, Kenelm. *The Two Dantes.* Berkeley: University of California Press, 1977.

———. "Tommaso d'Aquino." In *Enciclopedia dantesca,* vol. 5, 626–49.

Foster, Kenelm, and Patrick Boyde, eds. *Cambridge Readings in Dante's "Comedy."* Cambridge: Cambridge University Press, 1981.

Fraenkel, Hermann. *Ovid: A Poet between Two Worlds.* Berkeley: University of California Press, 1945.

Franchet d'Espèrey, Silvie. *Conflit, violence et non-violence dans la 'Tébaide' de Stace.* Paris: "Belles Lettres," 1999.

Franke, William. *Dante's Interpretive Journey.* Chicago: University of Chicago Press, 1996.

Freccero, John. *The Poetics of Conversion.* Edited by Rachel Jacoff. Cambridge, MA: Harvard University Press, 1986.

Frings, Irene. "Hypsipyle und Aeneas: Zur Vergilimitation in Thebais 5." In *EPICEDION: Hommage a P. Papinius Statius, 96–1996,* edited by Fernand Delarue, 145–60. Poitiers: La Licorne, 1996.

Fubini, Mario. "Catone." In *Enciclopedia dantesca,* vol. 1, 879–81.

Gadamer, Hans-Georg. *Truth and Method.* 2d ed. Translated by Joel Weinsheimer and Donald G. Marshall. New York: Continuum, 1996.

Galinsky, G. Karl. *Ovid's Metamorphoses: An Introduction to the Basic Aspects.* Oxford: Blackwell, 1975.

Ginsberg, Warren. *Dante's Aesthetics of Being.* Ann Arbor: University of Michigan Press, 1999.

Goar, Robert J. *The Legend of Cato Uticensis from the First Century B.C. to the Fifth Century A.D.: With an appendix on Dante and Cato.* Brussels: Latomus, 1987.

Gruen, Erich S. *The Last Generation of the Roman Republic.* Berkeley: University of California Press, 1974.

Hardie, Philip. *The Epic Successors of Virgil: A Study in the Dynamics of a Tradition.* Cambridge: Cambridge University Press, 1993.

Havely, Nick. "Brunetto and Palinurus." *Dante Studies* 108 (1990): 29–38.

Hawkins, Peter S. "Dido, Beatrice, and the Signs of Ancient Love." In *The Poetry of Allusion: Virgil and Ovid in Dante's "Commedia,"* edited by Rachel Jacoff and Jeffrey Schnapps, 113–30, 274–76. Stanford: Stanford University Press, 1991.

———. *Dante's Testaments: Essays in Scriptural Imagination.* Stanford: Stanford University Press, 1999.

———. "'Are You Here?' Surprise in the *Commedia*." In *Sparks and Seeds: Medieval Literature and Its Afterlife. Essays in Honor of John Freccero,* edited by Dana E. Stewart and Alison Cornish, 175–97. Turnhout: Brepols, 2000.

Hollander, Robert. "Dante's Use of *Aeneid* I in *Inferno* I and II." *Comparative Literature* 20 (1968): 142–56.

———. *Allegory in Dante's "Commedia."* Princeton: Princeton University Press, 1969.

———. "The Tragedy of the Diviners." In Hollander, *Studies in Dante,* 131–218. Ravenna: Longo, 1980.

———. *Il Virgilio dantesco: Tragedia nella "Commedia."* Florence: L. S. Olschki, 1983.

———. "Le opere di Virgilio nella *Commedia*." In *Dante e la "bella scola" della poesia: Autorità e sfida poetica,* edited by Amilcare A. Iannucci, 247–343. Ravenna: Longo, 1993.

Hopkins, David. "Dryden and Ovid's 'Wit out of Season.'" In *Ovid Renewed: Ovidian Influences on Literature and Art from the Middle Ages to the Twentieth Century,* edited by Charles Martindale, 167–90. Cambridge: Cambridge University Press, 1988.

Iannucci, Amilcare A., ed. *Dante e la "bella scola" della poesia: Autorità e sfida poetica.* Ravenna: Longo, 1993.

Jacoff, Rachel. "Intertextualities in Arcadia: *Purgatorio* 30.49–51." In *The Poetry of Allusion: Virgil and Ovid in Dante's "Commedia,"* edited by Rachel Jacoff and Jeffrey Schnapp, 131–44, 276–78. Stanford: Stanford University Press, 1991.

———. "The Rape/Rapture of Europa: *Paradiso* 27." In *The Poetry of Allusion: Virgil and Ovid in Dante's "Commedia,"* edited by Rachel Jacoff and Jeffrey Schnapp, 233–46, 294–95. Stanford: Stanford University Press, 1991.

————. ed. *The Cambridge Companion to Dante.* Cambridge: Cambridge University Press, 1993.

Jacoff, Rachel, and Jeffrey T. Schnapp, eds. *The Poetry of Allusion: Virgil and Ovid in Dante's "Commedia."* Stanford: Stanford University Press, 1991.

Johnson, W. R. "The Problem of the Counter-classical Sensibility and Its Critics." *California Studies in Classical Antiquity* 3 (1970): 123–52.

————. *Darkness Visible: A Study of Vergil's Aeneid.* Berkeley: University of California Press, 1976.

————. *Momentary Monsters: Lucan and His Heroes.* Ithaca: Cornell University Press, 1987.

Kay, Richard. "The Sin(s) of Brunetto Latini." *Dante Studies* 112 (1994): 19–31.

Kennedy, William J. *Authorizing Petrarch.* Ithaca: Cornell University Press, 1994.

Kirkpatrick, Robin. *Dante's "Inferno": Difficulty and Dead Poetry.* Cambridge: Cambridge University Press, 1987.

Kirkham, Victoria. "*Purgatorio* XXVIII." In *Lectura Dantis Virginiana* II. Dante's *Purgatorio*: Introductory Readings, 411–32. *Lectura Dantis* 12: Supplement, 1993.

Kleiner, John. *Mismapping the Underworld: Daring and Error in Dante's "Comedy."* Stanford: Stanford University Press, 1994.

————. "On Failing One's Teachers: Dante, Virgil, and the Ironies of Instruction." In *Sparks and Seeds: Medieval Literature and Its Afterlife. Essays in Honor of John Freccero,* edited by Dana E. Stewart and Alison Cornish, 61–74. Turnhout: Brepols, 2000.

Koffler, Richard. "The Last Wound: *Purgatorio* XXVI." *Italian Quarterly* 12 (1968): 27–43.

Lectura Dantis Virginiana I. Dante's *Inferno*: Introductory Readings. *Lectura Dantis* 6: Supplement, 1992.

Lectura Dantis Virginiana II. Dante's *Purgatorio*: Introductory Readings. *Lectura Dantis* 12: Supplement, 1993.

Lectura Dantis Virginiana III. Dante's *Paradiso*: Introductory Readings. *Lectura Dantis* 16–17, 1995.

Leigh, Matthew. *Lucan: Spectacle and Engagement.* Oxford: Oxford University Press, 1997.

Lewis, C. S. "Dante's Statius." *Medium Aevum* 25 (1956): 133–39.

Macfie, Pamela Royston. "Ovid, Arachne, and the Poetics of Paradise." In *The Poetry of Allusion: Virgil and Ovid in Dante's "Commedia,"* edited by Rachel Jacoff and Jeffrey Schnapp, 159–72, 280–82. Stanford: Stanford University Press, 1991.

Marder, Elissa. "Disarticulated Voices: Feminism and Philomela." *Hypatia* 7 (1992): 148–66.

Mariotti, Scevola. *Scritti medievali e umanistici.* Rome: Edizioni di Storia e Letteratura, 1976.

Marti, Mario. "Il canto XXVI del 'Purgatorio.'" In *Purgatorio: Letture degli anni 1976–'79,* 601–25. Rome: Casa di Dante in Roma, 1981.

Martinez, Ronald. "The Pilgrim's Answer to Bonagiunta and the Poetics of the Spirit." *Stanford Italian Review* 3 (1983): 327–63.

———. "La 'sacra fame dell'oro' ('Purgatorio' 22,41) tra Virgilio e Stazio: Dal testo all'interpretazione." *Letture Classensi* 18 (1989): 177–93.

———. "Dante and the Two Canons: Statius in Virgil's Fopotsteps." *Comparative Literature Studies* 32 (1995): 151–75.

———. "Lament and Lamentations in *Purgatorio* and the Case of Dante's Statius." *Dante Studies* 115 (1997): 45–88.

Masters, Jamie. *Poetry and Civil War in Lucan's Bellum Civile.* Cambridge: Cambridge University Press, 1992.

Mazzotta, Giuseppe. *Dante, Poet of the Desert.* Princeton: Princeton University Press, 1979.

———. *Dante's Vision and the Circle of Knowledge.* Princeton: Princeton University Press, 1993.

———. *The Worlds of Petrarch.* Duke Monographs in Medieval and Renaissance Studies 14. Durham, NC: Duke University Press, 1993.

Miller, Mark. *Philosophical Chaucer: Love, Sex, and Agency in the Canterbury Tales.* Cambridge: Cambridge Univesity Press, 2004.

Moevs, Christian. *The Metaphysics of Dante's "Comedy."* New York: Oxford University Press, 2005.

Momigliano, Attilio. *Dante, Manzoni, Verga.* Messina: G. d'Anna, 1955.

Moos, Peter von. "*Poeta* und *historicus* im Mittelalter. Zum mimesis Problem an Beispiel einiger Urteile über Lucan." *Beitrage zur Geschichte der Deutschen Sprache und Literatur* 98 (1976): 93–130.

Morford, M. P. O. *The Poet Lucan.* Oxford: Oxford University Press, 1967.

Musa, Mark. *Advent at the Gates: Dante's Comedy.* Bloomington: Indiana University Press, 1974.

Nardi, Bruno. *Studi di filosofia medievale.* Rome: Edizioni di Storia e Letteratura, 1960.

Narducci, Emauele. *La provvidenza crudele: Lucano e la distruzione dei miti augustei.* Pisa: Giardini, 1979.

O'Hara, James J. *Death and the Optimistic Prophecy in Virgil's Aeneid.* Princeton: Princeton University Press, 1990.

Padoan, Giorgio. "Il canto III dell' 'Inferno,'" *Nuove letture dantesche* 2 (1968): 47–103.

———. "Il canto XXI del 'Purgatorio.'" *Nuove letture dantesche* 4 (1970): 327–54.

———. "Teseo 'figura Redemptoris' e il cristianesimo di Stazio." In Padoan, *Il pio Enea, l'impio Ulisse: Tradizione classica e intendimento medievale in Dante,* 125–50. Ravenna: Longo, 1977.

———. "Ulisse 'fandi fictor' e le vi della sapienza." In Padoan, *Il pio Enea, l'impio Ulisse: Tradizione classica e intendimento medievale in Dante,* 170–99. Ravenna: Longo, 1977.

Paratore, Ettore. *Antico e nuovo.* Rome: S. Sciascia, 1965.

————. "Ovidio." Enciclopedia dantesca, vol. 4, 226–36.

————. "Canto III." In Lectura Dantis Neapolitana: Inferno, edited by Pompeo Giannantonio, 27–43. Naples: Loffredo, 1986.

Pasquazi, Silvio. "Virgilio." Enciclopedia dantesca, vol. 5, 1030–49.

Payton, Rodney. "Paradiso XXIX." In Lectura Dantis Virginiana III. Dante's Paradiso: Introductory Readings, 435–55. Lectura Dantis 16–17, 1995.

Pease, A. S., ed. Publi Vergili Maronis Aeneidos Liber Quartus. Darmstadt: Wissenschaftliche Buchgesellschaft, 1967.

Pertile, Lino. "Purgatorio XXVI." In Lectura Dantis Virginiana II. Dante's Purgatorio: Introductory Readings, 380–97. Lectura Dantis 12: Supplement, 1993.

————. "Paradiso IV." In Lectura Dantis Virginiana III. Dante's Paradiso: Introductory Readings, 46–67. Lectura Dantis 16–17, 1995.

Pézard, André. "Rencontres de Dante et de Stace." Bibliothèque d'humanisme et renaissance 14 (1952): 10–28.

Picone, Michelangelo. "Purgatorio XXVII: Passaggio rituale e translatio poetica." Medioevo romanzo 12 (1982): 389–402.

————. "Dante argonauta: La ricezione dei miti ovidiani nella Commedia." In Ovidius redivivus: Von Ovid zu Dante, edited by Michelangelo Picone, Bernhard Zimmermann, 173–204. Stuttgart: M & P, 1994.

————. "Dante, Ovidio, e la poesia dell'esilio." Rassegna europea di letteratura italiana 14 (1999): 7–23.

————. "Dante e i miti." In Dante: Mito e Poesia. Atti del secondo Seminario dantesco internazionale (Ascona, 1997), edited by Michelangelo Picone and Tatiana Crivelli, 211–32. Florence: F. Cesati, 1999.

————. "Canto XXVI." In Lectura Dantis Turicensis: Inferno, edited by Georges Güntert and Michelangelo Picone, 359–73. Florence: F. Cesati, 2001.

————. "Canto XIX." In Lectura Dantis Turicensis: Purgatorio, edited by Georges Güntert and Michelangelo Picone, 287–306. Florence: F. Cesati, 2001.

Picone, Michelangelo, and Tatiana Crivelli, eds. Dante: Mito e Poesia. Atti del secondo Seminario dantesco internazionale (Ascona, 1997). Florence: F. Cesati, 1999.

Pucci, Joseph. The Full-Knowing Reader: Allusion and the Power of the Reader in the Western Literary Tradition. New Haven: Yale University Press, 1998.

Purgatorio: Letture degli anni 1976–'79. Rome: Casa di Dante in Roma, 1981.

Putnam, Michael, The Poetry of the Aeneid. Ithaca: Cornell University Press, 1965.

————. "Virgil's Inferno." In The Poetry of Allusion: Virgil and Ovid in Dante's "Commedia," edited by Rachel Jacoff and Jeffrey Schnapp, 94–112, 270–74. Stanford: Stanford University Press, 1991.

Quint, David. "Epic Tradition and Inferno IX." Dante Studies 93 (1975): 201–7.

Richlin, Amy, "Reading Ovid's Rapes." In Pornography and Representation in Greece and Rome, edited by Amy Richlin, 158–79. New York: Oxford University Press, 1992.

Rigo, Paola. Memoria classica e memoria biblica in Dante. Florence: L. S. Olschki, 1994.

Robson, C. A. "Dante's Use in the *Divine Comedy* of the Medieval Allegories on Ovid." In *Centenary Essays on Dante by Members of the Oxford Dante Society,* 1–38. Oxford: Oxford University Press, 1965.

Ronconi, Alessandro. *Filología e linguistica.* Rome: Edizioni dell'Ateneo, 1968.

Sabbatino, Pasquale. *L'Eden della nuova poesia: Saggi sulla "Divina commedia."* Florence: L. S. Olschki, 1991.

Sanguineti, Eduardo. *Dante reazionario.* Rome: Editori Riuniti, 1992.

Sarolli, Gian Roberto. "Dante's Katabasis and Mission." In *The World of Dante: Six Studies in Language and Thought,* edited by S. Bernard Chandler and J. A. Molinaro, 80–116. Toronto: University of Toronto Press, 1966.

Savarese, Gennaro. "Dante e il mestiere di poeta (Intorno al XXVI del *Purgatorio*)." *Rassegna della letteratura italiana* 90 (1986): 365–81.

Scarry, Elaine. *The Body in Pain: The Making and Unmaking of the World.* New York: Oxford University Press, 1985.

Schnapp, Jeffrey T. *The Transfiguration of History at the Center of Dante's "Paradise."* Princeton: Princeton University Press, 1986.

———. "Dante's Ovidian Self-Correction in *Paradiso* 17." In *The Poetry of Allusion: Virgil and Ovid in Dante's "Commedia,"* edited by Rachel Jacoff and Jeffrey Schnapp, 214–23, 289–93. Stanford: Stanford University Press, 1991.

———. "Lucanian Estimations." In *Seminario Dantesco Internazionale—International Dante Seminar* 1, edited by Zygmunt G. Barański, 111–34. Società Dantesca Italiana, Quaderno 7. Florence: Società Dantesca Italiana, 1997.

Scott, John A. *Dante's Political Purgatory.* Philadelphia: University of Pennsylvania Press, 1996.

Scrivano, Riccardo. "Il Canto XXX del 'Purgatorio.'" In *Purgatorio: Letture degli anni 1976–'79,* 695–721. Rome: Casa di Dante in Roma, 1981.

———. "Stazio personaggio, poeta e cristiano." *Quaderni d'Italianistica* 13 (1992): 175–97.

Scullard, H. H. *From the Gracchi to Nero: A History of Rome from 133 B.C. to A.D. 68.* New York: Routledge, 1988.

Segal, Charles. *Landscape in Ovid's Metamorphoses: A Study in the Transformation of a Literary Symbol.* Hermes: Einzelschriften 23. Wiesbaden: F. Steiner Verlag, 1969.

Sinclair, John D., ed. *Divine Comedy.* Vol 1. *Inferno.* Oxford: Oxford University Press, 1939.

Solodow, Joseph B. *The World of Ovid's "Metamorphoses."* Chapel Hill: University of North Carolina Press, 1988.

Spillenger, Paul. "*Purgatorio* IX." In *Lectura Dantis Virginiana* II. Dante's *Purgatorio*: Introductory Readings, 128–41. *Lectura Dantis* 12: Supplement, 1993.

Spitzer, Leo. "The Farcical Elements in *Inferno,* Cantos XXI–XXIII." *MLN* 59 (1944): 83–88.

Stewart, Dana E., and Alison Cornish, eds. *Sparks and Seeds: Medieval Literature and Its Afterlife. Essays in Honor of John Freccero.* Turnhout: Brepols, 2000.

Stock, Brian. *Augustine the Reader.* Cambridge, MA: Harvard University Press, 1996.

Syme, Ronald. *The Roman Revolution.* Oxford: Oxford University Press, 2002.

Tambling, Jeremy. *Dante and Difference: Writing in the "Commedia."* Cambridge: Cambridge University Press, 1988.

Tavoni, Mirko. "Il nome di poeta in Dante." In *Studi offerti a Luigi Blasucci,* edited by Lucio Lugnani, Marco Santagata, and Alfredo Stussi, 545–77. Lucca: M. P. Fazzi, 1996.

Terdiman, Richard. "Problematical Virtuosity: Dante's Depiction of the Thieves, *Inf.* XXIV–XXV." *Dante Studies* 91 (1973): 27–45.

Teskey, Gordon. *Allegory and Violence.* Ithaca: Cornell University Press, 1996.

Took, John. "*Diligite iustitiam qui iudicatis terram*: Justice and the Just Ruler in Dante." In *Dante and Governance,* edited by John Woodhouse, 137–51. Oxford: Oxford University Press, 1997.

Vasoli, Cesare. *Otto saggi per Dante.* Florence: Lettere, 1995.

Vazzana, Steno. *Dante e "la bella scola."* Rome: Edizioni dell'Ateneo, 2002.

Vessey, David. *Statius and the Thebaid.* Cambridge: Cambridge University Press, 1973.

Whitfield, J. H. "Dante and Statius: *Purgatorio* XXI–XXII." In *Dante Soundings: Eight Literary and Historical Essays,* edited by David Nolan, 113–29. Dublin: Irish Academic Press, 1981.

Williams, Gordon. *Change and Decline: Roman Literature in the Early Empire.* Berkeley: University of California Press, 1978.

Wilson, Robert. "Prophecy by the Dead in Dante and Lucan." *Italian Studies* 52 (1987): 16–34.

Wilson, William. "*Paradiso* XXII." In *Lectura Dantis Virginiana* III. Dante's *Paradiso*: Introductory Readings, 318–28. *Lectura Dantis* 16–17, 1995.

Wind, Edgar. *Pagan Mysteries in the Renaissance.* New Haven: Yale University Press, 1958.

Woodhouse, John, ed. *Dante and Governance.* Oxford: Oxford University Press, 1997.

Index of Passages Discussed

General Index

Winthrop Wetherbee

is Professor of English and Avalon Foundation Professor
in the Humanities, Emeritus, at Cornell University.